# Researchers Hooked on Teaching

# FOUNDATIONS FOR ORGANIZATIONAL SCIENCE
A Sage Publications Series

### Series Editor

David Whetten, *Brigham Young University*

### Editors

Peter J. Frost, *University of British Columbia*
Anne S. Huff, *University of Colorado*
Benjamin Schneider, *University of Maryland*
M. Susan Taylor, *University of Maryland*

The FOUNDATIONS FOR ORGANIZATIONAL SCIENCE series supports the development of students, faculty, and prospective organizational science professionals through the publication of texts authored by leading organizational scientists. Each volume provides a highly personal, hands-on introduction to a core topic or theory and challenges the reader to explore promising avenues for future theory development and empirical application.

*Books in This Series*

PUBLISHING IN THE ORGANIZATIONAL SCIENCES, 2nd Edition
*Edited by* L. L. Cummings and Peter J. Frost

SENSEMAKING IN ORGANIZATIONS
Karl E. Weick

INSTITUTIONS AND ORGANIZATIONS
W. Richard Scott

RHYTHMS OF ACADEMIC LIFE
Peter J. Frost and M. Susan Taylor

RESEARCHERS HOOKED ON TEACHING:
Noted Scholars Discuss the Synergies of Teaching and Research
Rae André and Peter J. Frost

# Rae André
# Peter J. Frost

Editors

# Researchers Hooked on Teaching

## Noted Scholars Discuss the Synergies of Teaching and Research

Foundations for
Organizational
Science
A Sage Publications Series

**SAGE Publications**
*International Educational and Professional Publisher*
Thousand Oaks   London   New Delhi

*For information address:*

SAGE Publications, Inc.
2455 Teller Road
Thousand Oaks, California 91320
e-mail: order@sagepub.com

SAGE Publications Ltd.
6 Bonhill Street
London EC2A 4PU
United Kingdom

SAGE Publications India Pvt. Ltd.
M-32 Market
Greater Kailash I
New Delhi 110 048 India

Printed in the United States of America

*Library of Congress Cataloging-in-Publication Data*

Researchers hooked on teaching: noted scholars discuss the synergies
   of teaching and research / editors Rae André and Peter J. Frost.
       p. cm.—(Foundations for organizational science)
    Includes bibliographical references. ISBN 0-7619-0623-1 (pbk.: acid-free paper).
   —ISBN 0-7619-0622-3 (cloth : acid-fre paper)
    1. College teaching. 2. Research. I. Andre, Rae. II. Frost, Peter J. III. Series.
LB2331.R487   1996
378.1'25—dc20                                                              96-25240

This book is printed on acid-free paper.

97  98  99  00  01  10  9  8  7  6  5  4  3  2  1

| | |
|---|---|
| *Acquiring Editor:* | Marquita Flemming |
| *Editorial Assistant:* | Frances Borghi |
| *Production Editor:* | Diana E. Axelsen |
| *Production Assistant:* | Karen Wiley |
| *Typesetter:* | Rebecca Evans |
| *Print Buyer:* | Anna Chin |

# Contents

---

*To Miss Savalle (sic), who, during my freshman year at Cornell, with incredible, painstaking care, taught me so much about thinking and writing. And to all the untenured, dedicated Miss Savalles out there . . . Thank you so very much.*

Rae André

*To Mickey Bebb, Dick Sutton, Lily Gerdes, Joe Horner, and Tom Mahoney, who among many others, through their care and attention, have shaped my thinking and practice as a teacher and as a researcher.*

Peter J. Frost

# Introduction: Leading
# the Learning Experience

———————————————

Universities today need to do a better job explaining exactly what it is they contribute to society. They must address concerns that professors spend too much time on research and too little time on teaching. They must address the nature of research and its relevance to what is taught. The fundamentals of the professorial contribution—namely, teaching and research—are under attack, and universities must respond.

A few years ago, we had become concerned that the tension between research and teaching itself had, in some ways, become counterproductive, so we commissioned these chapters to learn more about what professors actually do and how they think about their work. Do they compartmentalize teaching and research as separate activities? Does the teaching-research paradigm even reflect their daily realities, and if not, what does? We were interested in seeing professors' work through their own eyes. We asked them to describe their jobs, keeping three ideas uppermost: teaching, research, and themselves as whole people who do both.

In the resulting collection, 19 professors describe what they do and why they do it. They write about themselves as whole persons who have developed a personal style that integrates both teaching and research. As a group, our contributors write in creative, holistic ways about learning, personal growth, love, dialogue, power, careers, customers, truth, enthusiasm, voice, refreshment, and commitment.

After reading these explorations, we believe that the contribution of these professors to society is abundantly clear. Each story is different, and each deserves to be read for its own particular merit. In general, however, these cases show that what professors can contribute to society is better students, individuals who think critically and broadly and who become enthusiastic about learning. Specifically, what those who have written here contribute is students interested in understanding individuals in organizations and organizations in society. If we want narrowly focused, passive learners who are organizational conformists and pallid citizens, then give them rote learning from a canned curriculum, not these professors. If we want organizational innovators and problem solvers, then expose students to people like these, who are themselves working enthusiastically at the cutting edge of their fields. Our contributors seem to have known instinctively that a crucial part of teaching students to learn is to model being a learner themselves through demonstrating, among other things, curiosity, passion, commitment of time and resources, and a spirit of playfulness. Professors who believe that their discipline is important empower students to see the world through a particular lens, and the experience of an aggregation of many lenses is an education.

We did not ask our contributors to tell us directly why their work contributes to the social good (nor should we have), but—each in his or her own way—they all did. We did not ask them to justify the importance of research, but their experience clearly does so.

## Our Contributors

Our contributors are a diverse group in terms of career stage, age, gender, nationality, race and ethnic origin, and type of institution. We chose them because we knew they excelled in both teaching and research, not that we knew how they had come to excel, or why. To know their research contribution was a relatively straightforward task, but to know the quality of their teaching, we had to learn about them through teaching with them ourselves, either in teams or at a common institution; through hearing of the teaching reputation they had developed in their institutions; or through sampling their teaching at conferences.

Disciplines vary greatly in how various scholarly activities are perceived, and caution should be taken in generalizing from our group to the professoriat as a whole. These professors work in the organizational sciences: organizational psychology and theory, business policy, economics, social philosophy and theory, education, social work, and sociology. Among them are many who have also held administrative positions as deans and associate deans and some who currently identify themselves as such.

We asked our authors to write about designing and living out lives that enable them to continue to work with the creative tension of doing teaching and research. We asked them to reflect on why striving for excellence in teaching and research have been professional and personal commitments for them. We encouraged them to include ways their academic work has nourished and discouraged their own intellectual development. We encouraged them to write in whatever style they chose, including anecdotes and illustrations and using alternative forms such as dialogue and poetry as they felt inspired to do so.

Many of our writers told us this was one of the most challenging writing assignments they had ever had, and one of the most satisfying. We think this impression suggests that the contributions made here challenge traditional modes of thinking about the experience of academicians and may lead to new ways of thinking about the role of the scholar and the role of the educator. One way of stating this is that one goal for this collection is a healing of the breach between research and teaching. Another goal is to search for new paradigms that enhance understanding of the complex realities of academic work.

Let's keep in mind that the challenge of writing this piece mirrors the challenge of academic work itself. Consider the job description that academia gives to new professors. It reads something like this: Your job includes two primary tasks. Task One will earn you an increased salary, will secure your professional mobility, will enhance the reputation of your employer, will result in invitations to attend interesting conferences nationally and internationally, and can be done on a flextime basis and at home. Task Two is unlikely to enhance your salary, save your tenure decision, or increase your professional mobility significantly and may, if pursued with too much enthusiasm, un-

dermine these. This task will tie you down to fixed hours at fixed lo-
cations to be determined, but increasingly, as the student body ages
and you gain enough experience to teach in graduate and executive
programs, it will include nights and weekends. Task Two may result in
your infrequent attendance at conferences held at out-of-the-way lo-
cations. Your challenge, should you decide to accept it, is to do both
of these tasks well and with enthusiasm.

This is how we describe our work. It is a reality. But is it the only
reality? The best reality?

## Challenging the Teaching-Research Paradigm

Our cases illustrate that experienced academics do not separate
teaching and research, but rather integrate them creatively, thought-
fully, and enthusiastically. Even professors who avow a disinterest in
teaching probably wish they could find a way to do it better and enjoy
it more. As Howard Aldrich writes in these pages:

> Scholars who go into their retirements living fragmented rather than inte-
> grated lives don't usually bother to record their misery. . . . When people
> complain about not being rewarded for efforts spent on teaching, my imme-
> diate response is always, "Good teaching is its own reward." I mean that a
> person's self-worth and sense of efficacy are bound up in what that person
> does for a living, and teaching consumes a large part of an academic's job,
> no matter how much he or she tries to escape it. Years of falling down on
> the job will take their toll, and that's no way to live.

The debate over the different contributions of teaching and research
is more a debate for administrators and those pre-tenure professors
who must meet defined standards than it is for seasoned professors.
And we find ourselves asking whether it is a healthy and helpful
dichotomizing of the academic role for those in the pre-tenure category as well.

It is an academic truism that research is more valued than teaching.
Why this should be so has as much to do with our culture as anything
else: It may be related to concepts of work and leisure as determined
by social class and to our valuing the written over the spoken word,
creativity over generativity, and individualism over collectivity. Whatever the reasons, this unequal valuation is reflected in a hierarchy of

institutions and, within institutions, of faculties. This book also suggests that, within the professorial role itself, the integration of teaching and research is crucial. The sum of these authors' experiences suggests that if professors are to be teachers, then their ability to integrate teaching and research is basic to their personal well-being over the course of their career, and it is probably a predictor of their classroom effectiveness. Not all teachers who do research will be good, but after reading these pieces, it is hard to imagine that teachers who do not do research will not be stale and disengaged. Although not suggesting that the converse is true, one implication is that all teachers should be researchers.

Administrators in many schools are wrestling with the teaching-research equation. Should researchers be trained to become better teachers? Should researchers be protected from teaching and their loads given to others who specialize in good teaching? Do two kinds of specialists, therefore, need to be identified, hired, and rewarded for excellence in their respective skill areas? On the basis of the exemplars here, we think the future path for most institutions should be to harness the twin talents of teaching and research in many, if not all, of their faculty. We have more to say about such issues in the final section of the book.

## Being Hooked on Teaching:
## How Professors Lead Learning

Among the main themes that emerge in these chapters are (a) teachers as models, for each other and for their students; (b) how the teaching-research paradigm frames careers, for better or worse; (c) teaching as learning and centering for the professor; (d) individualism versus collectivism in the institution and the classroom; (e) love for the profession and the people, *agape*—the overflowing love that seeks nothing in return; (f) dialogue and co-learning with students; (g) enthusiasm and even drama in the theater/classroom; (h) the essence of professional accomplishment; (i) the finding of one's voice; (j) critical thinking in oneself and one's students; (k) sensitivity to learning styles; (l) commitment to helping students develop deep, personal insights; (m) teaching versus research schools, and finding a best fit; (n) integration of individual research interests into the classroom; (o) love of one's subject; (p) truth; (q) entertaining versus teaching; and (r) intellectual and emotional refreshment.

Interesting as these themes are (and we cite them here so that readers can realize them as they explore the chapters), the stories of these professional lives are the essence of this book. After reading and reflecting on these stories in the aggregate, we note the following.

First, the context of the culture in which one works is an important factor in shaping the professor's ability to integrate teaching and research. The country or other overarching culture is basic. Although we made no systematic attempt here to be internationally representative, the contrast provided by our international contributors, along with their personal insights, reminds us that culture profoundly shapes institutions. For example, Nikita Pokrovsky (of Russia) reminds us of the role of intellectual historical context in shaping current thinking. Afsaneh Nahavandi (born in Iran) is the only writer who discusses the real, tangible net value of education, which was the main asset she could take with her from Iran. Peter Frost (a native South African) started his teaching in a training program designed to improve race relations in business organizations in his home country, and it shaped his thinking about the cultural complexity of the learning process.

Similarly, the culture of the educational institution matters enormously. The balanced support for teaching and research at one institution, the research emphasis at another, the teaching emphasis at a third—clearly these cultures shape the relationship of teaching and research and the jobs and lives of the professors within them. There is no unitary academia, and each professor must find an appropriate alignment for himself or herself. Of course, the typical progression is "down" the institutional hierarchy, from research institutions to balanced institutions.

Our authors have a commitment to people, for being fully present with and for them in their classrooms, and by and large, for championing them in their struggles in organizational life. In this, the research that each professor chooses frames his or her contribution. One studies organizational power, another studies organizational culture, a third studies learning styles. Whatever their research enthusiasm, however, many of them tell us and others demonstrate that, without it, they would be less interesting, certainly less informed, and less involved teachers. This idea obtains whether they are teaching basic, advanced, or special courses.

For this group of educators, to be less involved is intolerable. For most, however, teaching the specific interest of the professor is less important than encouraging an enthusiasm for the field and its methodologies, which in turn leads their students to find in the field the ideas they themselves want and need not only for the course but also for the future. Getting the students to think analytically as psychologists or sociologists or economists . . . or even, as Weick suggests, as complexly as possible, is the goal.

For the most part, our contributors are individualists. A few point this out specifically, considering it an attraction of the field. Others simply describe their work lives in terms of themselves in relation to their students and themselves in relation to their mentors, without saying much about themselves in relation to their colleagues. Seldom mentioned is an exciting team-teaching or research project, although these have clearly been undertaken by most on some occasions. This individualism corroborates the Boyer (1994) report finding that 6 of 90 academic departments studied had authentic collegiality, where people collaborated closely on decisions. This individualism may be explained, in part, by the fact that, in an individualistic society, it is most likely that enthusiasm—passion for a subject, relationships with other individuals—will emanate from personal rather than collective expression of an idea.

Today, in every large institution and in some small ones, there is pressure to standardize classes. We find merit in this for such reasons as fairness and continuity. Also, from a monetary (administrative) point of view, the more classes are standardized, the more academia can be bureaucratized: If the same thing is being taught to all the classes, then, in general, anyone can teach the class, including inexpensive part-time professors. Given these pressures, educators are bound to have some different views on the necessity of research. Does individuality—in particular, having a personal research agenda and developing a personal pedagogy—contribute to better education for the students? On the basis of the cases presented here, the answer is a resounding yes. In the balanced professor, idiosyncrasy combines with respect for the integrity of the field, including its main themes, tenets, and approaches, to yield an integrative classroom experience for the student. The cases presented here suggest that, at least in the organizational and related sciences, the unique professor as model learner and communicator is extremely important. We might even go so far as to say that if students get a good professor of the subject, whatever topics he or she covers in class, that is the main stimulus for their learning.

It may be that, in our society, team teaching cannot be psychically rewarding for most people and that, even where it is initially present, enthusiasm cannot be maintained in the face of group politics and resource constraints. Certainly, given the strength of the individual voices here, it seems that the professor's desire to make a unique contribution will be around for a long time. (Our notion of academic freedom itself may be derived from our need to preserve our individuality.) Interestingly, along the same lines, Boyer (1994) suggests that universities should move beyond standard assessments of professors to focus on such professional characteristics as honesty, courage, and persistence—all hallmarks of individual innovation. The upside of this is that students get great role models/teachers, and they love them and learn from them. The downside of this is, of course, that, in a society that increasingly needs teamwork, teamwork is not widely modeled for the students. We would note, however, that the chapter on collaborative teaching (Chapter 14, by Crary and Spelman) does suggest the considerable benefits (as well as the costs) to instructors who engage in intensive team teaching.

Finally, to be a professor is to work in a service profession in which burnout from constant interpersonal work and anonymous rejection by reviewers are occupational hazards, and professors must find strategies for renewal. Our writers here talk about doing something rather different once in a while and away from the classroom. There are two reasons for down time—that is, time not scheduled for teaching: (a) to put oneself into different settings to enhance intellectual learning (e.g., to see the world differently and more complexly) and (b) to find emotional renewal. In a department full of individualists, it is unlikely that people will find the social support they need. Professors tend to find support outside, especially from family, and renewal in formally sanctioned disengagements such as summers and sabbaticals without teaching.

In the final analysis, this book suggests that framing the debate about the contribution of universities in terms of "teaching" and "research" is an approach that is fundamentally flawed. The teaching-research paradigm is inadequate to the complexities of the realities of professors' professional lives. In this book, our contributors tell us repeatedly that, unless they are pre-tenure, they do not themselves separate teaching and research. Their stories illustrate over and over again that the terms do not adequately describe their job. Not that the job defies description, but what professors do is far more human, complex, and integrated. What good teachers do is develop a relationship with their students that is based on who they both are and what they both know. For such professors, teaching and research are part of a unified whole that is better described as a learning experience.

## Our Thanks

We give thanks to our authors for their individual contributions, especially for their willingness to do something completely different, and for their patience as they waited for others to bring their own chapters to fruition. We found the stories to be profound and interesting. They are sometimes very moving. One easily appreciates the human quality of the learning experience for each author. One can sense from each story some of the intellectual creativity of each author, and one can feel also the sense of excitement of the authors and their students as the ideas come alive, emerge, and flow within their teaching and research repertoires.

It has been a privilege to come to know our contributors. We looked forward so eagerly to each chapter, in part because this topic has not previously been discussed, really, and we were curious to know what they thought and, in part because we came to expect, on the basis of the first few chapters we read, that we would love each of them.

We were right!!!

## The Stories

It is time to move from the preamble to the play, to let those who were invited to participate tell their stories. Each author's experience is unique, and each is a complete statement that requires neither context nor embellishment. Yet, each is connected to the others through a passion for learning, a love of teaching, and an appreciation for research. Many themes and threads weave throughout the fabric of the collection. We invite you to explore, to discover, and to join us in the experience of learning that is provided in the pages that follow. Start where you like, dip into the chapters at will or whim. Read and reread some or all of the pieces. Bring to them your own interpretations fueled by your own life experiences as teachers, as researchers, as citizens.

Yet, we thought some readers might like some guidance too, so we divided the book into five sections. Read from front to back, the book may be seen loosely as a narrative about the teaching-research dilemma—the clarification of this dilemma, solutions to it as exemplified in scholars' lives, solutions laid out in the teaching craft, and finally, philosophical speculations about the nature of the problem itself.

We trust that you will enjoy the journey and that, along the way, you will find ideas, insights, and nuggets of wisdom that will make a difference in the way you learn and in how you teach others, whatever your roles are in life.

## Reference

Boyer, E. L. (1994, February 9). Report to focus on standards for assessing what professors do by Denise K. Magner. *Chronicle of Higher Education*, p. 22.

## Acknowledgments

We are most grateful to Constance Ackerman, Stacie Chappell, Vivien Clark, Eunice Davies, Maeve Frost, Marianne Penney St.-Andre, and Cynthia Ree for their fine administrative assistance on this project. We thank also those at Sage, including Marquita Flemming, Diana Axelsen, and copy editor Linda Poderski, for their roles in producing this book.

# I

# The Problem

## *Teaching on the*
## *Research Side of the Brain*

What is this craziness about the separation of teaching and research? What effect does this duality have on the people who live with it?

In this first section, we include several authors who, among other things, do an especially good job of clarifying the importance of teaching for all scholars and who suggest ways to live happily with both tasks.

Cynthia Fukami emphasizes the theme of balance in her reflections on career and life, work and home, feminine and masculine, teaching and research. "To work at something you love is an unbelievable privilege," she writes. "I keep running back and forth on my teeter-totter, looking for that magical balance. . . . Perhaps, the key is not the roles themselves . . . but the center: me. . . . My life is balanced because I'm 'centered.' "

Howard Aldrich reflects on a early career devoted to research and how later—but was it too late?—he discovered the essentiality of teaching. "Should my tale end as a tragedy? I have painted a nearly unrelenting picture of my unreflexive obedience to a mode of teaching that was taking me nowhere." Stay tuned.

Barbara Gutek directly attacks the teaching-research dichotomy and describes how teaching and research have been integrated in her work in a department of psychology and a school of business. From her perspective as both administrator and professor, she discusses some changes in academia that are having a profound effect on "the combined teaching-research enterprise." She writes, "Higher education . . . is facing competition on the teaching front. If we do not deliver the relationship between professors and students that has been the model of higher education for decades . . . students may take their tuition dollars elsewhere."

Rae André closes this section with a statement of the integration problem. She believes that *teaching* and *research* are simplistic terms for describing what we do. "We search for truth . . . we push for intellectual innovation, we share our truths and innovations with particular audiences, and we create environments that enhance learning." She argues further that the terms do not comprise a neutral dichotomy, but rather have become a basis for discriminating and ordering what we do and how we prosper in our profession, with the nod going clearly to research as being more important than teaching. She uses her own interdisciplinary experiences as an academic to critique this dichotomy and to suggest ways to begin to integrate its components.

# 1 Struggling With Balance

CYNTHIA V. FUKAMI

Integration. Balance. Having it all. A curse? A challenge? A lie? What made me think it could be done? Did I have role models? Only in the most backward sense. My role models were of what I didn't want—people who made choices across the various domains of their lives. My parents chose between work and home. My professors chose between teaching and research. Over the years, I haven't wanted to choose between my career and my life, between my work and my home, between my feminine side and my masculine side, between my left brain and my right brain, between my teaching and my research. As you experience life day to day, the tendency is to recall your history as a series of random walks. It's interesting, in hindsight, to see a pattern emerge. I guess this is a benefit of middle age.

Here is the main theme in my life—not extraordinary at any one thing, but pretty darn good at most everything, so why choose? From music and dancing lessons as a child to high school entrance examinations to college grade point averages to tenure decisions. My teachers used to comment on how well balanced I was. My dad still does. Am I too lazy to make choices? Too greedy? Too stupid? Too arrogant?

The stress literature is relatively clear. If you want to effectively cope with role conflict, the correct thing to do is choose. The last thing you want to do is "integrate," to bring everything you do with you everywhere you go. I have observed in wonder when a friend or colleague effectively "wears hats." I do not shift hats very easily. I have one hat that always gets worn wherever I go and no matter what I do.

A few years ago, Cathy Enz, Cindy Lindsay, and I ran a session at an Organizational Behavior Teaching Conference (OBTC) on balancing family and work. Cathy used a metaphor for the group to consider—a teeter-totter. Our participants were asked to close their eyes and to imagine being on one end of the teeter-totter. We all were then to imagine what object or person we might put on the other end of the teeter-totter—that is, what might bring us balance. When I participated in the exercise, this is what I imagined: I was keeping the teeter-totter in balance by running back and forth from end to end. This image has remained with me and explains much about me. If I run fast enough, perhaps I can do it all. This is also clear: The stress literature is right on. I have felt stress from this lifestyle. Those who choose have less stress. Nonetheless, this has been my choice—to not choose. Is there a greater reward from the greater investment, as Stacy Adams would predict? I'm too close to the situation to speculate on that; I'll leave that to others to judge. My task here is to be descriptive, not prescriptive. For whatever reason, this is what I do.

## Balancing Teaching and Research

When I was considered by my colleagues for promotion and tenure, I made the statement, "The philosophy guiding my work is that being an academic involves three equally important roles: first, teaching effectively; second, producing useful research; and third, providing service at the four traditional levels." Where did that philosophy come from?

Conventional wisdom might suggest I begin by discussing how good teaching and good research come from the same qualities. To be sure, there are similarities. They both require curiosity and the ability to break down a complex word into smaller chunks—to see complexity in simpler ways and to be able to communicate the simplicity to others. They both require the ability to see new issues in the routine and every day, and lots and lots of intrinsic motivation. Ironically, they both require humility—that is, a real appreciation for what you *don't* know. And, they both require confidence in what you think; sometimes the confidence is more important than the actual knowledge. So, some may conclude that teaching and research are merely two actions we take in playing out one role: a faculty member who creates and disseminates knowledge.

But the main point I'd like to make is that teaching and research can represent two different roles. Simply put, good teaching and good research can represent real differences as well. The three most important differences to me are, first, that teaching is immediate, whereas research is long-run. On the one hand, I know immediately, in real time, if my teaching is effective—if my students are learning, if process is good. On the other hand, I (along with my coauthor, Dave Hopkins) had a paper published in December 1993 on a project that was started in January 1988!

Second, teaching is forgiving, whereas research is cruel. On the one hand, it has been my experience that if I make a mistake in my teaching, perhaps in content but more likely in process, I can take time out and redirect. This can happen in the same session, the same week, the same term, the next term. In teaching, we get lots of points of contact. On the other hand, the research (or should I say publishing?) process can feel cold and cruel. We get a limited window within which to communicate to the editors and reviewers of our work. We worry about "offending" them. After waiting 6 anxious months for a review to return, we wonder whether we will anger the editor if we call and inquire about its status. When we're fortunate enough to get a "revise and resubmit," we walk a fine line between arguing with and capitulating to the reviewers.

Third, I feel confident that my teaching makes a very real impact, whereas research (at least in the way we currently perform it) may never affect anything real. I have no illusions about having an impact on every student who shares my class, but I am certain that a few in each class have been affected—some positively, some negatively. I know that my research has affected some of my colleagues who converse with me about their own research, but I don't have illusions about the world of managers. So, to me, teaching and research have represented different roles we play, as opposed to an integrated whole.

As I pause and reflect on this last paragraph, I have to say that, at one point or another in my career, I could have written exactly the opposite sentiments about teaching and research. In other words, at times teaching has been cruel and research forgiving; teaching has been long-run and research immediate; and my research has made an impact and it felt as if my teaching didn't matter. But this is my point. I believe that teaching and research have occupied separate but complementary roles in my life. When one was a source of pain, the other could be a source of pleasure. And vice versa. And, I think it is the dialectic that moves us from one to the other that creates a balance between them, much as Chris Argyris suggested years ago in his thinking about integrating the individual and the organization, or as a physicist might argue, that movement creates a momentum that overcomes the forces pushing us in different directions and allows for an equilibrium or a balance point. How has this played out in my own life?

I never knew that I wanted to teach or do research until I did each. The experience with research came earlier. Two important events gave me this experience at an early age. I entered the University of Illinois as a freshman "personnel psychology" major. (Yes, I am one of those boring people who never changed her major.) The only time I wondered about forks in the road was in my senior year in college. To my friends and fellow dorm residents, I had become a career counselor. Every semester, I would interpret the course schedule and degree requirements and counsel everyone on how to register. So, I wondered whether I would be better off in counseling than in personnel (in hindsight, I now understand that what I was really doing was teaching). At this point, I had absolutely no intention of attending graduate school. I decided to do an independent study at the counseling center to investigate that option. My sponsor at the center directed me toward a research project—validating an in-house career interest survey (a sort of Kuder preference test). I quickly learned two things. One, I didn't want to administer career interest surveys to people for my career, and two, I really liked doing the research. Because of this experience, I decided to attend graduate school but in a terminal master's program. I still had every intention of getting a "job" upon graduation, probably in personnel.

Once in the master's program, I was awarded a quarter-time research assistantship. My duties were to collect data, via structured interviews, on a sample of workers. During the first interview I conducted, I had an orgasmic experience. I discovered I could ask people questions, personal questions, probing questions, and they would answer me.

Having been a people-watcher all my life, this was an unbelievable experience. Talk about being a kid in a candy store! Then, I could take the data, perform statistical operations, and come to conclusions. I had completed my undergraduate stats class in a dense fog. Now, with research, it all made sense. I could use all these techniques and statistical tests to answer any questions I had (I was rather optimistic in those days). I knew I had found my future. I decided to enroll in a doctoral program and become a professor. Not only could I stay in college my entire life, but I also could get paid for it (albeit modestly). I will always have a warm spot in my heart for George Graen, who guided me through this part of my life.

Notice, though, we're only talking research here. Virtually every faculty member I encountered to this point in academia in my undergraduate and master's programs was a researcher, not a teacher. Can you tell I attended a publish-or-perish institution? In fact, some of my professors maneuvered endlessly to figure out how to avoid teaching entirely (à la *Impostors at the Temple*?). My early role models taught me that teaching was an inconvenience, something to be delegated to the slave-waged teaching assistants, something to be endured so that you could keep the big prize: the ability to get paid to do basic research.

I then went on to much of the same in my doctoral program. I was fortunate (though I didn't know it at the time) to attend a program under a fellowship with *no* teaching requirements and few research assistant responsibilities. I was actually empowered to do my *own* research, not to support someone else's. At the time, it was a tad frustrating. I was supposed to fly before I thought I could. But because of this system and with warm feelings for Tim Hall, who provided lots of rope, I was able to achieve a single-authored publication as a doctoral student—a paper that helped launch my research career.

So, research came first for me. Teaching came after I was well into my doctoral program. I didn't step in front of a class until Tim asked me to cover an introductory organizational behavior (OB) class for him while he was otherwise engaged. The topic was leadership, a topic for which I was well prepared from my earlier work with George Graen. The section was rather large, taught in a tiered classroom, and I pretty much lectured to the class. I interpreted and organized the text, much as I had the course schedules for my dorm mates in college. The students responded as my dorm mates had. They told me I was pretty good at conveying a body of knowledge. My skill at lecturing should not have been a surprise. I have always had a "presence" in front of large groups. I've attributed this presence to all those ballet and piano recitals as a child. I can perform in front of an audience. In fact, I remember one of my teachers in high school remarking, after I'd made a class presentation, that I'd make a wonderful college professor. I laughed then. I wonder what she would say now.

I did eventually teach several courses on my own during my doctoral program, at other area universities. I did it as a way of earning extra money and as a way of having the teaching experience to add to my résumé. I had good experiences, and I enjoyed it. In hindsight, I know the seed had been planted.

When I completed my degree, I was a well-behaved, well-socialized new Ph.D. in the publish-or-perish tradition. I interviewed for jobs in similar institutions, except for one. That one was a "more balanced" institution. They actually had me teach a class instead of present my dissertation research. When I turned down their offer, something was clear to me; the career path in academia moves from publish or perish to balance, but almost never in the reverse. I accepted the publish-or-perish offer. One thing was equally clear from the school I turned down: the prediction that I'd be back to balance eventually.

So, I moved on to the next logical step, the step for which I was groomed—a top-tier research university. What happened to me there was defining, both personally and professionally, because for the first time I felt in control. (Notice that this was a dangerous assumption. I was, in fact, *not* in control as an untenured new assistant professor, but I acted as if I were.)

My teaching continued to blossom. I continued to be a fine lecturer to large sections. I could still take the Bible and be the students' priest. I soon received the highest student evaluations in the whole school of business. Don't forget I had a contrast effect going here as I was surrounded by researchers, not teachers—the same types who had trained me in graduate school.

My research took much longer to root. Perhaps because of the rope in my doctoral program, perhaps because I'm a fuzzy thinker, perhaps because I couldn't fly as well as others thought I could (there's that presence again!), perhaps because 18 of 20 hypotheses in my dissertation were null, my research struggled. It was no fun being rejected. It was no fun trying to get null results published. I kept trying to recover the sunk costs of my dissertation and avoided the investment of collecting new data. Besides, my teaching gave me great pleasure. It was immediate, it was real, it was intrinsically rewarding, it was challenging, but I was up to the challenge. I didn't have a *clue* about publishing, though. My teaching effectiveness was noticed by the college's management training unit, and my schedule was soon filled with half-day, full-day, and multiple-day training gigs. Remember, I was at a publish-or-perish school and my senior colleagues were either not equipped or not motivated (with some exceptions, typically low status) to "press flesh" as one of them put it. So I did. It was lucrative, it was immediate, but it felt off-track.

I'll never forget the day I was giving a 2-hour seminar on conflict management to a group of visiting nurses. The lightning bolt struck: What was I doing there? Was this really why I went through my Ph.D.? To train nurses about collaborating? I left the seminar, drove immediately back to my office, put pencil to paper, and began the manuscript that became my first major post-Ph.D. publication. Thanks to Bob Guion, who herded me through this process and taught me how to write an article that was not a dissertation.

In short, I had started my career on the research end of the teeter-totter. That side felt forgiving and warm. Gradually, I had moved to the teaching side of the teeter-totter when research started feeling cruel and teaching became warm, but I stayed at that end too long and was losing my sense of balance. I started to regain my balance by moving back to the research end.

Unfortunately (or fortunately, actually), the lightning bolt struck too late and the teeter-totter started moving back to balance too late for that first job. Both my colleagues and I wondered whether I had time enough to "recover." Typical things happened: My late start at research was attributed to my *over*concern with teaching. I was actually told at one point by my colleagues to worsen as a teacher because it would look better on my record. When the president of the Undergraduate Student Association singled me out in his speech at graduation, my colleagues did not congratulate me. On the contrary, they "joked" about whether I had paid the student off. Eventually, I grew tired of being punished for being a good teacher. I was able to deal with not being rewarded for being a good teacher, but to be punished for it became intolerable. Throughout this time, I had begun to attend the Organizational Behavior Teaching Conferences and found great support there for the value of teaching. I tired of being at a school that didn't value what I valued. In all fairness to my colleagues, I think I caused them some grief because we were good friends. They simply didn't know how to interpret me from their frames of reference.

My fear at this point was whether I could find a school that valued both ends of the teeter-totter, as I did. The only schools with which I was familiar were either research schools or teaching schools. I didn't want to define myself either way, so I set about finding balance. Luckily, I found it, and 12 years later, here I am. As a private (high-tuition) school, we value teaching a great deal. As a result, our teaching load remains small, and best of all, our classes are also small. Scholarship is valued as well. We don't have the same requirements as publish-or-perish schools in either number or form, but we do expect (and accomplish) scholarship. Because the teaching load is reasonable, we have time to devote to scholarship. Because the scholarship expectations are reasonable, we have time to devote to teaching. I can't take credit for this system because it was in place well before I arrived, but I have enjoyed seeing it sustained over many deans and administrators, through rounds of strategic planning and curriculum development, and through promotion and tenure decisions. I think we were ahead of the game, as Boyer and others have described it.

Ironically, once I made the decision to leave the publish-or-perish school, the research side of the teeter-totter started getting bigger, and the reduced teaching load (in terms of number of students) helped this a great deal. My first major publication appeared, with several more in the queue, and I was elected to office in the OB Division of the Academy of Management. I was also asked to join the Editorial Board of the *Academy of Management Journal* (*AMJ*). The teaching side of the teeter-totter remained important as well. While I was on the board for the OB Division of the academy, I also served on the board for the Organizational Behavior Teaching Society. While I was on the *AMJ* editorial board, I was on the *Journal of Management Education* editorial board. At my current university, I simultaneously served on our Research Committee and on our Committee on Instruction. Several years ago, I received our university's award for teaching excellence and our college's Willemssen Distinguished Research Professorship. There is a life between the ends of the teeter-totter.

On reflection, I believe I had built momentum by running back and forth on the teeter-totter of teaching and research. By staying on one end too long, one runs the risk of losing momentum and, hence, one's balance. I am beginning to reach the conclusion that balance comes from movement, not from stillness. No wonder I'm dizzy.

## Balancing Life and Work

One real advantage of being a professor is that we have more flexibility within which to manage our whole lives. I know from firsthand comparisons that I can manage my life's demands—from the minor issues like dental appointments, visits to the veterinarian, and dropping off dry cleaning to the major issues like children's illnesses—much more easily than my secretary can. So, I'm starting from a position of flexibility.

I'm also distinguished by my spouse, who is unusual (if not a saint), and our relationship (which is atypical). We met as college freshmen who lived in the same dorm (so, not only did I never change majors in college, I also never changed partners). Simply put, we formed our partnership long before either of us knew what we would be doing with the rest of our lives. We just knew we would be together. He tells me he was attracted to me because he knew I would never expect him to take care of me. I tell him I was attracted to him because he knew how to have fun. So, just as the psychologists tell us, the bonds of attraction are strongest when one adds similar values with complementary needs. And, just as I described teaching and research, we have been able to balance out the good and the bad. He needed somebody to help make him serious. I needed somebody to help me be less serious. And so, here we are, 25 years later (and still counting).

We have never had to deal with issues of professional jealousy or whose career came first. I was more serious about my career; he was more portable as a graphic artist. More than that, he never had any difficulty with being partners with a strong woman. So, when I have told him that it was time to move for my career (three times up to now), he has said, "Let's go."

When it came time to have children and when we were concerned about child care alternatives, he said he would quit his job and stay home. And he has, for just over 6 years now. He *is* human; we both look forward to our youngest being enrolled in school full time. So much for stereotypes about men, Asian or otherwise. We have two daughters, so now he gets to be surrounded by strong women. Nonetheless, in the light of my profession and my partner, balancing work and life has not been as difficult as it might have been.

And yet, we have issues of balance to deal with. Although I am the breadwinner of our family, I have never aspired to be the "dad." Although Mark is the homemaker of our family, he has never aspired to be the "mom." Unfortunately, our society seems to want one of us to be mom and one of us to be dad. We find ourselves needing to navigate that space between the ends of that teeter-totter, as I have with teaching and research. We're still learning.

We have also never let work intrude too much on our lives. Of course, from time to time, demands are simply there and must be dealt with. But on the whole, we spend a lot of time together. A colleague once told me that I spent too much time with my husband, that I should be spending more time on my research. But here we go again with the main theme in my life: not to choose between the parts, but to try to seize the whole.

## Lessons Learned

Balance. Doesn't that sound calm, tranquil, settled—at peace? Is it? Observe the trading floor of the Board of Trade in Chicago as price is determined—the dynamic equilibrium of the marketplace. I wouldn't describe it as calm. Remember the performer on the *Ed Sullivan Show* with the spinning plates on the sticks? He wasn't taking a nap. Observe the ballerina as she rises on her toes and completes an arabesque. She is fighting strong forces of nature to achieve and remain in that position. If she dances an entire career, she may even cripple her body because of the unnatural positions she has attained. It's not very comfortable. Consider the teeter-totter. It's so much easier to move to one side than to keep both sides balanced.

Ironically, one early theme of my research was *multiple commitments*—the idea that an individual could be committed to more than one object or identity within one organizational membership. Obviously, my own life has shown that this can be true. We studied unionized workers and asked whether loyal union members could be loyal company employees at the same time. We found they could. In fact, performance was higher and turnover, absenteeism, and warnings were lower for those workers committed to both company and union when compared with workers committed to only one. We studied nurses and asked whether commitment to the profession interfered with commitment to the hospital or to coworkers. We found that commitment to the profession did interfere with commitment to the hospital but that commitment to coworkers complemented commitment to the hospital. We studied accountants in a public accounting firm and asked whether identification with the profession interfered with identification with the firm. This was my dissertation, and I still don't know what I found (remember the null results)! Dubin and others studied this same phenomenon as "central life interest," and others have studied these issues from the point of view of career development (e.g., Van Maanen, Bailyn, Schein). These researchers conclude there are different models for carving out one's life space. In short, I managed to research an issue that became important in my own life.

Perhaps, the key is not the roles themselves—teacher, researcher, administrator, colleague, partner, mom—but the center: me. The teeter-totter needs a fulcrum. My life is balanced because I'm "centered."

I love my work. My work is me. To work at something you love is an unbelievable privilege. Not that I'm willing to give my salary back. Not that it has always been easy. But I keep running back and forth on my teeter-totter, looking for that magical balance. In my dreams, I am a dancer, perched on my toes, in control, in deceptively tranquil balance.

# 2 My Career as a Teacher

*Promise, Failure, Redemption*

---

HOWARD E. ALDRICH

I remember the moment quite clearly. The emotional impact of that concluding sentence in my urban sociology class is as vivid today as it was back in the fall of 1969. I had just finished another hour of straight lecturing—which meant more or less reading out to the students the notes I had laboriously compiled the night before—when I turned to them and said, "But what does it all mean?" I shrugged my shoulders: "Who knows?" Momentarily stunned by this rather foolish revelation, the students did not respond, and I turned and walked out of the room. I knew something was wrong, but what? I wish I could say that I came up with a solution before the next class session, but alas, more than a decade passed before I finally came to my senses.

I want to tell you a story about my career as a teacher, using a simple life-course model. I've titled the first three sections of this chapter "Promise," "Failure," and "Redemption" because, as I look back, these periods in my life are so clearly demarcated. At the time I lived through them, however, I was almost completely unaware of the transformation I was undergoing. Thus, this chapter is an opportunity for me to make sense out of those changes and to make a few more general observations about teaching and its place in academic careers. The editors asked me about the link between my teaching and research interests, but for much of my career, the two have had a tenuous connection. Some signs of change are apparent, however.

## Promise

In high school, I was simultaneously a teacher's dream and a teacher's worst nightmare. I attended a very small school in the same corner of Ohio where Karl Weick (Chapter 17) enjoyed his formative years. Luckily, we never met as children, and so I can truthfully claim that my feelings about teaching developed completely independently from his! I was a teacher's dream because I not only did all the assigned work for classes but also read widely, brought outside material into class, and volunteered for extra assignments. I was also a teacher's worst nightmare because classes never went fast enough for me and my peers never got the point quickly enough. While my teachers lingered over fairly obvious points with my duller classmates, I was cutting up in the back row, drawing pictures of hot rods and spaceships and generally making a nuisance of myself.

Despite my disruptive behavior, several kindly teachers—perhaps they had taken courses in educational psychology?—spent time after class with me, suggesting additional readings and involving me in independent studies projects. Looking back now, it's impossible to overestimate the effect of that extra attention I received. I remember being driven home after one late-night school club meeting by a teacher who talked matter-of-factly about an assignment she was giving me for the club; it involved putting together the high school yearbook and clearly conveyed the message that I *could* do the job regardless of my inexperience.

I went off to college, thinking teachers had a pretty good thing going but never contemplating that I could do their job. U.S. colleges in the early 1960s were on the verge of entering a tumultuous era of societal transformation. During that decade, the public image of undergraduates changed from beer-swilling, party-going, politically conservative adolescents to politically radical, even dangerous, subversives who were a threat to the American way of life. The draft board sit-ins and the antiwar teach-ins at U.S. colleges in the mid-1960s now seem a lifetime away, and they are ancient history to today's student generation. I have long since learned not to toss off casual references to events from those days. Instead, I search for more contemporary references when I need examples of turbulent times!

Even though I only traveled 50 miles from my hometown to my university town, I might as well have been entering a parallel universe. Philosophy, political science, journalism, history, psychology, economics, and other social science courses became an all-consuming passion for me. By the second semester of my sophomore year, I'd decided to major in sociology. By my senior year, I'd taken all the undergraduate courses available in sociology and psychology and was taking graduate courses and independent studies courses with senior professors. As had happened in high school, a few faculty took a special interest in my intellectual development, inviting me to office hours and sponsoring my independent studies projects. Somewhere along the way, my intentions to become a lawyer evaporated. I still remember that fateful day when I decided not to mail in my application to take the LSAT; instead, I signed up for the GRE and the advanced test in sociology.

But when did *college teaching* become salient to me as a profession? I remember being incredibly impressed, even enthralled, by how patient and understanding my professors were. Sherm Stanage, Art Neal, Joe Balogh, and others worked in their offices, with their doors open, and it never occurred to me that I might be turned away, no matter when I sought them out. In my senior year, all my professors assumed I would go to graduate school, and so I began assuming the same thing. But I needed funding, and so I began investigating the scholarships available for graduate study in the social sciences. The Danforth Foundation and the Woodrow Wilson Foundation offered two of the best deals, and I obtained applications from them. The Woodrow Wilson Fellowship was explicitly for people intending to become college teachers; the Danforth Foundation sought people with a broadly humanitarian commitment to public life. In the process of writing applications for these fellowships, I discovered that I could make a pretty good case for my potential worth as a college instructor.

Graduate school at the University of Michigan in sociology was, in a sense, more of the same experience I'd had as an undergraduate. This was the mid-1960s, the federal government was lavishing money on the social sciences, huge survey research projects were being conducted at the Institute for Social Research, and Michigan formed a sort of "brain trust" for the social sciences. Talk of research and federal grants was always in the air, but talk of teaching was not. The incentive system was fairly clear, and I would have been a very dense graduate student indeed had I not realized that the best job offers were going to the students with the best research record in graduate school, not to those who'd done innovative teaching of undergraduates. Was anyone bitter about this? No. We all took it for granted; great scholars did great research and published great works and also gave a fair account of themselves in the classroom.

Michigan did have scholars who seemed to have extraordinary competence in both worlds. My classes with Ed Swanson, Dan Katz, Bill Gamson, George Katona, Phil Converse, and others were sometimes extraordinary learning experiences—and always interesting. As had happened to me as an undergraduate, several of my professors got me involved in their research projects, although very few of them maintained the open door policy I had enjoyed as an undergraduate.

But what of my own teaching experiences in all of this? Even though I turned down the Woodrow Wilson and Danforth Foundations to accept a National Science Foundation fellowship, I was still on their mailing lists and was invited to conferences, particularly by the Danforth Foundation. Thus, at least once a year, I engaged in rather abstract discussions with colleagues from other universities about theories of teaching. My only actual classroom experience, however, came as a result of my wife, insisting that because I would have to teach for a living, I ought to at least try it once before I left graduate school. As a teacher herself, she could see how unprepared I was, but she was amazingly good-natured about it. Accordingly, I volunteered as a TA for a large lecture class. Unfortunately, the class turned into the sort of free-form happening that, two decades later, would provide juicy examples for people like Bloom (1987) and Sykes (1988) when they wrote of the excesses of liberal education.

The class quickly spun out of control as the students took over the lecture stage or called out to the professor through bullhorns from the balcony. I stopped going to lectures and ran a guerrilla class on my own. As I was doing my dissertation on small businesses and how they were affected by the civil disorders of 1967 and 1968, I had plenty to talk about. Indeed, I had too much to talk about. I suspect I talked about 90% of the time. For a few months, my research actually informed my teaching because I used my preparations for the dissertation in choosing readings for the class. Because Detroit had experienced serious civil disorders in the preceding summer, the students were very curious about my dissertation plans.

Did I learn anything about teaching from that experience? I remember being vaguely sick to my stomach each morning before class, but I also remember the exhilarating feeling of having students pass me on the sidewalk in Ann Arbor and actually say, "Hello, Mr. Aldrich." As it turns out, I had learned very little that would be useful on my first job.

## Failure

When I went on the job market, in my final year of graduate school, I went through a process very typical of those times. Everywhere I visited, I was asked to talk about my research and about my long-term plans for publishing it. A few department chairs asked me about my teaching experience but in a very perfunctory way, and none of them asked to see my syllabus or teaching evaluations or even implied that I might be carrying them around with me. Because I'd never designed a course from scratch, I had only a vague idea of how to put together such a syllabus, anyway, and the one time I actually went into detail, I simply described the reading list from my one teaching experience at Michigan.

Totally unprepared, I thus walked into my first teaching experience at Cornell University's New York State School of Industrial and Labor Relations (ILR). I actually knew what a syllabus should look like and so spent several weeks during the summer preparing one for my only course in the fall—Urban Sociology. I don't recall any senior colleagues talking with me about what to expect, nor do I recall anyone actually making suggestions about what I might do in the course. A senior professor in another department had taught a course similar to mine, but no one sent me a syllabus, and my understanding was that I was on my own.

How shall I describe that first semester? The phrase "being thrown to the lions" does not quite capture my predicament because I went willingly into the arena, albeit completely unaware of how poorly armed I was. Through my high school and undergraduate days, the teachers and professors I admired had simply stood up at the front of the room, effortlessly spinning interesting tales and leading engaging discussions. I'd never really thought about how they managed it. I quickly discovered that observing and remembering good teaching did not provide me with the actual tools for accomplishing the tasks.

Looking back now, I can see that my favorite teachers were not great lecturers, but rather great discussion leaders and facilitators. At the time, however, the principles they used were opaque to me. Despite my undergraduate minor in psychology and my graduate minor in social psychology, I just didn't see the connection between leadership style, group process, and teaching outcomes.

Instead of thinking about how to facilitate discussions, I committed the cardinal sin of poorly prepared teachers everywhere: I lectured. For every class meeting, I prepared detailed lecture notes, often stretching to 10 or 15 single-spaced pages, completely scripting the hour. Worse still, these lecture notes were not prepared after serious reflection of what the hour ought to accomplish, but rather were a summary of what I had cobbled together from my outside readings. Preparing these massive lectures took me far into the night as my wife and infant son slept in the adjacent room. I had to find some material I thought was interesting and then copy the important passages out of the source into my lecture notes. I suppose the transitions between thoughts were mine, but they were often abrupt and disjointed.

My class meetings thus consisted of my walking into the class, asking about any questions from the previous class meeting, and then proceeding to "talk" my way through the lecture notes. My one saving grace was that I was a speed reader and could glance down at the page and absorb a paragraph worth of material at a time. I thus could give the impression—or so I thought—of actually speaking spontaneously, rather than of reading from a prepared script. Visualize, if you will, my situation: standing in front of 30 or so undergraduates who were mostly from the New York City or Long Island area, summarizing the work of authors who had written about happenings in cities I'd only briefly visited and completely unprepared to go a foot beyond the material I'd prepared. My alienation from the class was complete one day when I mispronounced a word and heard several students in the first row laugh.

Grading the class was a nightmare. Grade inflation at Cornell had pushed undergraduate expectations to incredible heights, with any grade lower than a B- eliciting howls of anguish and loud protests. I gave only essay exams, the one feature of the class that probably made some pedagogical sense. Because I had no idea how to objectively score such questions, however, the grading process took up just as much time as the lecture preparation process.

Rescuers appeared on the horizon several times, but after temporarily grasping the rope thrown to me, I always seemed to slip back into deeper waters. First, during my fall term, Lori, a very brave undergraduate woman, came to my office hours and more or less told me I was screwing up badly and asked if I realized what I was doing wrong. Lori's analysis was insightful, but she had no clear prescription for me other than loosen up a bit and try asking more questions in class. Her visit so stunned me that it has stuck with me ever since, and she is the only undergraduate from my Cornell teaching days with whom I still keep in touch. (She now owns her own small law firm in New York City.)

A second potential rescuer was William Foote Whyte, who was putting together his Human Affairs Program (HAP) that sent students out into the community to do fieldwork and public service. Through the HAP, my students did fieldwork-based term papers, rather than library papers. The HAP administrators did most of the initial contact work, but I also had to work with the voluntary associations and public agencies in which my students did their research, and I also had to meet fairly frequently with students to iron out problems. Fieldwork study was the most successful component of my undergraduate classes and is the only innovation I remember from those days that I've kept in my contemporary courses. Even though my own MA thesis at Michigan was based on participant observation, I never tried to turn any of the student projects into joint research that I could have written up. The idea occasionally occurred to me, but I didn't know how to follow through.

Nonetheless, despite these hopeful experiences, I was still floundering. My ignorance of the fundamentals of good teaching was compounded by my total absorption in the publishing game. I simply had no time, or so I thought, to figure out what I was doing wrong and fix it. Indeed, except for the severe alienation I felt from my teaching, I was enjoying myself. My research was going extremely well. I designed and carried out several large-scale surveys during my first few years at Cornell, and much of my time was spent in the field or at the computer center, collecting or analyzing data. I can't recall even imagining a link between what I was doing in the classroom and what I was doing in my research.

My colleagues didn't help. Many of my senior colleagues were quite cynical about the teaching process—William Foote Whyte stands out as a clear exception—and spent much of their time denigrating the undergraduate students. We had an Office of Resident Instruction, but its purpose was to keep records and counsel students on how to get jobs after they left Cornell. I don't recall anyone in a position of authority ever talking with me about teaching, good or bad. By contrast, my research was going incredibly well, and funding supplied by the ILR School allowed me to collect data for several projects.

To spare the reader further agony, I've kept my catalog of teaching woes rather short, but there is no escaping one obvious conclusion: The promise, if not the hope, of my undergraduate days had become a distant memory. Intellectual arrogance, lack of a support system, and a reward system totally focused on research and publication rather than on teaching were about to consign me to the massed ranks of lousy teachers. Fortunately, my story has a third chapter.


## Redemption

Should my tale end as a tragedy? I have painted a nearly unrelenting picture of my unreflexive obedience to a mode of teaching that was taking me nowhere. When opportunities came my way for possible changes in course, I let them slip through my fingers. And yet, I would never have accepted the challenge of being included in this book had matters not taken a turn for the better. Be forewarned, then; you are reading yet another example of selection bias in the literature on academic life. Scholars who go into their retirements living fragmented rather than integrated lives don't usually bother to record their misery. And misery is exactly what lay in store for me, had the teaching muse not begun to smile on me about 15 years ago. Thus, let me complete the third part of my tale; I've chosen the term *redemption* because of its deliberately ambiguous stance regarding agency. I can't claim to have pulled myself up by my own bootstraps, nor can I point decisively to any particular person or event that altered my course. Nonetheless, over that decade and a half, I became increasingly aware that things were getting better.

Cornell was not an unrelieved disaster on the teaching front for me. Several things happened that made quality teaching more salient to me: (a) dealing with renewal and promotion decisions and (b) designing new courses.

First, curiously enough, helping decide tenure cases made me reflect on the nature of public universities and what we owe our students. The ILR School, as a public college within a private university, occupied a rather ambiguous place in the ivory tower of the Ivy League. Elite status seemed to require low teaching loads and small classes for faculty so that they could get on with their important research, but public funding seemed to require some acknowledgment that many students were the first in their families to attend college and that the state was expecting some public service activities from the universities' land grant status. In debates over what standards to use in tenure cases, quantity/quality of publications dominated discussion, reducing talk of teaching competence to a whisper. Certainly, we carried out no systematic evaluations of teaching prowess for tenure decisions.

Second, because the administrative structure of the school was rather loose, faculty initiative played a large part in getting new courses onto the books. Accordingly, I was able to propose and teach a few courses for which I had no substantive preparation but a great deal of intellectual interest. Jane Weiss, a close friend who'd coauthored several papers with me, suggested I teach a course on World Systems Theory to follow up some ideas we'd worked on. I recruited a graduate student in geography for assistance, as well as the help of scholars in a few other upstate New York universities. I discovered that getting in over my head, acknowledging that fact, and asking other people for help can be a lot more fun than teaching the same old stuff over and over again.

The winter of 1982 marks the first time I was fully aware that I had become more concerned about teaching. The University of North Carolina had approached me about a possible job and invited me to make a visit to Chapel Hill. For reasons I cannot fully explain, I requested that I be allowed to visit several classes taught by senior professors. I recall only one clear motive: I was very concerned about the quality of students in North Carolina and whether they would measure up to the students I'd taught at Cornell. (Discerning readers will be thinking about the obvious asymmetry in the situation; my potential employers probably ought to have asked *me* to teach a class or two so that they could see whether I measured up *their* standards!) I think the department had never had such a request, but once they got over the shock, they sent me to two senior professors' classes. That was when another shock of recognition dawned on me: I had never sat in on any senior professors' classes at Cornell! Although neither of the men whose class I visited was a spellbinding lecturer, the confidence they exuded was mesmerizing, their students seemed competent, and I was convinced. I took the job.

In my new environment, I discovered that my department was one of the first in the country to offer a full-fledged graduate course on teaching. All graduate students who wished to teach their own courses first had to take a semester-long course on teaching methods. The course was pioneered by Ev Wilson, and I read his book (Goldsmid & Wilson, 1980) on teaching during my first winter in Chapel Hill. I began using some of the ideas he proposed, and I also began subscribing to the American Sociological Association's *Newsletter on Teaching* (since upgraded to a regular journal). I began experimenting in my classes with more in-class exercises and discussions and much sketchier lesson plans. I no longer walked into the classroom with my lecture already written out. Instead, following suggestions I had read in Goldsmid and Wilson and in other articles on teaching, I prepared discussion questions and general points I wanted to make. I began to understand the wisdom of the teaching tactics my wife had been telling me about and adapted them for my own classes.

After several years in my new department, I was asked to take over the teaching seminar that Ev Wilson had begun. In retrospect, that assignment was a rite of passage for me because I then had to take seriously my responsibility in helping educate future generations of teachers. Luckily, previous instructors in the course left me a strong legacy, and the university's new Center for Teaching and Learning (CTL) was looking for clients. In the first years of that course, Ed Neal, of the CTL, did many guest stints until I had the confidence to handle such topics as syllabus preparation, testing and grading, and instructor evaluation on my own. Colleagues in other departments who also cared about teaching quality set up "home and away" guest lectures with me. I talked about such things as constructing classroom exercises from an active learning point of view, in exchange for their doing sessions on educational psychology or leading good discussions.

My research interests also changed during this time; I became much more interested in human resource management practices, especially in business start-ups. Team-oriented practices were increasingly recommended to managers interested in unleashing employees' creativity, and many of the recommendations resonated well with developments in collaborative and cooperative learning. One great irony in my change of heart was that, in all my years at the ILR School, I had never seen the connection between employee participation schemes and active learning in the classroom. Now, as I read more about active learning schemes, I finally realized the generic principles underlying the "new" human resource management orientation and the "new" methods of teaching.

My students and colleagues helped me realize that I was putting into practice a central tenet of the "active learning" teaching philosophy: An instructor doesn't *teach* people anything; they have to *learn* it for themselves. I also began developing a position on the integration of teaching into one's career that has become a mantra for me in my class and in discussions with colleagues; namely, being an academic, even in the most prestigious, big-time research university, requires that most of us *teach* to earn a living. And if that's all that teaching is—meeting one's obligations to one's employer—then a faculty member is in for a long and bitter journey. People can fool themselves in the short term into thinking that the trade-off is worth it—tolerance of bad teaching so that one's real job is supported—but can the delusion be carried on over a lifetime?

I tell my students they should look around at senior professors who obviously teach with no joy and who scheme for ways to get out of the classroom. "Can you imagine a life like that?" "Wouldn't it be better to find ways to teach well and be rewarded for it, if nowhere else than in your own psyche?" Rewards from teaching flow on a different schedule than those from research and publishing; they come more quickly and more frequently! Thus, finding ways to actually enjoy teaching is, in a sense, a way of diversifying the sources of satisfaction we receive from our activities. Why settle for positive feedback that arrives only a few times a year, in printed form, when every class day can be a rewarding one?

When people complain about not being rewarded for efforts spent on teaching, my immediate response is always, "Good teaching is its own reward." I mean that a person's self-worth and sense of efficacy are bound up in what that person does for a living, and teaching consumes a large part of an academic's job, no matter how much he or she tries to escape it. Years of falling down on the job will take their toll, and that's no way to live.

## The Future

In addition to the new university environment at North Carolina that enabled me to throw off the inertia of my old ways, I have spent much more time overseas since the mid-1980s. Many of my overseas trips involve giving lectures or seminars to graduate and advanced undergraduate students, rather than to just other scholars. I find that having to explain myself in another culture poses a fundamental challenge of the taken-for-granted assumptions I have made about the way people learn. I work to get "local color" into my seminars, and I try to set aside time at the beginning of each overseas assignment to learn more about what students are looking for in the classes.

I regularly give seminars in Western Europe and have begun teaching in Japan. One of the most satisfying aspects of these ventures is my discovery that many of the active-learning strategies I use in the United States also work well in other countries. Team work assignments work well everywhere, so far, because they allow students to learn in their own language by talking with one another. Rather than have them listen to me for an entire period, I turn over responsibility for learning to the students, and they usually rise to the challenge. Indeed, I think the principle of *learning in their own language* applies not just to instruction in other countries but also to teaching in our native tongue. Students should be able to link what they are studying to examples from their own experiences, as well as to other course work. Thus, by teaching overseas, I have learned something about why active learning works in the United States!

Has my research become more closely connected to my teaching? Yes, directly and indirectly. *Directly* because I am now studying human resource management practices in new, small firms, where teamwork, motivation, and rapid skill acquisition are essential for business survival. Many of the practices I use in teaching have direct analogies to the practices found in growing firms. *Indirectly* because I am offered many opportunities to conduct research overseas through the seminars I offer. I discover a great deal about the flaws in my research designs and conceptualizations by trying to explain them to skeptical local students!

At last, more than three decades after starting college as an undergraduate, I can understand and appreciate those excellent teachers I had in my pre-graduate days. I think I can also now understand why they lived and taught as they did and why they had such a major impact on me. Although it took me more than a decade, I now see where I stand in the teaching lineage begun by those people. I'm doing what I can to pass on what I've learned about teaching to my graduate students and to my junior faculty colleagues. I must confess, though, I've just about given up on my senior colleagues, but that's another story.

## References

Bloom, A. D. (1987). *The closing of the American mind*. New York: Simon & Schuster.

Goldsmid, C. A., & Wilson, E. K. (1980). *Passing on sociology: The teaching of a discipline*. Belmont, CA: Wadsworth.

Sykes, C. J. (1988). *Profscam: Professors and the demise of higher education*. Washington, DC: Regnery Gateway.

# 3 Teaching and Research

*A Puzzling Dichotomy*

BARBARA A. GUTEK

For me, teaching and research have always been inexorably linked, and I cannot conceive of them in any other way. Thus, the current debate about research *versus* teaching—as if they were an either/or dichotomy—has me somewhat puzzled. Looking back on my career, I now think that when I started teaching, I viewed it as primarily a way to explain research to others. Once I started reading journal articles, it was abundantly clear to me that research findings would never be disseminated to the public through journals—nor were they ever intended to do that. They are too dull, boring, tedious, and difficult to understand for anyone not trained in research. As I learned a bit about the media, I became increasingly skeptical about their interest in conveying the results of research, at least in the areas in which I do research. But teaching presented real possibilities as a way to inform young minds about the progress being made on the research front. My views about the role and purpose for teaching have changed, but only recently. I am not sure I would have made any changes in thinking about research if I had not moved from psychology to a management department in the business school and become head of the department. But perhaps I would have—primarily because postsecondary training and education and universities themselves are changing. I now worry that the wonderful interplay of teaching and research is being threatened by changes in higher education. But I am getting ahead of myself in this story.

## How I Got Started

The first class I taught was at a community college after I had received my bachelor's degree. I was so proud of being able to teach in college that I did not bother to calculate my hourly wage until I had finished the course. (It was about $1.14 per hour!) I was puzzled when someone asked why people older than I was at the time would take a psychology class from me. What could they learn from me, this person asked, as they had lived longer than I had? Clearly, she and I had different views of learning psychology. She thought that psychology was one's accumulated experience with people and was learned by living; I thought that psychology was the sum of all the exciting research findings I had been learning about and that teaching psychology was a way of disseminating the results and conclusions of research.

I knew that I really loved doing research after I carried out a first research project as an undergraduate student at the University of Michigan at Flint, where research was not a high-status activity—or if it was, I never noticed. When I began graduate school in 1972, I felt honored to be able to do research at the Institute of Social Research at Michigan. I had already read many research monographs produced by scholars at the institute, and I was thrilled to be a part of the research enterprise that was the institute. I supported myself and my two preschool children by working with Dan Katz and Bob Kahn on a national sample survey of people's experiences with government bureaucracies (Katz, Gutek, Kahn, & Barton, 1975). As I look back, it is clear to me that my first interest in graduate school at the University of Michigan in the mid-1970s was research, not teaching.

In 1974, Jean Campbell, then the director of the Center for Continuing Education of Women (CEW) at the university, asked me to organize the literature on nontraditional careers for women by teaching a course on the topic. I enthusiastically accepted the offer. Thus, I started working in the area for which I am best known—women and work—by teaching a course on that subject, not by doing research. Of course, the course heavily relied on research, and subsequently as I have taught variations on this course for undergraduates and Ph.D. students, I have continued to rely heavily on research. I have always believed that any subject, even a controversial one, is amenable to research. In fact, research is especially important in controversial areas where opinions are typically strong and ideologically based and are often supported by firsthand experience or hearsay but not by research results. Research is what allows us to separate myth from fact, and it provides a solid basis for action.

As I put together the course, I read many research findings. At that time, I did not know how to put together a course syllabus in a new area except to go to the research literature. How could a nonresearcher even put together a course? I now know that many texts are not particularly research based and that textbooks containing information contrary to what we know from research are not uncommon.

Teaching is one way to start a new area of scholarship. Once I had put together the material for my course on women in nontraditional careers in the mid-1970s, I thought I might do more with the material. At the same time, Veronica Nieva, who was also finishing her Ph.D. at the University of Michigan, had also culled the research literature for articles for a course she co-taught with an attorney on women, work, and the law. As it turned out, she and I had uncovered many studies, but our combined list was reasonably impressive. So, we decided to write a book, a project that turned out to be considerably more work than either of us anticipated. The book was published in 1981 as *Women and Work: A Psychological Perspective.*

## A Developing Philosophy of Teaching

By the time I completed graduate school, I had developed an approach to teaching in which research served as a cornerstone: I believed that teaching was a means of disseminating research findings, that one could not teach a subject without knowing (and preferably doing) research in the area, and that teaching was a good way to stay current in an area of research. Content was clearly more important than process. I now think this philosophy of teaching was tied to my understanding of the twin roles of universities—to teach students and to generate new knowledge—which I viewed as interdependent, not independent, endeavors. This philosophy of the interplay between teaching and research that I developed in graduate school came with me when I started teaching and doing research at UCLA in 1976. I gave much thought to *what* to teach and almost no thought to *how* to teach. I spent much time finding studies I thought would appeal to students and ones they could readily understand and even replicate, in part or whole. For graduate students, I tried to find studies that embodied areas of research and were seminal or otherwise influential in their field. I explained how bodies of research develop, providing "family trees" of researchers (e.g., in the case of social motives, achievement motivation, and fear-of-success). Or, I provided a social context for understanding why a body of research develops at a particular time (e.g., the role of the women's movement in the development of research on sex discrimination, the role of the civil rights movement on the development of research on race discrimination). Or, I provided a geographic context for understanding a body of research (e.g., research on realistic job previews was done in Michigan near the automobile plants that, in the 1970s, experienced high turnover among new factory workers). When I read something new and interesting, I wanted to teach it, and that was true whether the students were Ph.D. candidates or undergraduates. I wanted students to get the same information I had (even when they didn't want it). Because I wanted to teach the latest thing that interested me, I was always changing courses. Until recently, when I began questioning my own teaching, I could not imagine having a set package of notes I would use over and over. Because I hated to leave anything out, my syllabi tended to become cluttered with too much material, and I typically assigned too much reading.

Looking back on my teaching, I realize just how much my approach to teaching was formed by my first teaching experience. I was asked to organize a body of literature by teaching a course. There were no textbooks, no readily identified body of literature, and no agreed-on set of topics that constituted the course I was going to teach. For better or worse, I tend to approach all courses in this same way. Even when there are hundreds of textbooks and a myriad of instructor's aids such as test banks, prepared overheads, packaged exercises, and videos, I have never used any of these. I can never find a package that agrees with me; I rarely even adopt a textbook, although I will use one on occasion. More often, using a textbook means cutting back on the original research I want covered or glossing over the work of particular scholars whose research and theories I wish to cover in depth. This approach to teaching—reviewing and summarizing a body of research— has been useful to me, and until recently, I believed it was useful and productive for students too. More on that later.

Because I focus on research, I do not like case teaching. Ideas have always seemed more useful to me than particular situations or dilemmas. I might quibble with the popular interpretation of Kurt Lewin's famous dictum "There's nothing so practical as a good theory" as it applies to research, but I genuinely believe it when it comes to teaching. Abstractions are so useful because they are generalizable; because they apply to many situations, teaching theory and concepts constitutes a parsimonious way of teaching. Professors can cover much more material by relaying concepts and abstractions to students that students could then apply to situations, as they deemed appropriate, than by focusing on particular situations.

Concepts and theories by themselves, however, are not sufficient. Research findings play several important roles in teaching. First, they support the utility of the concepts and theories that are presented. Second, empirical research is important to help persuade people of reality. It can help them get out of a set frame. Especially when I teach about gender issues, students often do not accept theories without research support. (Even then, they often prefer to stick with strongly held beliefs.) Third, they teach people to think critically about information presented to them and especially to question personal experience and anecdote as methods of learning. Personal experience, despite its vividness and salience, is not sufficient to understanding the world. If it were, a college education would not be so important. Furthermore, we can never replay an experience, can never be another person in the same experience. I often ponder how some particular experience would be different if I were male instead of female, African American instead of European American, 6' 3" instead of 5' 3", or 50 pounds overweight instead of within the recommended weight range. Likewise, my experience working with people who are on corporate boards and policy-making groups for professional organizations and universities has given me a keen understanding of the differing perspectives one has from the top versus the bottom, where so many of us started. I believe that, by exposing students to research, they will be able to draw on that research and thus temper and balance the role of personal experience in making inferences and drawing conclusions about the world in which they live.

Compared with many of my colleagues, I seem to make a lot of changes in course content, and so I have asked myself why I keep redoing classes so much, why I don't rely more on material that others have spent considerable time preparing, such as test banks, exercises, and overheads. I don't know whether it is a good answer, but the one I generated is that it seems as if I am shortchanging the students by not covering material I know and instead covering material someone else knows. It seems to me that students have some right to access the expertise of the professors whose classes they take. Thus, professors should convey their special and unique knowledge to students while adequately covering a body of knowledge encompassed by the title of the course. The same course taught by two professors will be a little different, not only because they use different teaching styles but also because they cover somewhat different material to take into account the topics each knows in detail.

## What Has Changed

The model of teaching I have described is based on an assumption of the professor as expert, with content being more important than the process of teaching. Professors pick the research they do (within limits), and that research is the basis for courses they teach. Students will be best served by learning what professors have studied. I believe that this approach has considerable merit, but it is far from perfect. It may not always meet the needs of students, and it often does not meet their expectations. From my vantage point in a College of Business and Public Administration, it is clear that the majority of our students are primarily interested in obtaining a job (rather than or in addition to obtaining an education). They view college as an investment in their economic future, they have some clear ideas about what they think they need to know to make themselves marketable, and knowledge of research plays a very small role in that knowledge. I have a lot of sympathy for today's students: Tuition rates have increased dramatically in the past two decades, and the quality and number of jobs available to the average new graduate seem to be going down. Colleges and universities have, it seems to me, gladly accepted the role of adding economic value to students in addition to or in place of educating them, and it is becoming difficult to deliver on that role. In the meantime, tuition continues to climb even though the payoff—a good job leading to a remunerative career—cannot be ensured. In the process, universities seem to be changing from primarily providing a broad education to primarily providing vocational training that has an economic payoff to its graduates. Not surprisingly, many students seem to stay in college until an attractive job possibility appears. What is the point of staying if one's goal—getting a good job—has been achieved?

An additional change is that the professor-as-expert model is under attack today from several quarters. Professors, along with other professionals (notably, physicians and attorneys), are increasingly viewed as more concerned with enhancing their own careers and incomes rather than with educating students. (Newt Gingrich [1995, chap. 4] is one such critic.) We are in danger of being viewed as dinosaurs who have outlived our usefulness, hopelessly outdated, teaching things that are not useful. It seems to me that many students are looking to their current employer and anticipating what a future employer will want, rather than trusting their professors to provide them with the knowledge to prepare them for life, including work life. Many students seem to believe that employers view work experience—any kind of work experience—as equally or more valuable than course work. Thus, many students hold jobs while they are full-time students. At the University of Arizona, over 80% of undergraduates are employed. Although many of them need to hold jobs to survive, others do so because they do not want to look like slackers and/or they think it will enhance their job prospects after they graduate. These additional reasons for having a job undermine any incentive to live more frugally in order to devote more time to academic progress. Furthermore, they help undermine or devalue the student role. When I asked each student in an undergraduate honors course earlier this year to tell whether he or she was employed and what kind of work he or she did for how many hours, the 2 students (out of 16 honors students) who were not employed appeared apologetic as several of their classmates teased them with comments like "Slacker!" and "Get a job!" And when graduate students and I surveyed Arizona students about several matters (as part of a graduate course on survey research methods), those students who were employed reported that having a job was an important source of self-esteem and that having a job seemed to contribute more to their self-esteem than being a student. The "just being a student" phenomenon reminded me of an earlier generation of women who apologized for "just being a housewife," as though that role alone was no longer sufficient to justify one's existence.

In addition, the public view of research itself seems to be undergoing a change. Research seems to be increasingly viewed as the esoteric and trivial pursuits of professors that are a considerable cost to overburdened taxpayers. There is some truth to this allegation. One negative effect of such a view is an increasing distrust of research itself by university students. Perhaps, we in academia facilitate the discrediting of research by being too narrow, too aloof, and too arrogant, although faculty are not wholly at fault. The cooptation of the research process and "data" by private interests to push particular ideologies or products probably contributes to public cynicism about research (see Crossen, 1994, for many examples, such as the infamous "research" taste-test battle between Coca-Cola and Pepsi-Cola, in which both sides argued that research data supported their product, a situation that often exists in more serious, academic research as well).

These trends—university education as investment in one's economic future, less reliance on professors to define and provide what students need to know, a devaluation of the student role, and a cynical view of research—(along with many other changes occurring in academia today) spell trouble for the academic enterprise as it has been practiced for the last 50 years or so, since the end of World War II.


## And the Future?

Today, I am changing my teaching, and I think teaching in general is changing as higher education is itself changing. Two very different events have made me rethink both the content and the process of teaching. Ironically, perhaps, one of them was becoming a department head in a business school. Through that role, I realized just how much the student experience has changed over the past several decades, in addition to changes in students' expectations. Whereas I recall taking just about any course I wanted to take with minimal requirements and prerequisites, students today at large universities have a daunting array of required courses, general education courses, prerequisites, and the like; and because not all the courses are available when students need them, students are not always able to graduate in 4 years. Meeting all the requirements in the time frame they have set for themselves (or until an attractive job emerges) preoccupies students to a much greater extent than when I was a student. As department head, I have worked to change the curriculum so that our majors have more exposure to the areas of expertise of the faculty, but many students have come to expect a uniform product from each faculty member teaching a class, and they seem to have little knowledge about or interest in special areas of expertise of the faculty.

I also realized, somewhat belatedly, I'm afraid, that teaching in a business school is not like teaching in psychology in that management is not simply the sum of research findings on the topic of management or organizational behavior or even gender and organizations. Students expect a "turnkey" education when they major in business (they expect to learn whatever they will need to know to start managing in an organization). They want prescriptions as much as or more than the descriptions provided by research findings. Research findings are a small part of what they find useful; current organizational practices, in contrast, loom large in importance. Furthermore, I believe that students are not the only ones to have these beliefs. Films provide one example: The films I remember both seeing and using in psychology 10 to 20 years ago featured prominent researchers explaining and illustrating psychological principles important for child rearing, for the workplace, and the like. Today, films about organizational behavior feature practices and procedures of firms, and if an expert is featured, he or she is likely a manager of a large corporation or a consultant. Rarely are professors and/or their research featured.

In response to these concerns and changes, I tried something entirely different this past year. In an undergraduate course on the legal, political, and social environment of business, I divided the class into two companies—General Motors and McDonald's—and covered various issues by comparing and contrasting these two companies. These were not case studies: Students were responsible for finding most of the information about each firm's history, current operations and standard operating procedures, and human resources. One of the most intriguing issues posed to the class was the following: Why is the pay of the production workers at GM about $18.50 per hour (plus generous fringe benefits), whereas the pay for production workers at McDonald's is minimum wage (with virtually no fringe benefits)? Although the course needs a lot of work and it departs dramatically from the class-as-research-story approach, I like the format. What students learn, however, is quite different from what they learn in my research-oriented classes. They get very little exposure to research, although they have ample opportunity for critical thinking—one of the skills I believe is developed by including research in the classroom. The class also sensitized me to just how much I don't know about organizations by knowing organizational research.

The second event that made me rethink my own teaching is, not surprisingly, an abstraction—this one, a perspective I have recently developed (Gutek, 1995). Several years ago, I had a real aha! experience, an insight into the ways interaction between a provider and a recipient of services or goods is structured. Here is the gist of it: In the distant past, recipients (or customers) received almost all their goods and services in "relationships"; that is, they received a particular kind of service or goods from a regular provider with whom they shared a history and expected to interact in the future. But today, more and more services and goods are dispensed in "encounters," wherein a customer sees a different provider, one of a group of functionally equivalent interchangeable providers, each time he or she seeks the same kind of service or goods. Having a regular hairstylist versus going to a walk-in chain salon or having a regular family physician versus going to the emergency room or student health center for medical care are examples of the distinction between the two ways customers and providers can interact. In my book, I argue that, increasingly, services are offered in encounters and that encounter systems are growing rapidly for a variety of reasons.

I believe that higher education is not immune to this trend, that higher education systems are increasingly moving in the direction of encounter systems to save costs and to compete with a variety of purveyors of adult education: corporate training firms, for-profit "universities," corporation-sponsored higher education, and soon, communication and other companies that are creating attractive multimedia "learning experiences." Encounter systems, in general, offer a uniform product, typically at the customer's convenience. Most important, each provider is expected to be functionally equivalent. Thus, a customer should be able to complete a satisfactory service transaction with any of a number of interchangeable providers. In buying a hamburger at McDonald's, getting a driver's license, ordering airline tickets from an airline reservation center, going to the emergency room or some HMOs to receive medical care, or going to a chain salon for a haircut, each time you get a different service provider; but in principle, it doesn't make any difference which one you get because all are supposedly trained to provide the same service. Furthermore, process or style of delivery supplants expertise as a key factor in evaluating the service. In relationships, customers or clients seek services from a provider because of his or her expertise (regardless of whether that expertise is hairstyling, medical care, or advice on graduate research). In encounters, in contrast, providers (who, in theory, do not differ in expertise because they are expected to be functionally equivalent) are evaluated by their delivery style. Are they courteous, friendly, engaging, entertaining? Do they deliver service promptly at a time convenient to the customer?

To the extent that the public and undergraduate students view faculty as interchangeable providers of service rather than as unique repositories of knowledge and to the extent that they evaluate delivery process as more important than content of the material covered, higher education can be expected to increasingly resemble the mass production of services characteristic of encounter systems. Being considered interchangeable will spell bad news for faculty, but will it spell equally bad news for students? I'm not so sure. In an elegant essay, Abbott (1988) argued that professionals could lose their "professional" position in the workforce, in part, because they have withdrawn from the clients they are intended to serve. The highest status often accrues to those who do not interact with customers directly, but who instead create knowledge or serve as consultants to other professionals who interact directly with customers. This is true of many professions, including medicine and higher education (see also Gutek, 1995, chaps. 5 and 11).

Certain aspects of higher education and training are beginning to resemble encounter systems. In many large public universities, students spend their first 2 years or so in classes of hundreds of students, and they may interact with one or more professors, lab assistants, teaching assistants, and/or study section leaders. They may receive advising from whomever is on duty that day and interact with dozens of people in financial services and other departments within the university. In short, many never establish a relationship with even a single professor. Although I am not convinced that this state of affairs is necessarily disastrous for students or higher education in general, I am not prepared to accept it wholeheartedly either.

Other innovative organizations competing with traditional university education have developed other aspects of encounter systems. For example, the University of Phoenix, which is a for-profit institution having more than 24 campuses throughout the country, relies on a bare-bones administration as full-time employees. "Faculty" are all contract workers, paid on a piece-rate (per course) basis. They are eligible to teach on the basis of their demonstrated teaching style, whereas expertise is assumed on the basis of reaching an educational threshold (a master's degree in some cases, a doctoral degree in others). This is in contrast to traditional universities, where ability to teach is assumed and hiring is based on demonstrated (not assumed) research ability.

I still believe that teaching and research are interdependent endeavors, not independent ones, and I see some dangers in separating them more than they are today. I am particularly fond of the research side of academia. But, I also believe that perhaps we have developed the research side much more than the teaching side. Not only do research methods and research topics change, but so do students and teaching methods. Not only is higher education being forced to face competition from private research firms and corporate research labs, but we are also facing competition on the teaching front. If we do not deliver the relationship between professors and students that has been the model of higher education for decades or deliver encounters in a way that is competitive with for-profit colleges, training firms, and others, public support for research universities may continue to decline and students may take their tuition dollars elsewhere—for example, to educational institutions having liberal admissions criteria and little bureaucratic hassle while offering classes at their corporation at a convenient time.

The University of Arizona, like many other universities, is betting heavily on new technology to improve students' experiences, but I am skeptical. If students no longer learn about research findings and the unique, informed perspectives of dedicated scholars in the classroom, they will be less educated, I believe, and we will have lost one of the most important ways of disseminating research results to a broad audience. This failure to learn about research being conducted in universities is particularly important because much of the research that is being done today is done in corporate laboratories or contract research firms. Privately funded research findings, if they are disseminated at all, are disseminated through news releases and advertising (see Crossen, 1994); furthermore, few researchers doing contract research have time to publish their findings in peer-reviewed journals. We and our students do not have much exposure to this body of research. But our students do have exposure to the research that is done in academia, and I hope this exposure makes them somewhat more critical judges of research findings as reported in advertisements and the popular press. Faculty and students both benefit, I think, by having research findings and the research process explained in the classroom, and I hope that point does not get lost in the current wave of enthusiasm to make universities more student-friendly.

## References

Abbott, A. (1988). *The system of professions: An essay on the division of expert labor*. Chicago: University of Chicago Press.

Crossen, C. (1994). *Tainted truth: The manipulation of fact in America*. New York: Simon & Schuster.

Gingrich, N. (1995). *To renew America*. New York: HarperCollins.

Gutek, B. A. (1995). *The dynamics of service: Reflections on the changing nature of customer/provider interaction*. San Francisco: Jossey-Bass.

Katz, D., Gutek, B. A., Kahn, R. L., & Barton, E. (1975). *Bureaucratic encounters*. Ann Arbor: University of Michigan, Institute for Social Research.

Nieva, V. F., & Gutek, B. A. (1981). *Women and work: A psychological perspective*. New York: Praeger.

# 4 If It's Not Teaching and Research, What Is It?

RAE ANDRÉ

Circa 1905, Great Aunt Ida was the teacher in a one-room school-house in Kansas. One snowy afternoon, she left school to ride home and was caught in a blizzard. As the story goes, the people near school thought she was safe at home, and the people at home thought she was safe at school. She spent the night out in the storm under her horse.

Being caught between teaching and research is a lot like being caught in the blizzard. You can get awfully cold out there, wondering why you're neither here nor there, thinking about whether you will survive the night. From the beginning of my career, I have believed that the modern intellectual convention (and practical realities) of separating teaching and research and describing our professional lives primarily in these terms is alienating.

Academics do not do teaching and research. At least, I hope we don't. These are but the superficial conceptualizations of our professional selves, of our thoughts and ideals and skills. No, what we do is deeper and more complex: We search for truth (in my case, about human behavior in organizations), we push for intellectual innovation, we share our truths and innovations with particular audiences, and we create environments that enhance learning. This is much more exciting and more involving and more relevant than mere teaching and research.

Of course, the traditional practice of cleaving our professional lives in two has evolved for a number of sensible, practical reasons. First, the words *teaching* and *research* do convey a rough sense of our primary audiences (we teach our students, we research for our peers). Second, the words are a convenient shorthand for our behavior. What we do on a daily basis is stand up before audiences and profess (we teach), and then we spend quiet time discovering, organizing, and committing our ideas to print (we do research). Third, we believe (or at least we acquiesce in the belief of our institutional leaders) that success in teaching and research is measurable. Although there are difficulties in such measurements, the alternatives may be worse (assuming that we maintain a competitive system of evaluation): Try measuring who is doing the "best" at telling the truth or at creating environments that enhance learning!

At the same time, using the teaching-research dichotomy to describe our work has created problems. First, it minimizes what we do in terms of complexity, ideals, and impact. It is a simplistic categorization, even an anti-intellectual view, of an intellectual pursuit. Continuing to rely on it suggests our own failure to communicate the complexities of what we do to the world beyond academe.

Second, in the profession at large, the words connote an unfortunate status bias, with teachers and teaching being ranked below researchers and writing. This perception may, in part, be a matter of class. In Western cultures, the upper class has always thought, read, and written, but it has seldom actually lowered itself to teach (Tolstoy notwithstanding). Producing intellectual work has been valued, whereas teaching it, aside from delivering the occasional invited lecture, has not. Perhaps, again, this is because, among the upper classes, leisure (or unscheduled time) has been more desirable than work (or scheduled time). Research is done on one's "own" time, whereas teaching requires conforming to an institution's schedule. Research suggests freedom and individuality, whereas teaching "someone else's ideas" suggests servitude and conformity.

Third, the teaching-research dichotomy today reveals who, in reality, we have become. It suggests how to succeed in the profession: Value research above teaching; produce one more piece of research regardless of whether it is innovative; and aim to score higher on teacher course evaluations regardless of whether the students learn more.

How did I get lost in this blizzard?

I hail from a long line of teachers and a short line of researchers. In addition to Great Aunt Ida, Great-Great Aunts Flo and Bess and Great-Great Grandmother Elizabeth were teachers in one-room schoolhouses of the frontier. Great Grandmother Birch journeyed by covered wagon from Kansas to Oklahoma to enter a land rush. There, she sold her Bible to buy a dictionary and, because the schools weren't good enough, led her family (including her husband, I am told) back again to Kansas. Her son, the family's first known researcher, was my grandfather Raymond R. Birch, a professor of veterinary medicine who made important contributions to the eradication of hog cholera and Bang's disease.

On the other side of the family, my Victorian grandparents were both in business. These grandparents went to school only through the eighth grade and then worked hard for many years; they emerged wealthy enough to send all five of their children through college and to pass on a company to the next generation.

I, the offspring of that next generation, am a TEACHER in a BUSINESS school. Some surprise!

If I, a professor, do not do teaching and research, what is it that I do? What is common to both teaching and research is the striving for truth and innovation in our field. What is different between them is they address different audiences through different modes.

For myself, a person who is excited by both teaching and research, my concerns are with truth, innovation, audience, and learning.


## Truth

In *Walden*, Thoreau wrote, "Rather than love, than money, than fame, give me truth" (1854, chap. 18, "Conclusion"). I have had this embroidered on a sampler in my home. Truth, like any other ethical concept, exists within a context. For Thoreau, an important form of truth was the sensual essence of living in the moment. Different people experience truth in different processes; one may find it in the scientific method, another in religious experience. Of course, a person may find different truths in more than one type of process.

As scholars, some of our notions of truth are embodied in our research methods. In the field of organizational behavior, for example, scholars respect the well-designed quantitative or qualitative study, and there is substantial convergence as to what is scientifically acceptable. Articles based on carefully honed theory are considered to be more important for career advancement than are books, which, it is argued, tend to be less grounded in the research of others and more loosely reasoned.

Truth is also a personal predilection. As an undergraduate, I weighed majors in psychology and English literature and took the latter. I had little notion of the real-world relevance of "all those rats," as I thought of psychology then, while in literature I was learning things that mattered to me, and I enjoyed the artistry of the language. Also, I had little idea of what I might do with a psychology degree. When I was choosing a major in 1964, college women were destined primarily to become teachers or nurses, and I wanted to get something practical out of my college education. I decided to get a credential to teach high-school English (which, in the end, I used for precisely 3 days of substitute teaching). A decade later, after a graduate degree in film studies and a few years making my living as an advertising writer/account executive in the film industry, I became restless with the subjective nature of literature and returned to psychology. Today, after 20 pleasant years imbued with a kind of truth based on psychology, I am drawn once more to the beauties and subtleties, the liveliness and holism, of literature.

I enjoy approaching reality wearing a variety of lenses. In recent years, I have had three long-term research projects in work simultaneously, each of which used a different approach to truth. One was my research on the design of economic development organizations, the most recent iteration having been based on a national database that took 2 years to assemble and from which I produced six articles on demographic representation and networking. I love mining these kinds of data; probing them for truth is an exploration akin to traveling in new places, searching for unique, unrecognized patterns of reality.

During the same time, a quite different project was my popular press book on solitude. It took 6 years to develop because my own life was the tutorial that suggested what topics to cover. I would experience an issue and then, using the frame of positive solitude rather than the more traditional frame of being in relationship, would work out how to deal with it. The book that emerged from this research has provided fresh insights that I and many appreciative readers live by every day.

The third simultaneous project has been my continuing work on intercultural negotiation and conflict. I am interested in understanding, from a psychological and social systems perspective, what creates bonds between people and what drives them into conflict. I have been learning and teaching on this topic for several years and really believe I am just beginning. One idea that has emerged is that people working in multicultural environments inevitably experience a kind of stress, which I call "diversity stress," and that part of creating effective multicultural organizations is understanding and managing this stress. So far, the new truth here has been in the naming, in identifying this phenomenon as discrete and important enough for us to pay attention to. I have published one academic article on this topic and am planning a book.

Each of these projects has used a different process of inquiry—data analysis, personal reflection, and theoretical speculation. On a daily basis, I enjoy working on several types of projects at once. Rotating among them is a mental refreshment, and I think I also accomplish more, or at least more that is interesting, than if I focus on one topic alone.

In addition, my work has always been interdisciplinary. Despite the annoyances of finding publication outlets for it and the time-consuming challenge of handling many points of view concurrently, for me the crucial connection between attending to real problems and doing research is clearer, the resulting work more instructive and accurate, when I view a problem from many perspectives. This unfortunate predisposition to be interdisciplinary emerged in my first book, which addressed quality of work life issues for homemakers. In the end, the project had three academic reviewers. As I recall, they were a sociologist, a psychologist, and an anthropologist. Or, maybe the anthropologist was an American studies specialist. Anyhow, I created the monster, and they read it, and they liked it, except that each one suggested I add more from his or her discipline (which I did, with a bit of difficulty). Fortunately, a few places (in this case, the University of Chicago Press) support such work. Likewise, before *Economic Development Quarterly* existed, my work on the design of economic development organizations fell between the two stools of business economics and public administration, and editors were hard-pressed to find a niche for it. I am enthusiastic about the newer and more experimental journals in our field today, which encourage a spectrum of academic theories and welcome the interdisciplinary thinker.

Who decides whether something is true? We academics tend to hold that truth is to be found somewhere in our peer review system, whereas in business schools we also give a nod to practitioners. In my writing, I have worked in a variety of forms—academic articles, popular articles, scholarly books, popular press books—and have found different audiences with different perspectives on truth in each. It is interesting to speculate what might happen if students or their parents were asked to review our academic work. Would they find it to be true for them? What would happen if we gave our work to CEOs or to union leaders? Writing for a variety of audiences keeps us on our intellectual toes; it makes us sensitive to the notion that truth is a negotiated reality.

Given these vagaries, it will not surprise you that I believe we academics have a responsibility to acquaint our students with a contextual view of truth. Certainly, when we are studying organizations, we are focusing on entities that are phenomonological along the crucial dimension of power, and we ourselves are also the embodiment of organizational power. What topics we teach and how we teach them matters immediately and centrally. For example, if we prepare students to critique business practices, rather than to learn business practices, we are molding their vision of the world. Or, if a businessperson tells us, as one told me at a recent conference, "You know what kind of help we need from you professors? We need you to improve our students' work ethic," we need to think deeply about the implications of this request. Why, exactly, should I do that? In a climate where corporations are seldom loyal to their employees, can I really justify telling my students that they should give their all to their companies? Or should I help them find some other sort of truth?

Certainly, power and values are spirits that energize—and haunt—our every classroom and our writing as well. We must acknowledge their presence.

## Innovation

I have a hunch that our field has an essential, defining problem: A lot of organizational behavior and theory has already been discovered.

It's right there in the textbooks, folks: the plethora and overlap of theories of motivation, the convergence of notions of leadership, the undying principles of group process, and the organizational designs of yesterday, today, and tomorrow. Will the phenomenon of groupthink be repudiated? Will the basic tenets of personality be overthrown? What are we teaching in organizational design—that an organic organization is a System 4 organization is a reengineered organization is a learning organization? Is there so much more out there that we can learn about these basic phenomena?

On a daily basis, I have to choose what to teach my students, I have real time constraints, and I have more than enough good material already for the basic courses, as does every experienced OB professor. I will add nuance, yes; detail, yes; basics, no. (Were I teaching in a doctoral program, that would be a different matter, of course, although the question of the ultimate audience—are we training doctoral students to teach undergrads and MBAs or each other?—remains.) Sure, there is great new stuff in *Academy of Management Review* and *Administrative Science Quarterly* and *American Psychologist* and so many other worthwhile journals. Just yesterday, I clipped three articles from *AMR* to read—one on organizational trust, one on the role of conversations in producing intentional change, and one explaining change in organizations. These articles will refine and influence my thinking. Yet, I do not have enough time to tell my students about a complicated model of organizational trust. I will not replace my effective unit on interpersonal communication with a complex, new set of ideas that would take at least 6 hours to teach. Every day, we teachers practice intellectual triage.

This problem is only going to get worse as, year after year, waves of graduate students and assistant professors hunt for paper topics on an increasingly well-worn path. Is this really a good use of valuable intellectual time and leadership?

Why do we do the article thing? Why do the numbers matter so much? And what happens after the article "game," as we all call it, is over? One reason is tenure and promotion. Good reason. Another is ego. A colleague once asked me enthusiastically, "So, who do you think is the greatest mind in our field today?" This was obviously a conversation he relished, whereas the answer in my own mind was, "Who cares?"

Doing minor work does not interest me. Deciding a professional pecking order does not interest me. What interests me is learning and teaching about how we can solve the plethora of problems in organizational life today. My view is not a rejection of research—far from it; rather, it is a call to rethink what sorts of research are responsible and useful.

As academics, we have the responsibility to call a new idea what is actually a new idea and to show the similarities behind ideas that are not actually innovations but rather are new vocabulary and modern examples of earlier thinking. We need to think more broadly about what kinds of research need doing. We should reexamine the content of our research in the light of the needs of our various audiences, with our students as a priority.

I admire the consistency of tenured professors who are still publishing in the academic journals. Their focus is rare enough. It seems that, after tenure, most professors move to doing consulting and writing books. If they remain active in the profession, they are drawn toward applied work, expansive work, lucrative work. Maybe they have something there. Leaving issues of income aside, I believe we need to create broader and deeper venues for intellectual life and expression that will hold people, not just through graduate school and the tenure process, but throughout their lives. Yet, I doubt that an apprenticeship devoted to writing articles is the best training one can have for the rest of one's career.

Our problem is really a wonderful opportunity. For one thing, it suggests that we might move more toward interdisciplinary thinking. For another, it suggests that we might move toward applying our knowledge and teaching our students how to apply it. We could think ever more seriously about validating consulting types of research, such as action research.

All my academic life, while I have been doing interdisciplinary work, I have also been writing about problem solving. In my first book, I tackled the work-life problems of 30 million women who had taken on homemaking as their primary occupation, and my students did interviews that changed their perceptions of their own lives. In my second book, I critiqued the flaws in a management theory that was widely discussed and perhaps practiced, and I did it in such a way that my critique would be read rather than shelved. In my third book, I wrote directly to people who contemplate personal solitude, bringing to them an integrated view of the existing research and some new ideas they could immediately apply. Also, my articles have usually had change in mind: Should small businesses and minorities get more involved in economic development? How can companies improve their training for international assignments?

Research has to have more impact. Although impact on other academics through basic research is important, our work should also be reviewed for classroom and organizational contribution. Meanwhile, we should honor the knowledge base that already exists, admitting that we already know some important stuff that isn't our own. We should assert that applying already existing theories to real-world problems may be just as important as putting our name on a new theory. Certainly, this assertion would make our field more relevant and perhaps more understood by the general public.

## Audience

All writing and speaking is teaching. All teaching is influence. Teaching is the act of convincing an audience to consider a point of view (if not to agree with it) and to learn a certain set of facts and/or ideas. *Teaching* is the buzzword for influencing students. *Research* is the buzzword for influencing colleagues.

Is there any wonder that students resist learning? Don't we all? As the lyrics to the Pink Floyd song "The Wall" suggest, students often regard education as useless and may consider it a form of "thought control." When I first heard these words, I was chilled by them. (I thought they heralded a loosening of the social ties of our democracy. I still do.) But, the students are correct about the purpose of education. The question is whether they can trust their teachers. To deny our influence is to deceive ourselves and our students. Instead, the responsible position is to describe it.

In becoming a professor of organizational psychology, I made distinct personal choices about influence. Having entered the graduate program in psychology at the University of Michigan with an interest in becoming a therapist, I became acquainted with this field called organizational psychology and decided that I could have more social impact working with organizations than with individuals. To my mind, organizations are where the action is. As someone (a Unitarian writer, if I recall correctly) has said, the measure of civilization is our ability to institutionalize humane values.

I also chose an egocentric versus an organocentric future for myself when I chose not to go to work for a particularly excellent corporation that, like most corporations, was clearly interested in my intelligence and knowledge rather than in my intellectual creativity and the expression of personal values. I don't kid myself that I today work for an organization that wants the latter either, but I have managed to put myself into the niche of academic freedom that suggests that who I am and what I teach are just as important as my abilities as a mental laborer. Academic institutions were designed to give us such choices, and we have a corresponding responsibility to serve our constituents there with the best education we can create. Teaching and research are two distinct modes of being. Teaching is analogous to being the general manager of an organization. On the one hand, I have to energize, motivate, and reward my students and to organize, direct, and strategize for my class. On the other hand, research requires a lot of concentration, contemplation, and solitude. It is not easy to find the love for both modes in the same person. Teachers must be involved in research to have a passion for their teaching, but the converse is not true. Researchers, like creative writers, may be passionately involved with their ideas, yet be content with reaching only a professional audience or even no audience at all.

For the teacher who is also a scholar, a crucial passage is finding one's voice. Where does the confidence to stand up in front of a class and say, "I know," come from? From direct experience? From "good" research? Or, simply, because we must do it because it is our job? Who am I that I have something true or worthwhile to teach? We should know what our own intellectual predilections and standards are and where they originated.

As a woman of my generation, I have had to make an explicit effort to claim my voice (see Gilligan, 1982). From overcoming the dictum not to concern myself with business in the first place, to figuring out how to take a leadership position in the field without being stigmatized as pushy, I, like all women, have been challenged in unique ways. No doubt, my respect for scientific approaches to management psychology and my strong desire to develop personal corporate experience derived, in part, from the need to establish credibility for my voice: Truth is always a friend of the less powerful.

We academics have the incredible privilege of being able to decide what research projects to work on and, within some limits, what topics and even what courses to teach. When my interest in international business grew out of my corporate experience of the 1980s, I created a new course—Managing People in International Settings—to frame the exploration, and when that interest developed into wanting to contribute to our understanding of conflict in multicultural organizations (to me, the essence of the diversity movement), I was able to create a course entitled "Intercultural Negotiation and Conflict." My research and teaching have complemented each other in both of these topic areas, although in both cases, the teaching came first: I developed the courses before I myself started to do research, a luxury I probably would not have had if I had been at a major research institution.

Likewise, my interest in economic development organizations came out of my experience of living in Flint, Michigan, during the 1981-1982 recession, watching the grocery stores close and observing the town fathers trying to deal with the crisis through an economic development policy that failed (the film *Roger and Me* had it right). When I have taught business policy, I have integrated this research there.

In short, I am my first audience. My work has life meaning for me in the sense that Victor Frankl described. In this, I am a very fortunate human being. It follows that who we are matters a great deal in what we teach our students. It matters that people bring different values to the classroom, that people choose different things to know (research) and to teach. It matters, and we should attend to our differences and how they affect our students.

My second audience is my students. I approach my students with an attitude of respect and love. They are my family in the manner suggested by Erich Fromm (1955, p. 362), who hoped that ties based on conscious relatedness may someday replace those of blood and soil. When my students are not learning, I am not happy.

My third audience for my ideas is my colleagues. It may sound condescending to say that we teach them, but that is, essentially, what we do through our research, presentations, and daily dialogue. Of course, a key question is whether our colleagues learn from us, and the answer is: only if they want to. Ideally, we are a community of scholars, a community of learners, but in my experience, colleagues seldom learn from each other. To learn from each other, we have to admit our own ignorance, and this is hard to do within systems that value knowing rather than learning, that celebrate experts rather than interactive teams, that are based on politics rather than on authentic process. The result is that we continue to reward what is measurable and to miss the interesting academic dialogue we yearn for. Yes, we do not practice what we preach.

I think we need to be frank with each other about who has been the target audience of our research. The primary audience has been other academics. They are, in fact, more than an audience; they are a constituency. We have assumed—and on the face of it, I would say it is generally true—that other academics are the best, if imperfect, judges of our research. They have the most commitment to the job of judging research—in contrast with practitioners, for example—and have more training than do students and practitioners. Yet, hoping that academics have the interests of students and practitioners at heart when they are doing research is like assuming that CEOs run their companies for the employees and stockholders.

We must always keep in mind that this academic audience defines truth rather narrowly and arbitrarily. Our field (OB) is dominated by 6 journals, for example. Contrast this with law, which has well over 100 journals. In our field, blind peer review by at least three reviewers is the norm. Contrast this with finance, in which the best journals typically send a piece out to one reviewer (commonly referred to as the person who "owns" the topic area), and we in OB seem positively democratic.

Understanding the business world is crucial to our profession, and I have personally made several career decisions (and some sacrifices) to get corporate experience. But we have to be careful about making business our target audience. Business isn't in my classroom every day, individuals are. Business isn't paying the tuition (interestingly, in France, it often does), parents and students are. Business doesn't always know what it wants and often doesn't have time to see the big picture. No, if there is any audience beyond my students, it is a multifaceted one: parents, society, businesses, non-profits, governments. I am not preparing my students for a job or even a career as much as I am preparing them to understand that society. I am not training them to fit in; I am educating them to understand their position in the world of organizations.

## Learning

My first book was an uncopyrighted work with an audience of two: At age 7, I wrote it to teach my twin brothers to read. I remember my thrill when they read it aloud, just as I remember the aha! experience when our collie learned at my hand to roll over. There was something truly delightful to me in these early experiences as a teacher, a delight that for me, still today, may be found just around the corner in any class. What is the nature of it, this "Hey, Mikey, he liked it!" effect? I think it is the elemental pleasure in connecting one on one with another learning being, an excitement about experiencing our mutual consciousness and aliveness. When an undergraduate student tells me, "Wow, this stuff on organizational design was great background for my job interview" (imagine that) or an accountant returning for his MBA tells me, "Gee, it is really interesting to learn that I am right-brained; now I know why I've always hated accounting!" I know why I am a teacher.

A colleague once asked me how I can stand to teach the same thing over and over, especially to undergraduates. Well, I don't teach the same thing over and over, year after year. But where there is repetition—and in my basic OB course there certainly is—I find that I simply have more mental time to pay attention to where the students are and to create the high I get when I realize they learn something. I imagine that an elementary school teacher must get her or his kicks the same way; it's not the material, it's the learning that counts.

This is not true for me in every class. Very often, I create new courses or new units in old courses, and in these instances it is indeed the material itself that captures me first. I imagine that having graduate students working with me on this kind of origination of ideas would be a lot of fun.

My research is an intense form of learning. I am constantly discovering new things in my research, and that is exciting. No one else knows it! I left graduate school with the full intention of keeping up on the literature in the field, and I admired one professor who kept "all the journals" neatly organized in his office. He was in cognitive psychology, not organizational psychology, so maybe that was a reasonable thing to do. But I soon found myself asking, "What field?" I found I had to specialize in my own research interests, and even then I could not keep up on all interesting developments. (Having only half a dozen top journals in the field does serve the humane purpose of reducing ambiguity to a tolerable level.) Beyond the journals, I keep up primarily by reading synthesizing kinds of works—leaning, for example, more toward *The Economist* and less toward *The Wall Street Journal*.

Lately, I have a strong desire to take my nose away from the grindstone of specificity and to let learning come more freely, to open myself to a broader range of inputs than only journal articles. In fact, I am planning my upcoming sabbatical around learning. First, I will spend 4 months in a very quiet place, reading broadly and writing. Then, I will be visiting at another university for 4 months, where I am "not teaching" (e.g., not scheduling time in a classroom, except for a few seminars), and again at least half my time will be spent in reading and writing and the other half in the congenial learning that comes from interacting with interesting colleagues in a different culture. (I am doing all this with the theme of intercultural negotiation and conflict in mind.)

I am learning a lot, too, from my new daughter, who is teaching me about human growth and learning—about the development of compassion, humor, and passion and about my own fear of failure in my connection with her. I am doing a bit more yoga, more staying in the present moment, more zen/unitarian/eastern explorations.

I used to attempt to make a class as comprehensive as possible, giving exams that required comprehensive knowledge; today, however, I strive to make a class as personal to students as possible so that they think about it, experience it, and integrate it according to their own ability to attend and to recall and to feel.

I think my involvement with my material models some good values: curiosity, steadiness, hard work, fun. It models integration of self and work, self and ideas, and such integration is central to learning. I think it is important to share with our students how we ourselves learn, to help them develop lifetime learning strategies. Not that I think mine have been particularly rich. I think I have not spent enough time learning. Were I to divide my life into producing, learning, and having fun, learning would be third on the list. (Well, maybe that's not all bad!) But life is annoyingly short: When I was about to enter Cornell as an undergraduate, I wrote out my ideal curriculum and it amounted to 7 years of study.

Fortunately for me, producing has involved a heavy component of learning. I would like to focus more on learning, to read more books and to listen more. I would wish the same for my students after they graduate, though I fear they will be as I have been for the last 20 years: busy.

## Learn This!

Truth . . . innovation . . . audience . . . learning. Think of these as the TRIAL of professing (sorry, it's my teacher gene), and you have one alternative to the teaching-research paradigm. If we used these categories to think about our work, wouldn't our dialogues be different? Wouldn't they be deeper, more complex, more holistic? To say nothing of more relevant?

They would also be more interpersonally difficult, and I'm not sure the profession could handle it. Our styles of discourse would have to be more participatory and supportive, more open to difference and diversity. We would have to be open to ambiguity rather than certainty, to collectivity rather than competition. This mode of thinking would challenge individuals. And it would challenge the existing hierarchy of schools: The notion of research school versus teaching school would have to be recast.

Did Great Aunt Ida get out of the blizzard alive? I thought you'd never ask. Well, yes and no. She survived the night, but her lungs were "weakened," as they used to say. Then, a friend of hers caught tuberculosis, and despite her mother's admonitions, she regularly cared for her. Still weak herself, she caught the disease and a few years later it caused her death.

I'm sorry I never had the pleasure of knowing her. I have a hunch we would have learned a lot from each other.

## References

Fromm, E. (1955). *The sane society.* New York: Rinehart.
Gilligan, C. (1982). *In a different voice.* Cambridge, MA: Harvard Universtity Press.
Thoreau, H. D. (1854). *Walden.* Boston: Ticknor and Fields.

# II

## One Solution

### *Lives That Integrate Teaching and Research*

In this section, we have included some interesting life stories that exemplify profoundly the integration of research and teaching.

Bill Van Buskirk calls this integration "getting a life" and, in a most charmingly written dialogue, answers a bunch of purely academic questions with a rich and human description of his personal and professional life choices.

David Boje's narrative of his career is frank, funny, and many other things, and it is thoroughly grounded in his research on storytelling, as well. He has been known to encourage his students to yell "I feel healthy, I feel happy, I feel terrific," and after reading this, you may inspired to do the same.

Peter Frost never wanted to teach, and today he cannot think of ever not teaching. In his chapter, Frost tells us how he was transformed from a budding inorganic chemist into an organic teacher-researcher-mask maker and reflects on how good teachers are developed.

Tom Mahoney's teaching and research interests have been a seemingly natural outgrowth of a lifelong career immersed in learning. He describes an easy intertwining of these two crafts in his own experiences and a Socratic style of teaching that seems well suited to the development of graduate students in course work and in their dissertation research. The latter is often overlooked as a rich arena for teaching, and it is clear that Mahoney not only enjoys doing it but also does it well.

Nikita Pokrovsky writes movingly about his experience as a scholar/teacher and professor of social philosophy and social theory in modern Russia. His ideas are a refreshing contrast to the American experience. For example, he writes, "In my opinion, upbringing, morals, and human relations are subsumed in learning and research work. All other aspects of teaching are secondary for me. . . . It also seems to me that a rationally organized academic research process has an enormous moral potential; it is as if it normalizes both a collective and individual consciousness." In a book that focuses on North American institutions, his chapter reminds us that our views on education are bound by history, tradition, and culture.

# 5 On Publish or Perish, Pedagogy, and Getting a Life—Synergies and Tensions

*An Interview With*
*Bill Van Buskirk*

BILL VAN BUSKIRK

D ear Reader, This has been a difficult piece to write because it is different from what I am used to. I have had the devil of a time getting the balance between different aspects of my life into the right perspective for this chapter. Also, the fact that this is my life, not somebody else's, weighed heavily on my mind. I wanted to address you as much as possible in my voice, to tell you what the academic life was like for me. In the end, the dialogic interview format seemed to allow the most authentic kind of talk to emerge. It allowed me to speak in a voice that is more informal and direct than is usual for me. For this interview, I imagined an interviewer with interests in management and organizational behavior.

Interviewer: This is an interview around how you balance your teaching, research, and life.

Me: And how I don't balance them. And how others help me balance them.

Interviewer: OK.

Me: Where do we start?

Interviewer: Let's start with the present. What are you working on now?

Me: Should we start with research?

Interviewer: OK.

Me: First, let me say that I finally got tenure about a year ago. Because this is my second university job since the Ph.D., I have labored as an untenured assistant professor for 10 years. Maybe we can get into that later, but the significance of tenure for my current work can't be overestimated. It has let me do some things I've always wanted to do but never had the confidence to try. I'm working on a series of cases with an old friend, Dennis McGrath. The common theme of these cases is how the symbolically embedded emotionality of organizational cultures empowers people in ways they hadn't thought possible. We're not sure how to pitch this yet, but we are envisioning a book on "the cultures of high performing non-profits."

Interviewer: So, you are plunging into a case-writing project in nonprofit organizations without having a clear sense of the publication outlets. Some would say that is a risky project.

Me: Maybe it is. But the pressure to do something like this has been building up for years. My dissertation was on how managers in three organizations symbolized their most intense experiences at work and on the impact of these representations on the organization. This was an addictive experience, and it was carried out with little sense of publication possibilities. But, I learned a lot in the process. I guess I don't worry about publication much. I just assume something will turn up. Anyhow, this is something I feel I have to do.

Interviewer: How is it going?

Me: Pretty well, so far. We've got one case done and are ready to start another one. The organization itself is quite fantastic, and that makes all the difference. The Community Women's Education Project (CWEP) in

Philadelphia is an organization that takes women on welfare with fifth-grade educations or better and gets them into college. Their success rate is quite impressive.

Interviewer: What is your interest as a researcher in an organization like this?

Me: The people there have very little in the way of resources, very little in the way of "management training," but they have evolved an organizational culture that is highly effective at emotional support, education, empowerment, and participative management. They do things that most job training programs have failed at dismally. We are trying to find out "what makes them tick" at the level of organizational culture. We believe that, by learning about organizations like this one, we will learn something about organizational culture that studying only for-profit organizations won't teach us.

Interviewer: Many management scholars would consider this quite a fringe activity for the field.

Me: I would agree with them. I have always thought that my interests are somewhat "fringy." I have never been very interested in rationality or cognition as a basis for understanding people and organizations. I came to the field out of community organization, drug counseling, and community mental health. I got an MA in clinical psychology before I entered doctoral study, and I chose Case Western Reserve University's OB program because of its emphasis on experiential learning. Before that, I had been at the Gestalt Institute of Cleveland and had participated in all kinds of encounter groups, T-groups, zen retreats, et cetera, et cetera. I had about 10 years of this kind of immersion before I started my Ph.D. Looking at managers through some kind of rational myth made no sense to me. It seems to me that we can never get away from our basic emotional nature, and I think the current work on organizational cultures is very congenial to this view.

Interviewer: You must have had an interesting time when you started to read organization theory.

Me: I'll say! Before hitting the Ph.D. program, I had read very little sociology, but at Case I got a crash course in Weber, Simon, and a whole bunch of others who looked at the world very differently from the way I had been trained. It was almost like culture shock. I was reading all about bureaucratic rationality and bound rationality when, at the same time, I was working as a consultant in organizations where rationality seemed scarce. This tension was what I wanted to explore in the dissertation, but for a while I had trouble finding either a literature to which to ground my interests or a methodology that would be acceptable. Then, I read Glaser and Strauss's *The Discovery of Grounded Theory* (1967), and I was home free, at least as far as doing the dissertation was concerned. Grounded theory involves research for the purpose of generating theory, not for verifying it. Theory generation was what I wanted to do, and the topic of "organizational emotionality" seemed tailor made. It was so vague. So little literature was published (this was 1979 or 1980) that a grounded study was the only way to go.

Interviewer:   But it wasn't all that easy, was it?

Me:   No. The whole process took 2½ years, I was disappointed in the final product, and my eyebrows turned white during the interviewing. I was actually under a level of stress that I never want to experience again.

Interviewer:   Why did you persist?

Me:   There were probably lots of reasons, but I'm not sure what they were. My dissertation advisor, Suresh Srivastva, said I would either have something special or I'd end up with a huge neurosis. He was probably right on both counts. In retrospect, I'm glad I did that dissertation. I learned a lot as a result. It has provided a lifelong interest that has structured much of my professional activity.

Interviewer:   What were your first few years after the Ph.D. like?

Me:   Pretty disoriented. I got a job teaching at Western Carolina University (at Cullowhee) in a part of the country I had never been. Aside from a few good colleagues—Bill Kane and Terry Kinnear in OB and John Adams in project management—I had very few people either within the school or in the surrounding community to share interests with. I had gone from the intense environment at Case to a very "laid back" one at WCU. I did get a much-needed opportunity to chill out after the dissertation.

Interviewer:   And you did get the chance to go to Japan.

Me:   Yes, that was a real adventure. My first trip was for a semester. It was called a Japan Center of North Carolina Fellowship. I had to agree to a summer of studying Japanese, which I considered a lot of fun. Then, we (14 academics from the North Carolina system) went to Japan for the purpose of studying or making contacts or just to immerse ourselves to see what would happen. Through contacts supplied by the faculty at WCU, I met with representatives from the engineering construction industry, and we agreed to apply for a research grant to study "Japanese project management." We got the grant, which led to a second trip in January 1985 for purposes of interviewing company representatives, government officials, and a few academics. Then, in 1987 and 1988, I did workshops in cross-cultural awareness for R&D professionals at the Canon Corporation.

Interviewer:   In retrospect, what did you get from the Japanese experience?

Me:   The clash of cultures was intense. Not being able to read the language gave me a feel for what it must be like to be illiterate. I was living in a society in which most of what went on every day was quite opaque to me. Also, the differences between the Japanese and myself were quite fascinating. Their gentleness and their politeness coexist with their competitive fierceness in business. As long as you are "inside the circle," you are considered family. I experienced some of this on trips where I came well recommended from the state of North Carolina or the Project Management Institute.

Interviewer:   Did the Japanese influence how you saw things in your professional life?

Me:   Yes. I guess the biggest influence was that they confirmed my instincts about the importance of the human factor in managing. They provided a model quite different from the American one in their organizations. They modeled how good human relations could be good business. They modeled a society in which success on Wall Street and human-centered forms of management could not only coexist but also reinforce one another. So, I guess you could say that, despite all the ways they were different from me, the Japanese reinforced the value that led me into organizational behavior in the first place: the concern for humanism in large-scale organizations.

Interviewer:   Yet, you didn't become a scholar of Japanese management.

Me:   Yes. All the while, in the back of my mind was the question, What has this got to do with what I started out to do? I wanted to get back to what I started in my dissertation, but it seemed I kept getting sidetracked. So, yes, I couldn't really get into the Japanese experience to the extent that I might have liked. I learned a lot, though. I coauthored an article on the "psychology of cross-cultural borrowing" with Kazuo Takeuchi, which was a great experience in cross-cultural communication, as well as an interesting thing to do. The work at Canon gave me an insight into what it was like for a Japanese person to confront American culture, sort of a mirror through which I could re-view my own culture shock experiences.

Interviewer: What was missing?

Me: Coherence. I was reading articles on symbolism one week and going to a conference on internationalization of the curriculum the next. I was very nervous because I wasn't publishing anything, although more and more work with which I could resonate was showing up in journals. Eventually, I just had to decide to let go of Japanese adventures so that I could focus.

Interviewer: How did you decide to do that?

Me: At the Academy of Management in 1986, I spoke with people at a consulting firm that did a lot of business in Japan. They needed someone to lecture their Japanese clients on equal opportunity legislation in the United States. They were interested in me because I spoke a little Japanese and was pretty comfortable living over there. They offered to cover my academic salary plus an increment, plus pay for all expenses, plus find me an apartment in the center of Tokyo (a rare and expensive perk). I was intrigued at first, and I asked my wife, who was a grad student at Penn, what she thought of the idea of my living in Japan for a year. Much to my surprise, she said, "Why not, if they will pay for me to come to Japan to visit a couple of times." So, I checked this out and was told this would be no problem. I went back to Gael, who said, "How about a couple of trips so that we could meet in Hawaii?" I felt a little sheepish but was told that this would be no problem either. Then, instead of being excited about this prospect, a little voice turned on inside my head and said, "Nope, you are not going to do this. You are through being an academic tourist. You are not even interested in equal opportunity legislation. It's time for you to build your life around your real interests."

Interviewer: So then what happened?

Me: I came to work at La Salle [La Salle University, Philadelphia] in 1987. La Salle was my alma mater, and it was a little weird to come home again after 20 years, but the real reasons I came were the colleagues and the city. Colleagues at La Salle were much more plentiful than they were in Carolina, especially Steve Meisel and Joe Seltzer, who shared my interests in experiential approaches to the classroom. From La Salle, it was easy to make contacts in Philly and in other cities. In Philly, there is an incredible richness for a student of organizational behavior. In Philly, there are thousands of organizations that one can almost walk into anytime one pleases. I needed an environment like this if I was to continue to do the kind of case studies of organizational cultures and grounded theorizing I did in grad school.

Interviewer: What about the best paper awards? How did they affect you?

Me: They came along at just the right time. Before the Academy of Management award, I had published a few pieces in small journals, but my confidence level was not particularly high, especially because these articles were about Japan-related topics. That my colleagues in the OD Division would actually like something I did was very affirming. And because the award was given for work rooted in my dissertation, I got a strong shot of courage to continue to follow my instincts. When I found out about the Roethligsberger Award from the *Journal of Management Education,* I felt welcomed into the field. I felt that I had a kind of place amid scholars whose work I had long admired. I needed this boost at the time because my wife had gotten sick and I had very little time to devote to research. But in the back of my mind I thought that if I had been able to do this much, I would be able to pick up the pieces somewhere down the road. My wife died in 1991, and I am trying to pick up those pieces right now. But we'll talk more about this later.

Interviewer: So, you were going through all this and it was publish-or-perish time.

Me: That's right. La Salle was going for AACSB accreditation at the time, and it needed people who could publish. I was focused on getting articles out the door whenever I had time to do so.

Interviewer: How was that? How did you adjust to the pressure of suddenly being at a publish-or-perish job?

Me: The pressure subsided after the first few journal "hits." La Salle is a Catholic university oriented toward liberal arts that makes modest demands on research. So, I had nothing like the kinds of expectations present at a large research-oriented place. Nevertheless, I felt the pressure to get lots of stuff into the pipeline. The awards went a long way toward easing the stress. They gave me confidence and impressed the folks at La Salle that I was "for real."

Interviewer: Let's talk about the content of your work. A number of your pieces are training or pedagogically oriented.

Me: Yes, I guess that is inevitable, given my background. In my travels in Japan, I had many experiences in culture shock. Being an inveterate journal writer, I wrote about many of them. As I reflected on these, a number of possible classroom exercises suggested themselves. I read books on Japanese psychology and group life to bolster my understanding (especially helpful were *The Anatomy of Dependence* by Takeo Doi [1972] and *Japanese Society* by Chie Nakane [1970]) and devised exercises that I field-tested in the classroom. When I was satisfied, I wrote them up for the *Journal of Management Education.*

Interviewer: How do you get from there to your pieces on symbol sensitivity?

Me: I'm not sure there is a direct connection. I have always been a devotee of T-group-like technologies for learning about the human side of management. When I began reading a lot of literature on organizational cultures and then on symbols, I began to wonder whether some of that technology couldn't be adapted to learning about corporate cultures from the inside. By the time I came to La Salle, I was ready to try a course in symbol sensitivity with MBAs. I had no idea how it would go, so I talked about it with my dean, Joe Kane. I said, "I'm trying this course that's a real stretch. If I screw it up, I won't do it again." He said, "Fine." The course went well, and it ended up as an article in *JME.*

Interviewer: You build a lot off your T-group experience. Your work is either pedagogically oriented or theorizing about emotionality in the workplace.

Me: Yes. I spent about 10 years in various kinds of training and therapy groups as a participant, trainer, and therapist. Most of this occurred before I had any formal graduate training. It has shaped everything I do professionally. Most of the challenge of writing has involved finding publishable topics that are in synch with these interests. Most recently, I did a piece on using T-groups to learn about organizational culture, rather than just interpersonal relationships.

Interviewer: Besides pedagogy, do you have any theoretical or empirical interests?

Me: Oh, yes. I've gotten a start on lots of things. My interest in organizational cultures has taken me more and more into looking at the work of D. W. Winnicott and Robert Kegan on the one hand and some of the post-modernists (especially Ken Gergen) on the other. Winnicott's notion of the holding environment is quite suggestive for looking at what goes on in organizations at a deeper level.

First, we want to ask what organizational cultures do for their members. I think, first and foremost, they provide a set of symbolic scenarios through which members can imagine themselves in a world that is too subtle, remote, distant, complex, hidden, or dynamic to ever be grasped with concepts and logic. The effect of these self-world images is to "hold" an individual by triggering spontaneous images that are constitutive of the individual's spontaneous perception of well-being. If the world is benign, I don't have to worry about it. I don't have to be hypervigilant around the edges of my life. I can plunge in and concentrate on, even become lost in, the work at hand. When organizational cultures are at their best, they seem to be playful. Individual members from top to bottom are able to imagine themselves as playful. This is just what Winnicott is concerned about in children: the extent to which their human and symbolic environments allow them to trust, relax, and play.

Interviewer: And what is the organizational consequence of all this?

Me: If you switch the lens from the individual to the organization, you realize that only certain kinds of identities can be held by any given cultures. Some organizations hold test pilots better than accountants. Others hold men better than women. A given culture can't hold everything. But what an organization *can* hold, the ways in which it allows its people to imagine themselves in the world, will go a long way toward the kinds of competencies it can develop, invoke, and draw on. Dennis and I have been impressed lately with the work on social capital (Putnam, Coleman) and cultural capital (Bourdieu). I hope to digest this work soon and start writing about it.

Interviewer: How does this interest influence research?

Me: Let's take the instance of CWEP. It is an educational organization—sort of. It is a social service agency—sort of. It doesn't fit any category very easily because it evolved over time as the CWEP staff and board interacted with the students. One of the first things that hits you when you go there is how poor everyone is yet how energized they are. CWEP students typically have multiple children, no husbands, a pile of defaulted student loans, a history of failure in jobs, and a history of unsuccessful educational experiences. On top of this, many of them are reading at the fifth-grade level.

With all this difficulty in keeping things together day to day, you wonder how in the world these people would ever be able to focus on classroom work. Then, you look around the CWEP environment and see that every issue that threatens to distract students from schoolwork is dealt with (or is attempted to be dealt with) in one way or another. Much of the support is structural. Affordable day care is on the premises. Social workers on staff interview about 80 students a month just to keep in touch with what is going on. Faculty are selected for their ability to work with this population. The organization has built contacts at colleges, corporations, and foundations in the area so that as students graduate, they are supported in whatever way makes sense. The point is that, at CWEP, the identity of "being a student" can be embraced by students. They can believe in themselves as students, and they can act on this identity because of the unique network of supports the organization supplies. Students say that they have seen agencies that do one or another of these things well but that nowhere else have they experienced the whole package.

Interviewer:   What about the culture of the place?

Me:   It is so thick, you can cut it with a knife. Every new teacher is given Paulo Freire's book on literacy, *Pedagogy of the Oppressed* (1982). As students learn to read, they read material that helps them see their position in society in nonblaming terms. Many of the students blame themselves for their problems, so this new view is very important. The heart of the culture seems to be a message that every CWEP staffer puts out— namely, that the key to financial security is long-term education that gets you through at least 1 year of college. The organization's staff are not into "quick-fix" jobs at McDonald's. They are uncompromising about this line, and they go to great pains to convince their students that this is the case.

What strikes me about all this is that once a student really buys the "CWEP line," a significant change comes about in her identity (how she sees herself in the world). She now has a future, a long-term future. She has a role—a student. She has an altered relationship to her children— no longer a failing mother, but a woman struggling with hope for her children's future. The CWEP line seems to function like a kind of mantra that students can say to themselves when times get tough. The overall lesson is that, to educate disadvantaged populations, you may need to create schools with organizational cultures that help them bridge the gap between pasts characterized by failures and a credible, powerfully imagined, positive future. We hope that, by exploring CWEP and some other organizations like them in an appreciative fashion and in exhaustive detail, we will learn something about the interface between organizational cultures and educational processes.

Interviewer: Do you have any interest in what would be considered mainstream activities in the field of management?

Me: Yes. I teach business strategy and policy to undergrads and management skills to MBAs. I've done research and consulting in Japan. I've even studied Japanese, although I'm far from conversationally fluent. I like the diversity of what I do, and I see no reason to change it. It seems like there is something new to learn every day.

Interviewer: How about the future? Are you at all ambitious to move on to a bigger university where you could maybe get more support for your work?

Me: Maybe someday. But not right now. Maybe if I get so deeply into research that I want to make it the center of my working life, I'll need to change. But, for a lot of reasons, I'm still "getting it together." I don't want to make traditional research expectations the driving force behind what I do. I don't want to make "what the journals will currently publish" the final arbiter of my professional experience.

Interviewer: Anything else before we move on?

Me: Yes, I would like to say something about the support I get. I think that, too often, research productivity is imagined as an individual achievement. But that is not true for me.

Interviewer: What specific supports mean the most?

Me: La Salle has few resources, compared with a big state school, but much of what I've been able to do has been because I'm here. Experimentation in the classroom is really encouraged, and there is a fair willingness to tolerate experiments that don't work so well. This makes the classroom a great laboratory.

There is a real willingness to use faculty interests. The provost invited me in to do a symbol sensitivity/team building day with the Council of Deans at the school. Interest has been expressed to expand the training to other administrators and to the School of Nursing. I like being appreciated locally.

La Salle's culture is quite self-reflective. *Culture* is not a foreign word here, and there is a fair amount of talk about the La Sallian values that go back to the 17th century . . . a quite congenial place for an organizational culture vulture.

Finally, just being in Philadelphia is a terrific support. The Non-Profit Management Development Center at La Salle has worked with more than 3,500 organizations, and we are working with staffers to define a research role for the faculty. So, there is a virtually unlimited number of potential research sites. I have friends here with whom I write and who read my stuff with very little coaxing. Most noteworthy is my relationship with Dennis McGrath. We were undergrads together in the late 1960s, and when I left town, he went to New York to get a Ph.D. in sociology from the New School for Social Research. He got immersed in the European critical tradition of scholarship, a very different experience from mine in applied behavioral sciences. But when I returned to Philadelphia, we discovered that our interests matched and that our differences were a powerful resource. We've worked together on a number of projects, the most recent of which is the CWEP case.

## Teaching

Interviewer: Speaking of supports, what are the main supports for your pedagogy?

Me:  I think getting tenure has freed me up to think more expansively. While I was under the gun of publish or perish, I always felt rushed. I usually got good ratings from the students, but I thought that if I really invested myself in teaching, I could do a fantastic job. I was fortunate, in a way, in that much of what I had done in training and counseling transferred over into the classroom. All the role playing, simulation gaming, and workshop designing I had done in the past provided a lot of background useful for the classroom. Also, the Japanese adventures made for great exercises and course content.

Interviewer:  And just plain stories, I would think.

Me:  Yes. This background freed me up for writing time. I could usually be improvisational in the classroom. Because of my background, I needed less prep time for classes.

Interviewer:  So, where are you now?

Me:  I still feel some of the tension between teaching and research. I have never believed that to do one well means you do the other well. I continue to look for ways to kill several birds with one stone.

Interviewer:  Some examples?

Me:  I think the whole CWEP experience has insinuated itself into my mind as a metaphor. I begin to ask, How well does the culture of La Salle hold its students? Do we have anything like the mantra that gets instilled at CWEP? Even closer to home, what about the culture I create in my classroom? What does CWEP suggest? After going to CWEP, I began to get excited about challenging myself. Can I create something really special, really exciting in my strategy class, for example? What would Paulo Friere say about teaching strategy and policy?

I think the first step is to richly imagine the students. What is the place of the strategy class in their lives? How do they use it to make sense of their worlds? I know my students are either first- or second-semester seniors. They are always on the job market. They are nervous about the turns the world economy has taken, and they don't understand much about what is happening to them. If they are constructing their worlds in ways that are nerve-wracking and depressing, can I, without watering down the course content, arrange things such that their natural symbolic flow turns exciting? In the words of Winnicott, can I fashion a holding environment in that classroom such that students can relax into play as they engage the material of the course? Can they play at the work of the course? If this is to happen, the course needs to be well designed experientially, and the content needs to simultaneously educate and respond to the dramatic scenarios of the world that students are spinning as they sit in class.

Interviewer:   How do you do all that?

Me:   I have no final answer. I'm just starting to experiment. I have four ideas that I am ready to try: (a) selecting cases as a dramaturgical act, (b) resurrecting the strategy simulation, (c) getting judiciously involved with students who are having trouble, and (d) using the final exam to put students in touch with their own questions. I'll talk about each in turn.

As for selecting cases as a dramaturgical act, when I was looking for cases to include in the strategy course, I looked for everything I could find that would bear on the competitive battles between U.S. and Asian competitors. There was no master plan in this. I just wanted to stick to what I was interested in and to what would allow my Japanese experience into the discussions. As the semester wore on, however, I began to realize that these cases sparked a kind of a drama in the minds of the students. They were able to surface many of their own questions about the Japanese and their own fears about going out into a world that was somewhat dominated by foreign competitors. These concerns surfaced without distracting from the case discussions. Rather, they seemed to energize them. Students were using the cases to "imagine themselves into their futures" (see Denzin, 1991, for more discussion on this). If cases, in addition to being pedagogical resources, are also raw material that seniors use to imagine their futures, then selecting them has dramaturgical as well as pedagogical significance.

Interviewer:  So, something symbolic is going on. As students discuss the cases, they are altering the way they are "held." The class becomes a kind of "holding environment."

Me:  Exactly. Students can symbolize their dilemmas and begin to play with them. This capacity to play is Winnicott's definition of good holding.

Interviewer:  What else?

Me:  Resurrecting the simulation and making it more central in the course. I have been impressed with the power of simulations to involve students in a dynamic way in the actual process of strategy formulation. I have seen undergraduates get involved way out of proportion to the percentage of the grade attached to the game. They care immensely about whether they are first or second. Where is this energy coming from? Is something dramaturgical going on here too? I think so. I think the keys are activity, competition, and using one's own intelligence to do more than reflect on what others have done in the past, which is the dramaturgical structure of case analysis. As students make decisions, they either discover that they may have better judgment than their fellow students or, if things go wrong, that they are capable of learning from their own experience. I think a decent strategy simulation can make a real contribution to the holding environment of the classroom as students discover that their own abilities can make a real difference in a dynamic, albeit simulated, business environment. Their coping resources become more vividly imagined into the wider world of business experience.

Interviewer:  What about getting more involved with students?

Me:  This is a bit dicey. If I get too involved, I lose the ability to give research and consulting their due. If I am serious about trying to strengthen the classroom as a holding environment, however, I have to take cognizance that no matter how cleverly I arrange things, some students are just not going to "get it." In the past, I have been content to let these students go their own way and take responsibility for their behavior. Now, I have a "research reason" to interview those who seem to have trouble or who seem disaffected. Precisely here, the holding environment of the classroom is not working. For whatever reason, the students are unable or unwilling to focus on the work of the class. CWEP gave me the idea to aggressively go after these folks to find out specifically what the difficulties are. I know that this is not an original idea and that many other conscientious teachers do this already, but conceptualizing it in terms of the holding environment motivates me to do it.

Interviewer:   So, seeing the classroom as a setting where your research interests are played out makes you a better teacher.

Me:   Yes, I guess so. I'm beginning to understand that the more synergy I find between teaching and scholarship the better.

Interviewer:   What about having students ask the questions in the final exam?

Me:   I have always been bummed out by the structure of the final exam. After students have worked all semester, when they know more about the subject than they ever will, the final exam often puts them in an infantilized position where they have to psyche out the professor to see what he or she wants. Especially with college seniors, this approach seems unnecessary. I'd like to see the process of preparing for a final really give the students a value-added boost as they leave the class. So, together with Evonne Kruger at La Salle and Mary Ann Hazen at the University of Detroit–Mercy, I've devised an exam in which students come to the professor in small groups and ask questions that they genuinely want to know the answers to. Students are evaluated on the basis of their questions, rather than on their answers to the professor's questions. We are working through the review process at *JME* on this one.

Interviewer:   How does this exam affect the culture you are trying to build in the classroom?

Me:   I have some data on this. We have interviewed about 200 students on how the process has affected their learning, and we have been surprised by the results. Students say that they work harder preparing for this exam than they do for others but that there is less stress and they enjoy the process.

Interviewer:   How do you account for this?

Me:   From the interviews, I think students, without realizing it at first, replace cramming with reflection. They are permitted to work in groups, so the experience becomes a social one. They control the actual shape of the questioning and answering, so they find they are empowered rather than intimidated. And, finally, they get a much more nuanced sense of the connections between their questions and the material of the course. Each question they formulate is a specific connection made explicit and carefully articulated. Having formulated their own questions allows them to own the whole course, and they are much more able to think critically about the course because they have a place to stand vis-à-vis the material.

Interviewer:  How do you evaluate the questions?

Me:  I don't want to get into that here. The *JME* piece tries to deal with evaluation issues. I'm interested in how this contributes to the emotional culture of the class.

Interviewer:  OK, so what is its contribution?

Me:  It takes much of the fear out of the course as long as students do the work. Students discover—some for the first time—that the intellectual enterprise is more than telling some authority figure what he or she wants to hear. Students are able to experience what, to me, is a central process of academic inquiry, formulating one's own questions. In a sense, it is an exercise in helping students find their own minds, their own sense of intellectual excitement. I don't mean to say that other approaches are always totalitarian or anything of the sort, but I have found that, even in group projects, case analyses, or verbal presentations, students carry much of the baggage of their previous educational experiences, which were usually anything but empowering.

Interviewer:  So, how do all these things fit together?

Me:  I don't know. I've never tried them all in the same semester. Together, they constitute a vision of what I want to do next.

Interviewer:  You also teach a course in management skills in the MBA program.

Me:  Yes. I enjoy the course a lot. It enables me to follow some of the themes I've outlined above but with a different slant.

Interviewer:  What is your slant on management skills?

Me:  I think it is a terrific way to teach organizational behavior to working MBAs. Reconceptualizing OB as management skills allows students to customize the discipline to their own career strategies. At the same time, I suspect the approach has some major flaws. I was impressed with Peter Vaill's (1989) critique of the management skills movement when he pointed out that more was involved in management skills than just application. First, researchers reified the skills from the contexts in which they were identified and practiced. Next, we classroom teachers are supposed to teach them, and students are supposed to "apply" them in their own settings. The difficulty I have with this way of imagining management skills is the same as I had with the old T-groups. To the extent that we create an environment that is conducive to trust, feedback, risk taking, and psychological safety, we create an environment that is most unlike the environment that is present in many organizations. The application of management skills often involves negotiating some pretty tricky space in the back-home organization. The point is not to trash management skills, but rather to say that awareness of the context within which the skill is to be applied is an important skill in and of itself.

Interviewer: And this gets you back to . . .

Me: You got it . . . cultural awareness and symbol sensitivity, especially the more emotional sides of the issue.

Interviewer: So for you, symbol sensitivity is a management skill.

Me: Yes. I try to inoculate students from some of the chilling effects of their back-home cultures. Writing assignments involve reports of student attempts to "make something happen" in their organizations, cultural analyses of their back-home organizational cultures, or imaginative scenarios of their futures as managers.

Interviewer: Do you have synergies between teaching and research in the MBA course?

Me: Yes, two. First, students who opt for cultural analyses follow a step-by-step process in which they start by identifying 100 to 200 symbols in their organizations (a version of this process can be found in Van Buskirk, 1991). We have classroom exercises that make this easy. Next, students cluster their symbols, articulate the personal meaning of each cluster, and write a final statement. Each paper is essentially a small case of the person in his or her organizational culture. We intend to analyze these in terms of how each student is "held" by the organizational culture. Second, we have a very large group of students who have taken our course and currently work in organizations. We hope, one of these days, to do a big interview project to generate rich descriptions of exactly what stayed with students and what did not. Because the vast majority of our students stay in Philadelphia, we should be able to do this.

Interviewer: So, it seems that you not only teach a course but also follow a line of inquiry within it. And you look for synergies with research and publication.

Me:  I almost have to. Following a line of inquiry (culture creation in the strategy course and transferability in the skills course) keeps me interested in what is going on. Otherwise, things tend to get routine. This is a difficulty especially because I teach the same courses semester after semester. Instead of getting boring, each section I teach is a kind of different lens that reflects emergent interests in a different way. Usually, each section changes the interests in some way. In addition, finding synergies between the classroom and intellectual interests is absolutely essential because I do not have much support for research and I have to find a way to envision almost any setting I'm in as a research setting.

## Life

Interviewer:  So, you seem to look for synergy between teaching and research. How does this professional activity blend or create tension with your wider life?

Me:  The one big overarching event in my life has been my marriage to Gael Mathews and her subsequent illness and death. I've done a lot of thinking about this during the past 3 years, but not until now have I thought about it as it relates to professional activity.

Interviewer:  So, you see connections?

Me:  Yes. Gael got sick in December 1989, and from that time on I was primarily a nurse/general support person until she died in February 1991. For about a year and a half after that, mourning was my "full-time job." Almost everything else went on automatic pilot.

Interviewer:  What do you mean by mourning being a full-time job?

Me:  After Gael's death, I was exhausted, I was torn apart with a lot of conflicting feelings, lots of voices, longing, regret, guilt. I didn't know what to do. So, with a lot of help from friends, I put the professional world on hold for quite a while. I taught my classes. I even wrote a little. But my energy for really plunging into research and teaching was gone. So, I took a page from my old Gestalt/Jungian training. If I was surrounded by voices, I would let them all speak. I began to write a journal, and I sought out situations and people who would bring up all the feelings and memories relative to Gael and me. I went to California where she lived and grew up and spent considerable time with my in-laws. I went back to Berkeley where we used to live and revisited our old house—stuff like that.

Interviewer:  How did that work out?

Me:  I've gotten a great deal from that experience.

Interviewer:  Have you been able to move on?

Me:  Yes. The seeds of moving on were there in the mourning process, in my relationship with Gael right there at the end of her life. The day after she died, her mother and I opened a little pouch that Gael wore around her neck. Inside were a few crystals and a little button that said "spiritual warrior." When I saw that, I experienced an incredible shock of recognition. I recognized her, her attempts to reach out to others even when she was so sick she could barely stand, her pursuit of graduate studies until about a week before she died, her incredible commitment and intensity about how she lived her life. Then, an aftershock hit, a second shock. I recognized myself in her. This button could have been worn by me too! This is what I've always wanted to be in some way, a spiritual warrior. I think I've taken on that metaphor (don't ask me what it means) in some sense for my life. A lot of work took place between that moment and now. It's more than 2 years after her death, and I am just now moving out of the house we lived in. But, the seeds of moving on were always present. From early on, I could see a connection between living my life in the best, most intense way I knew how and doing honor to my wife. This was the beginning of moving on. I realized this over and over during the mourning process, and the movement back into a busy professional life has been quite organic.

Interviewer:  How would you characterize that movement?

Me:  The most important aspects were reconnecting to a loving relationship; accepting the support of friends, many of whom are in the same academic field; reading in Jungian literature; and practicing a kind of cobbled-together spiritual practice of meditation, journal writing, and poetry.

Interviewer:  Talk about the new relationship.

Me:  I can't say enough, really. Without Susan, I don't know where I'd be. We met at the Organizational Behavior Teaching Conference when both of our spouses were very ill with cancer. A mutual friend, Chris Paulson, introduced us. We talked for several hours about strategies for managing our situations. Then, we went our separate ways. Susan's husband died in September 1990; Gael, 5 months later. We met at the conference the next year and talked all week. I guess we moved together through the grieving process. It was so very nice not to have to do everything alone. As time went on, the relationship deepened. We are currently working at a long-distance relationship and trying to balance work and life together.

Interviewer:  Has the mourning process affected the way you understand symbolism?

Me:  Yes. One odd effect from this whole thing is that my involvement with and understanding of symbols has really deepened. As this is happening, I come closer to the themes I was beginning to explore before Gael got sick. The Jungian reading has complemented the Winnicott/Kegan work I spoke about earlier. I'm excited about working with these ideas in the context of qualitative research. I've just gotten the Ethnograph software, and I'm beginning to play with it. Very exciting possibilities.

Interviewer:  So, you've cycled through mourning, staying close to the people and places from your marriage, spiritual practices, and poetry, and somehow you are back where you started, sort of.

Me:  Sort of, yes. Getting involved in poetry has been a real delight. I've always been a kind of closet poet, but one thing I've done is to read "Gael poems" to people who knew her. They kind of bring her back into the room as a photograph does sometimes. It started at her memorial service when I read a poem I wrote about meeting her. Her mother came up and asked me whether I had written anything else. I said, yes, I had. She said, "I want everything you write about this." I said OK. This started a slow process of "going public."

Interviewer:  Why not share one with us?

Me:  Oh God! I can't *believe* you asked that.

Interviewer:  Why not?

Me:  Oh, go ahead, twist my arm!

Interviewer:  Twist, twist.

Me:  OK, OK. That's enough.

Gael's Gift

I wake up. The fog clears.
I see like my fathers did,
Those big shouldered Rockies,
Golden and rosy in the dawn:
Mute, immobile, eternal, challenging,
Standing stern and beautiful
In the outback of our minds.

When, choking and chilled with sweat,
I witnessed your final shuddering agony,

The ground opened up beneath my feet
Like a trap door. I landed hard,
Muddled and blinking in a world
Out of focus, night and day reversed,
Surrounded by a brave new population.

Here, in this place, spirits burn everywhere
Like yours did at the end; eyes shine
Even when the flesh is in decay,
And everything that's fragile is important.

Interviewer:   So, why is this activity so special to you?

Me:   It alters my stance toward culture. Instead of reflecting on it, poetry involves me, in however small a way, in the creation of it. I enjoy this activity immensely.

Interviewer:   So, life is being pretty good to you.

Me:   Oh, yes. Work is going well, I'm past the tenure worries, I've got a terrific new woman whom I love very deeply, I'm connecting to community and friends, I'm past the tenure hurdle, I'm reading and writing in areas I'm excited about, and I've come to terms with Gael's death. I imagine that she has liberated me, that she has encouraged me to go on. Without really knowing what has happened to me, I have "gotten a life," it seems.

Interviewer:   What about the future?

Me:   Nothing special. Just more of the same, I hope. A lot more of the same. I like Walt Whitman's line:

I, now thirty-seven years old in perfect health begin,
Hoping to cease not till death.

Interviewer:   Seems like a pretty good place to end.

## References

Denzin, N. (1991). *Images of postmodern society: Social theory and contemporary cinema.* Newbury Park, CA: Sage.

Doi, T. (1972). *The anatomy of dependence.* Berkeley: University of California Press.

Freire, P. (1982). *Pedagogy of the oppressed.* New York: Continuum.

Glaser, B., & Strauss, A. (1967). *The discovery of grounded theory.* Chicago: Aldine.

Nakane, C. (1970). *Japanese society.* Berkeley: University of California Press.

Vaill, P. (1989). *Managing as a performing art: New ideas for a world of chaotic changes.* San Francisco: Jossey-Bass.

Van Buskirk, B. (1991, May). Enhancing sensitivity to organizational symbols and culture. *Journal of Management Education, 15*(2).

# 6 From Outcast to Postmodernist

DAVID M. BOJE

When I did not publish many things in the right journals, I perished at UCLA. I was a failure as a teacher and as a writer. I remember moving all my unfinished research projects into boxes, piling all those student papers I thought important to save into the hallway so that the janitor could cart them away the next day. I had struggled to get my career off the ground for 7 years in this fifth-floor office. After the 4-year review, I was told I was not a good teacher and had not established myself as a national scholar. It was like being in a nightmare. One student evaluation had something nasty to say about me, and naturally the committee quoted that one disgruntled student in the cover letter of my evaluation. When I met with the dean, he suggested I resign and not go any further with the tenure process. I assured him I would work even harder and get some results. I worked harder, but the teaching did not improve and the publications were not what I needed to succeed. I knew my fate was sealed when, after conducting (with Michael Jones) the first Organizational Folklore Conference in Santa Monica with name folklorists and organizational behavior people along with executives in attendance, I asked the dean what he thought of the conference. "Please do not encourage the folklorists; we are trying to move them out of the business building. We need the space for the computer lab." I was stunned. I had achieved national, even international, recognition for doing cross-paradigm bridge building, and this guy was counting beans. Once again, the dean advised me to withdraw my tenure application so that, in this way, I could avoid putting UCLA in the embarrassing position of having to turn me down. If I left now, I would not have this black mark on my record. But, emotionally, I was in no shape to go anywhere. I was such a workaholic that my family had left me; I was incapable of relaxing. I wrote and wrote and worked and worked. As I continued to work into the sixth year, the tenure committee handed down its inevitable recommendation: "No." I was given the option of staying on during the seventh year while I looked for another job or of just leaving immediately. Such a choice! I thought about my option and decided to stay the seventh year.

During my sixth and seventh years at UCLA, a curious thing happened: My teaching scores became excellent. During that time, I began jogging, watching my diet, and getting myself into shape. I weighed in at over 210 pounds. I now weigh 155. I managed to get my wife and children back, but we eventually divorced. During the 6th and 7th years at UCLA, because I knew I did not have tenure, I settled down in the classroom. I began to teach my way without constantly trying to teach for the ratings. The pressure was off, and I acted naturally. I stopped submitting articles for rejection. When I was not teaching, I went to the library and started reading. I read about the history of printing. I read for 2 years. It was glorious. I loved history. I traced the industry from Gutenberg to the present. I went out and interviewed the oldest printers I could find in Los Angeles, including the Chandlers, who had founded the *Los Angeles Times*. I transcribed each interview myself and tried to make sense of the history. I did have a relapse, sending my analysis of printing history to *Administrative Science Quarterly* (*ASQ*). An editor sent back a short letter saying it was not the kind of thing the journal would send out for review. That was that.

In my study of printing, I met some people who invited me to go into business with them. I did. We eventually founded an agency specializing in recruiting personnel in the quick and commercial printing markets. We did quite well, but I was bored. I began to write monthly columns for the *Printing Journal*. A wonderful thing happened. I could write and publish each month, and all the editor did was thank me for my submission. I got an acceptance letter every month and not one rejection in 2 years. She encouraged me to stop citing other people. Stop quoting others. Stop using all those fancy words. Every month, my article went to 30,000 readers. Can you believe it? That is a lot more than ever read the articles I managed to publish in *Administrative Science Quarterly* (*ASQ*), *Management Science* (*MS*), and *Journal of Applied Behavioral Psychology* (*JABP*).

I had learned a lesson. When the evaluation pressure was off my teaching, my teaching and my writing got better. I began to wonder whether I could make it in academia. The business had reached a point where the partners were ready to split. I called Tony Raia, and he called Edmond Grey at Loyola Marymount, and like the wave of a magic wand, I was being interviewed to be a visiting professor.

I was scared to death. All those negative messages kept ringing in my ears. "You can't teach. You should resign. You cannot write. You are not going to make it." On my first day of classes, I was scheduled to teach three management sections, one at 10 a.m., one at 11 a.m., and the third at noon. To prepare for this day, I had done several things. During the summer, I had spent 2 weeks going to the campus and reading the archives. I read about the history of Loyola University and its merger with Marymount College. I also interviewed a number of students during an OBTC conference at Loyola Marymount. At this conference, I met my friend and frequent coauthor Bob Dennehy. "What works in the classroom?" "What does not work?" From the students, I heard stories about unprepared instructors, about instructors who read from the book, and about what options students had used to get a bad teacher removed from the classroom. "There are too many classes with just a midterm and a final."

Another thing I did to prepare for my reentry into teaching was to get some coaching from a great teacher. Her name was Eleanor Brigand. I always call her "Lady Eleanor." Lady Eleanor taught art to elementary school art teachers. She taught them how to teach. Now, I was born left-handed and never quite adapted to this right-handed world. My handwriting sucks. She had me practice striate lines and little circles the way first graders still do. Then, step by step, she taught me calligraphy. I never got past the first few exercises, but I learned so much from this woman that I cannot ever thank her enough. She taught me about the aesthetics of harmony. "Harmony principles for visual design? What is that?" I asked. "Oh, harmony is variety in unity. It is a basic law of the universe. It is everywhere." "Really? I studied design—well, organizational design." "It applies to that, but for you right now it applies to your teaching." Take the basic components of harmony.

"First, there is rhythm. You have to watch the rhythm. Students like to have some repetition, but you have to have interval too. Without interval, repetition gets dull and boring. But, with you, you need more repetition to calm some of the chaos you bring into the room. If you have rhythm plus contrast with emphasis in balance, then you can be a great teacher. For example, look at emphasis. You have to have an emphasis, a major point of focus in your teaching. You cannot teach all over the place. You have to be able to build up a lesson and bring emphasis into your teaching."

As I took art classes from Lady Eleanor, I crafted my syllabus. For emphasis, I chose storytelling. I would tell stories to make my points, and I would ask students to collect short stories to fit each of the five modules of the course. I did up a diagram, using the calligraphy pens Eleanor had taught me to use. Students could see the entire course, and I would be able to focus on a subset of the course model every few weeks. It is a simple structure, but structure has never been an easy thing for me.

One thing I decided to do was dress for students and not for faculty. I was going to have institutional spirit. I would wear LMU clothing until I had a tenured job at LMU. I wore an LMU cap until the very meeting that the management faculty recommended me for tenure at LMU. At UCLA, I wore suits and ties, tried to do the conservative walk, and kept my mouth shut. I felt I was not part of UCLA and never bought a single item of clothing that said *UCLA* on it. I never felt I belonged at UCLA. In fact, during the 1½ years I waited for my 4-year review to be completed, I stopped speaking altogether. The fear was crippling. Walking across the sculpture garden, past all the nude stat-ues of women in contorted and bizarre stances, I prayed that no one would notice me, that no student would speak to me, that no faculty would interact with me. I was inside my body somewhere; I could climb up into my brain and peer out of my eyes to facilitate a class discussion, but my self was hiding somewhere in my left leg, just above my ankle. When the dean told me the bad news, I did not shudder or stutter. I had already delivered the news a thousand times as I walked from the parking lot, through the sculpture garden, past the nudes, into my office, and turned on my computer screen to stare at the words.

The last thing I did was teach with more enthusiasm. "Up on your chairs!" I yelled, as I looked the room of 40 students in the eye. One by one, the students stood on their desk seats until the very last person was off the ground. Knowing of my fear of reentering the classroom, my pastor came to my first class. He also jumped up on his chair. "This will be a different course. We will be learning by doing. This is my philosophy of learning:

> I hear and I forget
> I see and I remember
> I do and I understand!"

The students were chuckling. A few were serious. It was an electric moment. "How do you feel?" I asked. A few students replied, "Fine." "Wrong answer," I replied. "In this class, we will practice enthusiasm. Let me demonstrate:

> I feel healthy
> I feel happy
> I feel terrific!"

I shouted out the reply I wanted, and on *terrific*, I jumped to the floor. "Now it is your turn. How do you feel?" They gave the reply but were not in unison in their words or actions. "Let's do it one more time." By the third time, the response was in unison, and it was loud. I introduced my pastor and then started my storytelling.

"Let me tell you the story behind this cheer. I met a man named Richard Chavez when I was running my personnel recruiting business. Richard Chavez was born in Mexico, and his parents had a poor farm and lived in a shack with dirt floors. They immigrated to the United States, but Richard had polio, and each year the doctors said he would be dead very soon. Yet, Richard kept a positive mental attitude. He went through the rehabilitation schools, those schools for people with disabilities. After high school, he decided to be a detective. He rolled his wheelchair to the only detective school in the area, but the steps prevented him from going inside to take any classes. He hung out there until the teachers sat on the steps for their lunch. 'Would you help me become a detective?' he asked one teacher after another. Finally, one said, 'Yes, if you come here before and after school and during lunch, I will sit out here and teach you what you need to know.' He did just that. He was successful and opened up his own detective school. Here is a man who sleeps in an iron lung at night, drags around an oxygen tank with a tube stuck in his nose during the day, and look at what he has done. As Napoleon Hill and W. Clement Stone put it:

> Whatever the mind of man
> can conceive and believe,
> it can achieve with a
> positive mental attitude."

I then handed out index cards with blue writing that had the "I feel healthy, I feel happy, I feel terrific!" cheer on them. "This is the theme of our course. I want each of you to learn to lead and to manage with a positive attitude. It begins with managing yourself. I want each of you to learn to tell stories, like my Richard Chavez story." I asked each student to bring in a 1- to 2-page story, following the outline in the syllabus, that captured a management experience.

At the next class period, I thought about how to begin the class. Should I do another cheer? Should I tell another story? Would students get into this? Again, my pastor came to class to give me moral support. I needed his support because when I left UCLA, I left teaching. Now, I was facing up to all my inner voices. I needed to act positively and enthusiastically to calm the inner storm. "Stand up. I want you to hold the hand of the person next to you in each row and form two chains, one on this side and the other on that side of the room. When I say, 'How do you feel?' I want you to squeeze the hand of the person next to you, and when it gets to the very last person, that person will say, 'I feel healthy.'" We did just that. The left side of the room finished first. We went back the other way for "I feel happy." This time, the right side of the room finished. It was now a contest, and energy was in the air. "OK, this is for all the money. How do you feel?" Both chains jerked as left and right hands squeezed each partner's hands in rapid succession, and members shouted, "Hurry up!" It was close, but the left side won. I then had a problem. We had 40 people and only 45 minutes left in which they could tell their stories.

"How many of you brought your stories today?" Most of the hands in the room shot up. That was neat. At UCLA, with my sheepish style, hardly anyone did an assignment on time. "Everyone with a story, please go to the front of the room and tell your story without notes." They followed directions, leaving six guys in the back of the room. "You guys are the peanut gallery. You applaud after each story." At the front of the room were 34 students huddled across the length of the black-board. After an interminable silence, one stepped forward and told her story. "Thank you. Let's hear some applause," as I smiled at the peanut gallery. "Next!" Each student told his or her story. Some were long, but as people began to shuffle and tire from standing, the stories got briefer and briefer until, just as class was over, the last person finished. As students sat in their seats after their telling, they too applauded the performance of the storytellers. I pointed out examples of good per-formances. "Good use of dialogue. I felt I was there with you. I liked your eye contact." Students began modeling those aspects of the tell-ing. My plan was to have students bring in a story each week that would fit with the topic I was to cover.

After 2 weeks of cheers and spirited exercises, a group of students corralled me at the door as I looked in the hall for those last few scur-rying students before I began class. "Professor Boje." "Call me David." "Oh, yeah. We wanted to tell you, we talked it over and decided you are very strange, but we like your class and the cheer is cool." At the beginning of my first semester, the course evaluations came to my office. I took a peek and could not find any hateful comments. I usually dreaded getting course evaluations. I was not big on rejection. Every evaluation had good things to say. "Best course I ever had." "Best teacher I ever had." "I learned to be more assertive and to stand up for myself." It just went on like that. Not a lemon in the bunch. I had connected with the students of Loyola Marymount.

I had reentered the academic life of a business professor. I was only a visiting professor, with no prospects for tenure and no invitation from anyone to be considered for tenure. Still, it felt great to be in the classroom. My nerves calmed, my pastor stopped accompanying me to the classroom, and I kept up my enthusiasm. In the second semester, the demand for my course was crazy. Fifty people per section signed up, and the dean said, "There are people lined up here trying to get into your section. Can you take two more per section and that will be all?" As the second semester came to a close, a curious thing happened.

The student body took a vote and elected me teacher of the year for the university and for the College of Business. I was recognized with two plaques and invited to all kinds of events.

Within the week, the Management Department asked me to apply for an open, tenure-track position. I had avoided making any connection with my colleagues. In fact, I had made up my mind just to focus on students and my teaching and not to have anything to do with the academic side of Loyola Marymount or the Academy of Management. The writing I did was for my students, not for those people. I no longer trusted professors.

I was at a cocktail party, and a few professors and graduate students from UCLA were there. "Oh, David, I heard you got teacher of the year at LMU. Poor guy! I guess that means you won't be getting tenure again!" (said with lots of laughter ringing in my ears). Wow, was this true? Would I be typecast as a nonserious academic because I was having success as a teacher? A few weeks later, I heard the same message from my colleagues. "You know, Dave, people are saying you are a good teacher, but with all your devotion to teaching, you won't have time to publish."

Decisions. Decisions. Hal Leavitt called me and asked me to help him put together the fourth edition of *Readings in Managerial Psychology*. I accepted. This was difficult for me because my original involvement in the project was with Lou Pondy. In graduate school, he made me a coauthor of the third edition. Lou told me, "When Hal Leavitt asked me to be a coeditor, no one knew who I was. Now, I am going to do the same for you." I worked up the final list of articles in 1988, and the book was released in 1989. Because Lou had died of cancer in 1987, we decided to dedicate the book to him.

From his grave, Lou Pondy gave me a second shove to get back into writing. Larry Pate, my upper classman at the University of Illinois, invited me to edit a special issue of the *Journal of Organizational Change Management* (*JOCM*) that would be dedicated to Louis Pondy. Lou always caught me being good at something. In graduate school, he encouraged me to take risks with my teaching and to tell stories. Working with him encouraged me, and I admired his ability to put passion into his lessons, to feel the weight of humanity in his words, and to masterfully orchestrate the forms of Thompson, Simon, March, and Kuhn. He gave lectures the way musicians played classical scores. He improvised on their scores, and he made his own original music. He wanted to reform organizational behavior. He was never satisfied with the status quo. I was an apprentice to the master, who in turn was passing along the wisdom of the ages. The special issue included notes from his diary, ideas he had about mentoring doctoral students, and unfinished papers begun with former students and colleagues.

I finished the Pondy special issue but still had writer's block. Just the thought of writing for top-tier journals still made me ill. I was totally discouraged about doing any research and publishing. Still, my interview with the academic vice president had been good: "With two *Administrative Science Quarterly*s, a *Management Science,* and other journal articles, the *Readings in Managerial Psychology* book, and this special issue, you already have more than is needed for tenure." For most people, I guess this would take the pressure off, but for me the pressure about tenure came from my past at UCLA, not from my current life at Loyola Marymount. I had to prove something to myself.

I had some serious thinking to do. I reread my rejection letter from UCLA. "David Boje has only published with other people. He has not shown he can write and publish on his own." As one esteemed faculty member put it in his anonymous comment to the committee, "This guy gives qualitative research a bad name." This was a low blow. At UCLA, they did not value my type of research, and they certainly did not value working with others. I often worked with others to find out how to tame my prose, structure my arguments, and get the style down. Reviewer after reviewer liked my ideas but could not stand my grammar. One reviewer even cited Homer to me and suggested I give up any aspiration of ever being a writer. Writing the magazine articles for 2 years had taught me a lot, but I still had major emotional blocks about writing for refereed journals.

I decided to do the article that would have given me tenure at UCLA. It would be a single-authored article and be published in *ASQ.* It would focus on stories and storytelling in an organization. I would do everything in the article myself. This was a good choice because Loyola Marymount did not have hoards of doctoral students to help me anyway. The computer consultants knew about spreadsheets but could not tell me the nuances of multivariate statistics. No, here at LMU, I was on my own.

For a site, I chose an office supply distributor. It's funny that a marketing professor asked me to help him with a consulting project. Norm is a character. He is so Type A that he gets out of his car at traffic lights, goes to the crosswalk and pushes the pedestrian button, runs back to the car, and jams the gearshift into drive just as the light turns green. I tried 50 times to tell him about my project, but he just never could hear me. Norm couldn't care less about academic writing. He had been a marketing executive before doing some visiting teaching at Loyola Marymount. Several days each week for the better part of a year, he and I went to the Stationers Company. When we got there, I turned on my tape recorder. When the CEO and the board asked us to tour all the sites and to talk with all the managers, I kept the recorder running. When we went to lunch, drove in a car, or talked by the cooler, I kept the recorder running. Everyone knew it was running. Some were curious; none seemed to mind. Sometimes a CEO, VP, or manager would ask me to turn it off for a moment. They would tell me a story or a joke or make some gossipy comment about someone else. I wrote all these items into my field notes. They had Norm and me conduct focus groups with vendors, customers, and employees. My recorder stayed on.

I wanted to capture how people told stories as part of doing their work. Stories were my focus in my teaching. I wanted to keep it the focus in my research as well. Each week, I transcribed my tapes and tried to identify the stories. It was difficult for me to see where conversation left off and a story began. It was difficult to pinpoint who was speaking in a nine-person conversation. I tried to understand everything I could about the context of each story fragment. I looked for variations in how the stories got told by different people across different contexts.

To overcome writer's block, I got into therapy. As I wrote, I learned to speak affirmations to my inner child. "You can do this. Once you put down a sentence, another one will follow. Do a little at a time. You can do it." As I held and nurtured my inner child, my creative self surfaced and I was able to write. If I did not do my inner-child work, I would write defensively and end up not doing it correctly.

I drafted the article and sent it off to experts in folklore and organizational storytelling. They liked some of the ideas. They suggested I use a more journalistic style in pulling the article together, be more analytic in my interpretations, drop the myth-making sections ("too subjective, focus in on the more objective data"), and watch my grammar. I took my draft to the tutoring lab for students at Loyola Marymount. I found a terrific lady who knew all about writing. She took out her red pencil and stitched a tapestry of red embroidery onto my work. I went back and made the corrections and brought it to her a second time. Finally, after a year of data collection and a year of rewriting, the manuscript was ready to send to *ASQ*. After 4 months of waiting, the reviews came back with a letter from the editor. They turned down the article. It was not acceptable for publication. The editor thought the article needed so much rework that it just would not be possible to do it. At first, I took this as a rejection, but after a few weeks I decided I could take it up as a challenge, rewrite the article from top to bottom, and answer point by point the challenges of the reviewers. I worked about 4 months on the rewrite and resubmitted the article. The editor sent it back out for review.

The reviewers thought the article was a dead issue but, in their reviews, noted how the author had addressed their concerns seriously. They sent back another rejection but left me a stronger invitation to rewrite the article. On the third submission, the editor and two reviewers liked that version, and the third reviewer said that the article was weak but that because others seemed to see something in it, she or he could go along with the majority. I was asked to address each comment, and if I could satisfy the editor that my revisions were substantial, they might take the piece. I had months of work to be done. Two weeks into my fourth revision, I got a telephone call. "We have a space in the next issue. If you can get your paper rewritten by next week, you can be considered." I worked around the clock and met the deadline. The article was published in the *ASQ* in 1991.

During the time I had begun this project, I became editor of *JOCM* and took on the role of track chair for the International Academy of Business Disciplines (IABD). These are a journal and a conference that UCLA would have given me no credit at all for participating in. Only first-tier journals and conferences count at first-tier universities. I decided they could go to hell. What had they done for me anyway? I did a special issue on storytelling and consulting for *JOCM* and recruited storytelling submissions for the organizational theory track at IABD. I decided that my role would be to help other marginalized players in the Academy of Management have an outlet to discuss and publish their work. In 1991, I timed my publications so that *ASQ*, the IABD track, the storytelling special issue for *JOCM*, and an article on teaching storytelling for the *Journal of Management Education* hit in that same year.

Bob Winsor and I began working on deconstructing total quality management (TQM). I studied ancient histories of Japan; Bob attacked

Alvin Toffler and Michael Bell's postindustrialization thesis. We both decided that real differences existed between that and postmodernism. We think TQM has historical roots in Taylorism in ways that do not get brought out in the Lean Production or the Demings story of TQM. He and I did a bunch of conference presentations and papers attacking TQM as Taylorism.

Bob Dennehy and I have playful spirits. We were playing around with the book exhibitors in Washington. "Say, have you heard the latest?" "No, what?" "These textbooks are passé; people are using the newer storytelling methods to teach their OB classes." Of course, we had no plan at all for a book of our own. But at the next conference, we played the same game, and several publishers called our bluff and asked for an outline and prospectus. We finally did a contract with Kendall/Hunt to write a book on storytelling and management.

The book project took a postmodern turn. I wanted to find the next level of analyzing stories and storytelling and to find some way to use this analysis in managerial education. As I pursued the storytelling trek, I kept running into discourse analysis. Finally, Bill Hetrick, another marketing professor, introduced me to Michel Foucault, Frederic Jameson, and Stewart Clegg. I read Foucault's *Discipline and Punish* in a weekend and filled several tablets with notes. My friend Dale Fitzgibbon sent me stacks of articles from journals from every discipline. And I added the Alta Conference, a group of organizational combination theorists, such as Leonard Hawes, Eric Eisenberg, and Larry Browning. It was like being back in graduate school. When I got exposed to Lyotard, Baudrillard, Derrida, and Bakhtin, my head was bursting with ideas. Here were theorists, particularly Foucault, who took historical analysis seriously, analyzed stories, and challenged the status quo. This was too much fun to pass up. During one Christmas break, I sat down at the computer and did nothing but write for 14 hours a day. When I finished, I sent the drafts to Bob Dennehy for criticism and revision and for him to add his own ideas. When we finished, we had written *Managing in the Postmodern World: America's Revolution Against Exploitation* (1993). I did not wait for the publisher and began teaching from the book the very next semester.

Students were asked to compare premodern, modern, and postmodern interpretations of traditional management. I asked students to learn the framework and to apply it to a team analysis of a local corporation. Their task was to collect stories and taped interviews, transcribe their data, and use the perspectives as content analysis categories. Then, I asked them to deconstruct their collected stories by using a story deconstruction methodology Bob and I had put together. Students were challenged. "We are working harder in this class than in our 4-unit accounting course. I cannot believe all the work." I learned to back off a bit, but my enthusiasm and theirs made for some of the richest and most insightful analyses I have ever seen any undergraduate students accomplish.

In writing the postmodern book and articles, I began to see how I had grown up in a modernist society, worshipped a modernist academy, and worked in a modernist (and premodernist) university. I decided I would make *JOCM* an outlet for postmodern writers. I began contacting people like Stewart Clegg, Hugh Wilmott, and others to write for the journal. My friends Bob Gephart, Bob Dennehy, Bill Hetrick,  and I planned a showcase symposium to feature Stewart Clegg. Stewart was relocating from England to Australia, and I arranged a distinguished lecturer visit for him at my university. Stewart wrote the foreword to the postmodern book and invited Bob Dennehy and me to the European Group on Organizational Symbolism (EGOS) meetings in Paris. We met Gibson Burrell, Hugh Wilmott, John Hussard, Bruno LaTour, and many other people in the postmodern movement.

The teacher of the year awards continued for 4 straight years. I published more at Loyola Marymount than at UCLA. I got tenure and full professor. *JOCM* became a well-respected journal in academy circles, as well as internationally. People ask me to autograph my book. I met Grace Ann Rosile at an OBTC seminar I was conducting on the book that Bob Dennehy and I wrote. We gave her a copy, and she agreed to teach with it in her management course. She also joined the organizing team for the postmodern track of the IABD conference. Grace Ann Rosile and I began to write together and fell in love in the middle of an OBTC T-group. Who would have thought such wonders were possible?

I decided to become a leader in the postmodern movement. It changed the way I do my scholarship. I want to transform the way we publish, teach, and do organizational behavior and change. I am a rebel and a revolutionary. Grace Ann Rosile and I are working at becoming writing and life partners. In our teaching, we have switched from having students study the premodern, modern, and postmodern aspects of an organization to doing the "Greenback Company." In Greenback, students invest $10 per person and organize themselves into a premodern guild, which becomes a modernist pyramid and finally a postmodern company. The idea of Greenback is to let the students manage their money, invest in a fund-raiser, and use that money and sweat equity to do something about their community and Mother Earth. We have painted rooms in inner-city schools, built a garden for a babies-with-AIDS shelter, fed the homeless, put on celebrity basketball games and AIDS awareness dances, and done other projects. In this way, students get to experience being postmodern in a modernist world.

In terms of scholarship, my friends and I want to change the academy, the nation, and the world. We go to academy meetings and distribute campaign buttons, campaign literature, and information on how to write postmodern articles in journals we control, how to get papers accepted at an annual postmodern conference (umbrella-ed within IABD), and how to do postmodern dancing. In the words of Paul Newman, playing the role of Fast Eddie in *The Color of Money,* "I'm back!" Another one of those curious things happened. Academy of Management division members began to invite me to their conferences. Sage Publications invited Bob Gephart, Tojo Joseph, and me to do a book on postmodern management and organization theory. Grace Ann Rosile, Deborah Summers, Bob Dennehy, and I decided to collaborate a postmodern OB text. Other journal editors asked me to write invited articles for their special issues. People with book projects wanted to publish my stories. Peter and Rae asked me to write this chapter.

My good friend Kurt Motomedi told me something about myself: "David, you are like the guy who walks up and down the beach in Santa Monica, wearing all these medals. You publish and you hang another medal on your jacket. But the jacket is full, so you hang more medals on your bathing trunks. But no matter how many medals you pin on, it will never be enough. My grandmother told me this: 'In the end, after you retire, the janitor at the library will pull all your books and articles from the shelf and put them in the dumpster.' In the end, we will perish, no matter how much we publish. The key is to find some people to have fun with."

# Bibliography

Boje, D. M. (1989). Bringing performance back in. *Journal of Organizational Change Management*, 81-93.

Boje, D. M. (1989). Louis R. Pondy (1938-1987): A mentor and his magic [Special issue]. *Journal of Organizational Change Management*, 1(2).

Boje, D. M. (1991). Consulting and change in the storytelling organization. *Journal of Organizational Change Management*, 4(3), 7-17.

Boje, D. M. (1991). Organizations as storytelling networks: A study of story performance in an office-supply firm. *Administrative Science Quarterly*, 36(1), 106-126.

Boje, D. M. (1991). Teaching storytelling in management education. *Journal of Management Education*, 279-294.

Boje, D. M. (1993). On being postmodern in the academy: An interview with Stewart Clegg. *Journal of Management Inquiry*, 2(2), 191-200.

Boje, D. M. (1993). The university is a panoptic cage: Disciplining the student and faculty bodies. In C. Grey & R. French (Eds.), *Critical perspectives on management education*. London: Sage International.

Boje, D. M. (1994). Organizational storytelling: The struggles of premodern, modern, and postmodern organizational learning discourses. *Management Learning Journal*, 25(3), 433-461.

Boje, D. M. (1994). Premodern, modern, and postmodern: Which way is up? In G. Palmer & S. Clegg (Eds.), *Constituting management markets, meanings, and identities*. London: Sage International.

Boje, D. M. (1994). Stories of the storytelling organization: A postmodern analysis of Disney as "Tamara-land." *Academy of Management Journal*, 38(4): 997-1035.

Boje, D. M., & Dennehy, R. (1992). Postmodern management principles: Just the opposite of Fordist principles. *Proceedings of International Academy of Business Disciplines*, 442-448.

Boje, D. M., & Dennehy, R. (1994). *Managing in the postmodern world: America's revolution against exploitation* (2nd ed.). Dubuque, IA: Kendall/Hunt.

Boje, D. M., & Rosile, G. A. (1994). Diversities, differences, and authors' voices. *Journal of Organizational Change Management*, 7(6), 8-17.

Boje, D. M., White, J., & Wolfe, T. (1994). The consultant's dilemma: A multiple frame analysis of a public housing community. In R. W. Woodman & B. Passmore (Eds.), *Research in organizational change and development* (Vol. 8). Greenwich, CN: JAI.

Boje, D. M., & Winsor, R. (1993). The resurrection of Taylorism: Total quality management's hidden agenda. *Journal of Organizational Change Management*, 6(4), 57-70.

Boje, D. M., & Winsor, R. (1994). The globalization and rediscovery of the American system. In *Business research yearbook: Global business perspectives: Vol. 1. Publication of International Academy of Business Disciplines*. New York: Lanham.

Diagnoses, T. K., & Boje, D. M. (1993). Interorganizational networks: A meaning-based perspective. *International Journal of Organizational Analysis*, 1(2), 161-183.

Hetrick, W. P., & Boje, D. M. (1992). Postmodernity and organization: The body and post-Fordist control. *Journal of Organizational Change Management*, 5(1), 48-57.

Leavitt, H., Pondy, L. R., & Boje, D. M. (1989). *Readings in managerial psychology* (4th ed.). Chicago: University of Chicago Press.

Pate, L., & Boje, D. M. (1989). Retrospective sensemaking on a mentor and his magic: An introduction to the contributions of Louis R. Pondy, 1938-1987. *Journal of Organizational Change Management*, 2(2), 5-12.

# 7 Learning to Teach

*Lessons From a Life in
Business and Academia*

PETER J. FROST

*There is much learning to be derived from the teaching process. But the teacher must remain the student if the teacher is to grow.*

Rodegast & Stanton, 1985, p. 60

It is 7:45 a.m., and in 45 minutes, students will come into the room for the final class of the term on the topic of leadership. I move around the room, checking on things, while an audiotape is playing on the deck. It is a set of popular tunes with the theme of endings and "good-byes"; right now, the Beatles are singing, "You say good-bye and I say hello." I check the video machine and try out the two clips I will be presenting at some point during the session, adjusting the tracking to ensure that the images are clear. The

AUTHOR'S NOTE: My grateful thanks to Rae André, Vivien Clark, Janice Foley, Maeve Frost, and Keith Murnighan for their comments and assistance.

music feeds my mood. I have been mulling what I might do to start the session; how I will facilitate the student presentations of their work, which will form a large part of the whole session; and how the closing ceremony I have planned with the students is expected to unfold. Now that the session is at hand, my adrenaline is flowing, and as usual, I see ways to tinker with some aspects of flow of the class and with the presentation of my ideas that I had not considered earlier in the week. I make changes to notes and sequences I have sketched on a few cards. I sit for a while, just living with the anticipation of the session; then, I go to the chalkboard and write on it a few affirmations. This time, I use "This is no dress rehearsal, this is it!" and Viktor Frankl's (1959/1984) words: "Everything can be taken from a [person] but one thing: the last of the human freedoms—to choose one's attitude in any given set of circumstances, to choose one's own way" (p. 86). It is 8:25 a.m., and students come into the room. They notice the music; some smile and comment, and others tap their feet or move their bodies a bit to the beat. In a few minutes, I turn down the music, the noise level drops, and the class formally begins.

## Starting Out in Science

In the beginning, I never wanted to teach! In my teens and early 20s, I was consciously against the idea despite the fact that both parents were gifted teachers. I originally trained to be an industrial chemist. I completed a BSc (Honors) in chemistry at the University of the Witwatersrand, in Johannesburg, South Africa, the city and country of my birth. Actually, I had wanted to be a journalist when I was in high school, but it wasn't a strong urge and my family showed little support for it.

I chose a science degree because it seemed a sensible thing to do. After all, my father was a science teacher (and at that time a high school principal), I had done well in science and math in my graduating examinations, and physics and chemistry were glamour subjects with promising career prospects for university graduates in the late 1950s and early 1960s. Absent from this decision-making exercise was any real self-awareness about my career interests and aptitudes.

My 4 years studying for the honors degree in chemistry were more about getting an education in life than about preparing to enter a profession. I spent quite a bit of time going to the movies, hanging out with new friends, taking part in social and somewhat political events, and discussing all sorts of subjects unrelated to my field . . . and then cramming like mad at exam time. I did well in my courses, but even though I signed up just before graduation for a master's degree in inorganic chemistry, I don't think I had seriously envisioned what it meant to pursue a career in this profession.

I delayed my start in this program for 1 year. Like many others of my age from Commonwealth countries such as South Africa, Australia, Canada, and New Zealand, I made my "pilgrimage" to London and the European Continent. I worked at odd jobs in London for short periods and traveled around for the rest of the time. That experience changed me in many ways, and after I returned to South Africa and went to discuss an MSc program with my designated advisor, I immediately felt the wrongness of the decision. I felt sick at the thought of doing more work in this area, of spending the rest of my life in a laboratory. I left the advisor's office and never returned! I was 22 years old and in need of some career advice. I received some professional guidance that identified me as being oriented toward ideas and people. I would be suited, the report said, to working in personnel, in psychology, in teaching, or as a journalist.

## Finding a Career

I joined Unilever as a management trainee a few weeks later. I was too late to be included in the formal management training program for university graduates, but I persuaded the recruiters to place me in the personnel department of the Lever Brother's plant in Boksburg, my hometown. I think I was accommodated because the company had a major chemical laboratory at that factory and the recruiters figured I would soon tire of this personnel kick.

I never looked back! I took to the personnel activities assigned to me like a duck takes to water! For the first time in my life, I had a sense of purpose, and Lever Brothers was a great place to start. I enjoyed being in a factory setting, I liked the idea of working on people-related issues, I could see the relevance of the issues being raised, and I had a sense that what I was doing could make a difference to others. Mickey Bebb, several years my senior, was my supervisor and my mentor. He constantly forced me to push the limits of what I could learn and do on the job. He afforded me a great deal of freedom to go well beyond my job description (which was in itself very vague and might be roughly designated as "running around" the factory and the offices doing what came my way). We talked for hours about personnel issues, about applied psychology, and about training. He functioned as a demanding coach and gave me confidence in my abilities and in my choice of career. I absorbed more learning in my 15 or so months at Lever Brothers than in all 4 years as an undergraduate in the science program.

Dick Sutton was the senior personnel executive of Edgar's Stores Limited, a fast-growing family outfitting chain that soon recruited me away from Lever Brothers into a management training program. I found myself within a few months, at 24 years of age, a personnel manager responsible for all the retail outlets in the geographic heartland of South Africa and located in a major political center of Afrikaans culture. (Afrikaans is one of the two "white" languages in South Africa and, at that time, was the language of the ruling party in the country. English is the other "white" language.) I had just married, and my wife, Nola, and I found ourselves far from our roots.

Edgar's Stores was another great training ground for me. It was much more hard-edged and rough-and-tumble than Lever Brothers, and the pace of growth and change was frenetic. Dick Sutton injected a strategic dimension to my understanding of the personnel function. I started to look to academic literature for ideas about personnel practice, and I began to think about models and frameworks to develop practical solutions to managerial problems. (The literature at that time had few well-researched ideas.)

This was taking place around 1963. While at Lever Brothers, I had enrolled in a psychology degree program at the remarkable, newly emerging University of South Africa (UNISA). It was the only institution in South Africa that provided adults of all races with the opportunity to pursue a university degree, and its mechanism for education was through correspondence. (Nelson Mandela, the current president of South Africa, is one of its graduates.) Its standards were high, and it offered courses in subjects I needed to further my education in personnel management. I was able to "start over" academically while continuing to work full time. It proved to be a major bridge to my future as an academic. I continued my studies on an accelerated basis while at Edgar's Stores. As I began work on a master's degree in psychology in 1966, however, I realized I needed more time to attend to my studies than was possible given the demands of my managerial role, and I saw further study as a key to continued flexibility in my career. Despite the attractiveness of the work I was doing at Edgar's Stores, I reluctantly quit this job and accepted an offer by Lynn Shaw to work as an industrial psychologist in a consulting division she had founded in PUTCO, a Johannesburg transportation company. It was a "9 to 5" job and provided the change of pace I needed to be able to concentrate on my graduate training. It also subsequently provided the site and the data for my MSc thesis.

My advisor at UNISA, Lily Gerdes, taught me about the value of supportive (patient yet demanding) academic mentorship. Completing a research-based degree while working full time and raising a young family (our new preoccupation) was enormously challenging. There were so many things to attend to and to enjoy in my work and personal arenas that staying the pace to complete the graduate degree was difficult. Lily Gerdes was the right person to help me keep focused, and I learned a great deal from her about doing research and about working with students in a mentoring/advising role.

## Stepping Out of the Box

During the mid-1960s, my wife and I decided to live outside South Africa, at least for a while. We wanted to experience other cultures, and I wanted to further my academic training in personnel in a different context. We chose to go to the United States. As a result of a meeting and a series of conversations in South Africa with Tom Mahoney (Chapter 8), then a professor at the Industrial Relations Center (IRC) at the University of Minnesota, we applied for admission to that school. I enrolled, on borrowed money, at the University of Minnesota in March 1969, intending to spend 1 year (or so) working on a master's degree in personnel. My wife and I had neither the financial resources nor the time, with responsibilities for two very small children, to stay out of the labor market for long. After my first semester in the program, however, I was invited to join the Ph.D. program in the IRC. With the aid of a fellowship and some creative budgeting, we made it through the next 4 years to complete the program. (My wife was not permitted to work, given my international student status, but over the years she filled many hours as a one-person "day-care" center, and her efforts helped us financially get through the days and months of the program.)

I was exposed to many good teachers, undoubtedly the most influential being Tom Mahoney. Like Bebb, Sutton, and Gerdes, my earlier
mentors, he challenged and trusted me to rise to the occasion: He drew
the best out of those who responded even though this was sometimes
a painful and frustrating experience for his students and perhaps for
him. He expected that his students know the literature intimately; ask
intelligent, probing questions on issues; forge points of view that are
intellectually honest; and learn to develop their own scholarly voices.
I doubt that any of us who were his advisees will forget this shaping
experience. It happened in classroom and advising, one-on-one situations. I absorbed from this exposure many lessons about ways to communicate ideas and to inspire others to learn. I realized, only much
later, that emerging from this exposure to Tom and to my earlier teachers, I was developing a sensitivity to and an interest in the processes
of learning. It has become a preoccupation of mine. For me, the process of communication is as important as its content. I think it also is
a legacy of growing up in a family of teachers in which I absorbed,
almost by osmosis, an appreciation for teaching and learning despite
my apparent indifference to this influence in my early years. Now, I
spend large blocks of time thinking about how something can be taught
differently and better, with how students can be engaged and stretched,
and with how to make a lesson more interesting. (As an aside, I love
movies and books that provide the story about the making of the movie
or of some other product or of some event.)

We returned to South Africa in 1973 and stayed about 18 months
before we emigrated to Canada and I joined the University of British
Columbia (UBC) in Vancouver, where I am today. In South Africa, I
rejoined Dick Sutton as a personnel consultant in a different organization, South African Breweries, a large consumer goods conglomer-
ate. I worked with Dick Sutton and three other consultants to create
modules to teach communication and negotiation skills to supervisors
and employees. We took the then new ideas of behavior modeling and
its applications and created a program that was very successful in helping
resolve conflicts and build bridges between white supervisors and pre-
dominately black employees. I learned to teach by doing such programs
over and over, often in quite explosive situations. One such program
immediately followed the settling of a wildcat strike in the hotel industry in Durban. I was part of a small team of professionals involved
in settling the strike, and within hours I was implementing an inten-

sive week-long conflict resolution and communications training program involving the managers and employees from the Durban hotels.

I got feedback on my performances in the classroom quickly and explicitly from participants and from my colleagues. It was an invaluable preparation for later teaching when I became a full-time academic. It was the only somewhat formal (structured and monitored) training I ever received to become a teacher.

## A New Career, A New Country

We arrived as a family of four in Vancouver, British Columbia, Canada, on December 16, 1974, to start a new life. I had been offered a post as assistant professor while still in South Africa, and although it was a bittersweet decision to accept (Frost, 1990), it was a wonderful opportunity that we simply could not pass up, given our intent to emigrate eventually from South Africa. We landed with five suitcases and few other possessions. I was slated to teach three courses starting in the first week of January 1975. Two were graduate courses—one on organizational theory and one on organizational behavior. A third course was a section of the core mandatory undergraduate course on organizational behavior. To say that I was stretched in teaching these courses would be an understatement! I was barely minutes ahead of any class each day, and particularly in the graduate courses, I was forced to improvise a great deal and to draw on the energy (and goodwill) of the students to get the material covered in a coherent and interesting manner. These two courses went very well; we had a great deal of fun. I think we all learned a lot, and I loved the experience of teaching at this level. One lesson I internalized was that, at least for complex, ambiguous material and reasonably sophisticated, reflective audiences, learning can be very effective if the instructor is also learning and if he or she acts as a facilitator rather than as an authoritative dispenser of truth. It is akin to trapezing without a net.

Teaching the undergraduate course was a different experience altogether. My senior colleagues had advised me to enjoy the graduate courses and to just grin and bear the other one—it was not going to be a positive experience. Many students resented having to take the course and thought the material was trivial, irrelevant, or, at best, common sense. My colleagues were right about it being an unrewarding experience. We were all in a straightjacket (the students and I). The textbook was uninspiring (true of most textbooks, I believe), scant real experiential learning was going on, and no practical, applied material was provided to ground the concepts. The material did not bring the topics alive for these 18- to 20-year-old students. I remember lying in the bath one night, thinking, "There has to be a better way to teach this stuff!" and realizing that, at least for that school term, I was powerless to change much. My section needed to be in synch with others. There were simply too many constraints to be able to make it different. I was stuck with my lot, at least for the term.

I learned something from this experience—that I hate to have a poor experience in class, where the students and I are not connecting and opportunities to learn are lost. I go through all kinds of emotional discomfort when this happens, and I become preoccupied with figuring out what went wrong and with how to create ways to get back on track in the next class. I can barely wait to get back into the class to recoup the momentum. It is a draining experience—one shared, I suspect, by some other instructors who care about their teaching. I have also learned (sometimes painfully) that, at times, I have no way to avoid a class that doesn't work out as I had hoped and that it's OK for this to be so. In fact, my experience with the two graduate courses and with a course I will describe next suggests that effective teaching has little to do with "having control" of the outcome. The best I seem able to do is to facilitate the process that unfolds from my designs and to get out of the way of the learning that actually takes place.

## Bridging Teaching and Research

Following my first experience teaching the undergraduate course, I volunteered to coordinate and revamp the course with others who might be interested in the project. It was perhaps a somewhat reckless move for an untenured professor on a 5-year tenure clock, but I could not go back into that environment again and stay sane. My project team included Vance Mitchell, the division chair who had hired me; Thad Barnowe, a fellow assistant professor; Diana Cawood, an instructor and graduate student in the program; and Ron Ruhl, a visiting instructor. Over a period of 3 years, we transformed the course into one of the most popular and well-respected offerings in the faculty. The course design later contributed to a faculty award I received for pedagogical innovations. The course included some organizational simulations we created. We used novels, an array of experiential exercises, and readings chosen for their relevance to current issues. We later used The Organization Game, the simulation developed by Bob Miles and Alan Randolph (1979).

My interest in developing this course, my experiences as a manager and as a consultant, my research interest in organizational politics, and my association with Vance Mitchell and Walter Nord led to the creation of the book *Organizational Reality: Reports From the Firing Line* (Frost, Mitchell, & Nord, 1992.) Now in its fourth edition, it is a collage of short and long stories, articles, poems, news clippings, and the like that represent our sense of interesting and provocative ways to communicate ideas about organizational life. It emerged from the collective view of Vance, Walter, and me that texts of that time were out of touch with lived experience in organizations as we knew it. Our instincts sent us in search of supportive evidence, though in mainly non-academic outlets. We produced a text that could be used in the classroom to supplement other materials. It has been quite widely used in business schools. As a compendium of stories about life in organizations, it also found a home in the field of organizational communication. It was a project that also tapped my journalistic leanings. I have found that seeking out and drawing on stories or reports of organizational participants and creating frameworks and story lines through which to present them is a useful way for me to communicate ideas and insights about organizational issues. (Other examples are *Rhythms of Academic Life* [Frost & Taylor, 1996], *Publishing in the Organizational Sciences* [Cummings & Frost, 1995], *Doing Exemplary Research* [Frost & Stablrin, 1992], and this volume, with Rae André.) Creating and editing the *Organizational Reality* book also steered me toward literatures and scholars in the organizational culture and symbolism arenas and provided an important frame-breaking experience that helped me begin research work in these arenas.

A second product can be traced directly from my teaching this undergraduate course. It stemmed from an observation and a hypothesis I was starting to formulate, shared by Thad Barnowe, that one problem with communicating with and teaching young undergraduate students about the concepts and practices of organizational behavior was it required a different orientation to the way the world works than does an orientation toward concepts in finance, accounting, and more broadly, the physical sciences. Despite the positive changes we had made to the introductory course in organizational behavior, I kept encountering indifference and even cynicism from some students to the ideas. I was not troubled by students' critiques of the ideas; this was encouraged and welcomed. The problem was that some students just did not seem to be able to "get it" at all when we talked about and experimented with such concepts as interpersonal skills, conflict, the effects of organizational design, or motivation. What made it a puzzle for me, one I kept failing to resolve, was that many people in this "tuned out" category were dean's honor list students. They were bright and articulate people. They were in the course because it was required of them, but they could not "see" the point of it at all. At the same time, the eyes of others in the class were lighting up; enthusiasm for the topic was high.

Thad Barnowe was having a similar experience and making similar observations when he taught this course. Together, we developed the notion of "Thing Specialists" and "People Specialists" to distinguish between two hypothesized orientations to the way individuals see and respond to their world. We developed sets of scales to measure these orientations and tested them on student samples. Interestingly and somewhat disconcertingly, just as we were ready to explore initial effects of our scales, we discovered that someone else, the psychologist Brian Little, had developed a virtually identical concept, with a richer conceptual orientation than ours and similar instrumentation. He had published his work some years earlier (Little, 1972). Brian lived and worked in Vancouver. We had not known of his existence, nor had our literature reviews turned up his work. There is often a simultaneity to the observation, naming, and publication of new ideas in science, and we had become another statistic in this pattern! We met with Brian, incorporated aspects of his instruments with ours, and proceeded with our studies with a better handle on the concept and a more useful measurement tool. We published some of our findings in *Occupational Psychology* (Barnowe, Frost, & Jamal, 1979).

## Teaching Without a Net . . . Almost!

In the fall term of 1982, I was assigned to teach an undergraduate elective course on organizational analysis. Craig Pinder had previously taught the course, which focused on such issues as organizational design and structure. Although I designed it differently, I benefited from his excellent reputation as a teacher, in that the course retained its drawing power and many excellent students were enrolled. I decided to try something entirely different in both the design and delivery of this course—different, that is, from the rather structured core course I had coordinated and taught in the previous several years. I needed a change and a challenge. I decided to use *The Invisible War* by Samuel Culbert and Jack McDonough (1980) as one class text, and I adapted the pedagogy that Culbert and McDonough had used to teach the concepts and that was described in the book and in other materials they shared with me. Their focus was on the politics of organizational life and on the subjectivity of the enactment and impacts of organizational structures and events. Their pedagogy included requirements that students keep personal journals and that the instructor adopt a largely nondirective approach to teaching the course. (The nondirectiveness of the instructor was punctuated by probing questions designed to get the students to think more deeply about the material being discussed.) The tensions that emerged from this probing and from the apparent lack of structure in the course became the source of students' journal entries. The insights that came, often late in the course, from processing these tensions and frustrations provided a basis for the learning about organizational issues in much more visceral ways than might occur from an exclusively intellectual treatment of topics.

I adopted the text and much of this orientation to learning in my course, although I added another text and readings that provided other sources of information helpful to organizational analysis. I wasn't sold on an exclusively interpretive approach to learning, and more to the point, I was unsure of my ability to run this course in such a clinical and "unstructured" way. I was teaching without a net, and it was unnerving to students and to me. My reputation as a good teacher ("He's won awards, hasn't he?") served as a double-edged sword. In the early days of the course, as the students and I struggled with this process, the students were waiting for direction. The expectation was that they would be impressed by my performance, and it was not happening. I was low key, unobtrusively probing for ideas, and there was a lot of down time—at least in the form of instructor-led discussions. Culbert and McDonough (1980) were correct; this approach surfaced frustrations and controversy in the classroom, and it showed up to a considerable degree in students' journals, which I read but did not grade. (I wrote comments in the margins that established a dialogue with each student, but I did not evaluate their contributions. At most, I urged them to search more intensively for understandings about what was happening in the content and the processes of class sessions.) The course was somewhat like a sensitivity training session and was intended to build for students a strong connection to organizational as well as personal understandings.

Later, the class began to get a second wind. I think this happened partly because students surmised, "Because this guy is supposed to be a good teacher, this must be something he intends and there must be lessons in what is happening, so let's get involved ourselves and take the experience seriously!" This attitude showed up to an extent in the journals. In addition, this shift is imbedded in the Culbert and McDonough design. In the absence of someone directing the show, students gradually take ownership of the learning and start to move forward. I felt that I was wobbling on the tightrope until this shift appeared. I was feeling internal pressure to revert to a more direct instructional role until the shift took place.

The course did not "come together" as a whole learning experience about organizations and organizational life until the last week of the term, right after students had completed their papers based on journal entries. Getting through that project had necessitated my extending office hours for 2 weeks prior to the paper deadline. I helped students wrestle with the meaning of their journal entries, and in nondirective ways I tried to facilitate their choice of a way to write a paper that was stimulated by their journal entries.

The closing week in this course was remarkable! (I observed the same experience in subsequent offerings of the course.) Students seemed to have grasped, in quite evocative ways, some subtleties of organizational issues and practices, and they were excited and energized by the experience. The journal-to-paper exercise seemed to be pivotal for many students. One student came to my office shortly before the deadline, paper in hand, and said to me, "You bastard! I finally caught on to what this was all about at 2 a.m. this morning—after being frustrated for weeks—and when I did, I figured out what I wanted to say. I was blown away by the experience. It's the best thing I've ever written!" She talked about realizing that she had to take ownership of her understandings about organizational events and processes and about developing her own voice on the material, rather than give all the authority to texts, instructors, and other "experts."

The students' papers were among the best I had ever read. The challenge was how to grade them, because each paper was different. Each paper reflected organizational and personal issues presented in a unique and idiosyncratic way. I evolved a way of assessing the papers that required several readings of each one. It was an admittedly very subjective and time-consuming evaluation of how much the paper reflected understanding of organizational issues and personal growth and insight about themselves as organizational participants. I wrote detailed comments and explanations on each paper and gave mostly A's and B's because I believed these to be appropriate. Very few people came back to challenge their grades, and I changed hardly any of them after we'd talked about the paper and the course.

## Lessons Learned From the Experiment

Many students did come back in the first week of the next term. They would say hi and then hang around for a bit, without any apparent agenda. Only some time later, when I had observed this to be a fairly common phenomenon in the first week of the next term, did I tumble to the thought that courses like this—in fact, I believe, most courses— need some marker, some process, some symbolic event to close them, or they need some way to deal with incompleteness as another organizational reality. The need is for instructors to help students let go, perhaps even grieve the end of an intense experience that has spanned several weeks and that involves the dissolution of a temporary organization and community. I had been working on organizational culture and symbolism issues in my research at the time, and I was reading about dying organizations and the need for ceremony and symbols to help members of the organization cope with such endings. I started to build attention to symbolic closings into all my courses. Together with Carolyn Egri and Ken Keleman, I worked out a way to communicate this insight to others, and we eventually published our work in the *Journal of Management Education* (in press).

I took two other insights from this particular teaching experience. One was a recognition that I had replicated, in some important ways, the kind of teaching experience I had received from Tom Mahoney. Although teaching a different topic (compensation and reward theory and administration) and using somewhat different classroom techniques, Mahoney had created the same deeply stretching learning experience for his students and provoked in them the similar kinds of frustration, exhilaration, and breakthroughs. I was reproducing in my own way as a teacher what had been for me a profound personal learning experience!

The other lesson was that fairly deep personal insights can be taught alongside more abstract learnings even and perhaps especially in a course aimed at macro concepts of organizational analysis. We need to incorporate this connection more extensively into our teaching students about organizations. The danger is that when talking about organizations, they can become reified so that the active involvement and emotional investment of participants in organizational outcomes is forgotten or trivialized. (As an example, reengineering may be a way to improve the effectiveness of an organization. It may also be a failure. Either way, it affects all those who come into contact with it, and they have thoughts, feelings, and experiences that feed into its enactment and that occur as a result of its introduction.) Interestingly, as I continued to experiment with the organizational analysis course over the years, I found that the undergraduates could work through some quite sophisticated and challenging reading materials on organizational issues because they had a way to "ground" the material in their personal contexts. For example, by paying attention to the lessons learned from adapting the Culbert and McDonough (1980) pedagogy, I successfully used, for several years, Gareth Morgan's *Images of Organization* (1986), which in my opinion is more naturally a graduate-level text and might usually be read with little interest or comprehension by business school undergraduates.

I made a conscious decision, as a result of my experiences with this course, to incorporate into my teaching, wherever I could, a personal learning dimension to accompany whatever is being explored on the organizational dimension. Taking this stance has led me to find and develop learning experiences that might reveal personal dimensions that link to organizational life. Techniques have included creating masks, creating personal mission statements, keeping a personal journal, and working with video images that tap emotional issues in organizations (e.g., Marx, Jick, & Frost, 1991).

## Revisiting Links Between Teaching and Research

I learn a great deal by presenting what I am working on as a research idea—a report or paper—and then hearing what I say and what others provide as feedback. I benefited from presenting ideas and findings about the politics of innovation with Carolyn Egri at a 1988 Conference on Appreciative Management at Case Western Reserve University, in Cleveland. We reconfigured an important aspect of our conceptualization of executive leadership as a direct result of our own late-night rehashing of the feedback we received from the audience in our conference session. It led to a genuine aha! experience and made the subsequent publication a better piece (Frost & Egri, 1990). I find that this breakthrough effect frequently happens when I take seriously the task of communicating my ideas to an audience—that is, when I am thinking like a teacher as well as like a researcher.

The origin of the people-thing orientation of students also flowed out of observations and lessons from the classroom. We noticed the difficulties that bright students had with organizational concepts and developed our dichotomy of personal orientations. I have found that working through difficult or challenging research ideas also sharpens my teaching skills. Needing to communicate clearly to students the slippery constructs of organizational power and politics, I was helped by the time I had spent wrestling with ways to define and understand the concepts for research papers on these phenomena. My recognition of the need to include closing ceremonies for course endings might not have happened had I not been working at the time with symbolism literature that introduced the concepts of collective grieving and organizational transition.

## Enhancing the Academic Credibility of Teaching

I like Walter Nord's way of thinking about research and teaching as processes characterized by "continuous learning" (Nord, 1996). I think that as long as one is working with an open mind on research or teaching and one has an expectation that one is creating, discovering, improving, and coming upon different understandings when doing research or teaching, learning is taking place. It is then possible for each of these crafts to feed and enhance the other.

If this is true, why is teaching still regarded so lightly in many major business schools even as more attention is being given to this craft? In part, this lack of credibility is because of a belief in some quarters that good teachers are born, not made, and because many researchers think it is easy to do—as in: "If you're good, it's easy to do and it doesn't require a great deal of time/as much time as doing good research!" I think it is more accurate to think of it as a craft that can be learned; one can get better at it with practice and feedback. Furthermore, it takes enormous investments of an individual's time, energy, and attention if we are talking about delivering good teaching.

In part, teaching lacks credibility because we have not yet created a strong set of means to measure its performance, although the introduction of evidence in the form of teaching dossiers is a step in the right direction. We need an evaluation procedure for promotion and tenure decisions at universities that includes a clear set of criteria and the use of external referees to assess this issue. In part, teaching lacks credibility because we do not acknowledge and know the body of intellectual and empirical knowledge that exists about teaching and because we don't have one of our own.

When we teach about teaching, the emphasis typically is on techniques: Not much is said or studied about the philosophy and "science" of teaching. So, the doubters and skeptics can downgrade its importance. "This is not about knowledge, about something with academic substance." We haven't addressed this issue in our field, and more needs to be done by those who can bring research or teaching skills to bear on the topic. Perhaps, this chapter as well as a forthcoming special research forum in the *Academy of Management Journal* will help move the appreciation and practice of teaching to a more sophisticated level in our field.

## Taking Stock

I've been traveling a journey from a stage when I did not want to teach, to a life in which I love to teach. When I am teaching, I feel truly present. It is a time when I am very focused and attentive, when I feel very much alive. I am drawn to the joy, the excitement, and the challenge of designing ways to communicate knowledge and to the performance, mine and others', that occurs in the theater of the classroom.

When the performance goes well in this theater, a bond develops between teacher and participant; it has an intimacy that, if managed with integrity and sensitivity, expands the learning of everyone to an extraordinary degree. I have taught classes in which this happens and have felt stretched and challenged by others in the class to learn and to reveal knowledge, ideas, connections, inferences, and solutions, some that I did not know existed. Sometimes, I feel as if I am reaching into some deep, hidden pockets in my teacher's costume to find inspiration and insights that are "miraculously" there. As a teacher, as a co-learner, I feed off such experiences. When things don't work out, it is draining to manage the process, and in the aftermath I feel humbled and even discouraged. This is painful, but it helps keep a balance; it helps me develop a healthy sense of myself as a teacher. The possibility that one might make a difference to the understandings that others have about themselves and about organizational life is all I need to keep the flame of my enthusiasm alive.

I love to teach, but I would not want only to teach. If I were required to teach every day, all academic year long, I know I would lose my passion for it rather quickly. I like to write; I like to create new knowledge that will find its way into journals and books. I like to be immersed in my teaching for a time and then to work on other things, to get back to writing and investigating ideas, to spend time collaborating with colleagues on interesting projects

## At the End of the Day

In 1991, I was teaching a management seminar in South Africa for the School of Business Leadership of the University of South Africa. The 2-day session was held at a hotel that was, interestingly, across the street from the church where my parents were married in 1938. At the end of the first day, one participant came up to me, introduced himself to me, and said, "Are you Felix Frost's son? He taught me years ago in high school. He was my favorite teacher, and he made a huge impression on me. I've never forgotten him." I said that I was his son and that my father was living in a nursing home in North Vancouver. He had had several minor strokes and, over several years, had lost much of his capacity to look after himself and needed constant supervised care. The participant and I talked for a while about my father, and I discovered anew his impact on students he had taught long ago. The manager asked me to convey his best wishes to my parents, and we each moved on to other tasks.

I was profoundly moved by the encounter, and when I returned to Vancouver and visited my father, I told him the story. I am not sure how much of it he took in. On some days, he was more lucid than on others. I like to think that he did absorb the message, that it mattered to him, and that somewhere he registered with pleasure that someone had acknowledged his significance as a teacher.

If someone communicated such an opinion to me, one day, in my twilight years, I think it would have special significance for me. Although teaching in academia might not yet be accorded the institutional and professional significance given to doing research, I think that when teaching is done well, it contributes to learning where it counts the most—in the hearts and minds of others, of the students with whom one works. To teach others so that they learn to be more competent, to be wiser, to be better human beings is what it is all about. To be remembered for having spent oneself in the service of learning and of improving the human condition through teaching would be a worthy epitaph, I think, for an academic. It is one I would cherish!

## References

Barnowe, J. T., Frost, P. J., & Jamal, M. (1979). When personality meets situation: Exploring influences on choice of business major. *Occupational Psychology, 52,* 167-176.

Culbert, S. A., & McDonough, J. J. (1980). *The invisible war: Pursuing self-interests at work.* New York: John Wiley.

Cummings, L. L., & Frost, P. J. (1995). *Publishing in the organizational sciences.* Thousand Oaks, CA: Sage.

Egri, C., Keleman, K. S., & Frost, P. J. (in press). Breaking up is hard to do: Building separation and transitions at the end of the course. *Journal of Management Education.*

Frankl, V. E. (1984). *Man's search for meaning.* New York: Pocket Books. (Original work published in 1959)

Frost, P. J. (1990). Creating scholarship and journeying through academia: Reflections and interpretations from the field. *Journal of Applied Behavioral Science, 25*(4), 399-418.

Frost, P. J., & Egri, C. (1990). Appreciating executive action. In S. Srivastva, D. Cooperrider, & Associates (Eds.), *The power of positive thought and action in organizations* (pp. 284-322). San Francisco: Jossey-Bass.

Frost, P. J., Mitchell, V. F., & Nord, W. R. (Eds.). (1992). *Organizational reality: Reports from the firing line* (4th ed.). New York: HarperCollins.

Frost, P. J., & Stablrin, R. (1992). *Doing exemplary research.* Newbury Park, CA: Sage.

Frost, P. J., & Taylor, M. S. (1996). *Rhythms of academic life.* Thousand Oaks, CA: Sage.

Little, B. R. (1972). *Person-thing orientation: A provisional manual for the T-P Scale.* Cambridge, UK: Oxford University, Department of Experimental Psychology.

Marx, R., Jick, T., & Frost, P. J. (1991). *Management live: The video book.* Englewood Cliffs, NJ: Prentice Hall.

Miles, R. H., & Randolph, W. A. (1979). *The organization game.* Santa Monica, CA: Goodyear.

Morgan, G. (1986). *Images of organization.* Newbury Park, CA: Sage.

Nord, W. R. (1996). Research/teaching boundaries. In P. J. Frost & M. S. Taylor (Eds.), *Rhythms of academic life.* Newbury Park: Sage.

Rodegast, P., & Stanton, J. (Comps.). (1985). *Emmanuel's book.* Toronto: Bantam Books.

# 8 Scholarship as a Career of Learning Through Research and Teaching

THOMAS A. MAHONEY

It is common to conceive of a career as a progressive succession of experiences building toward an integrated whole, different stages of experiences elaborating on and developing the potential revealed through prior experiences. A career plan, in this sense, can be likened to a map detailing the direction necessary to achieve or realize some desired end stage. Career planning often is urged as beneficial in the development of one's potential to realize some desired end.

Yet, a career may also be cast as a retrospective rationalization of past experiences, a making sense of what may have occurred as unplanned and unpredicted experiences that accumulate and build toward some realized end. Viewed in this manner, a series of experiences may yield a meaningful sense of development that would have been unlikely to emerge from a prospective analysis of potential experiences. Often, what may have occurred as unlikely and unpredictable experiences emerge as the most telling and significant stages in a series of developmental experiences.

I find the retrospective analysis most useful in the analysis of my own personal career in a life of scholarship. That career was unselected, unplanned, and emerged over time "doing what came naturally." The various stages that occurred make sense in retrospect, and their contribution to the entire experience can be perceived with far greater clarity than would have been revealed in any attempted prospective career planning.

Although that career might be labeled as one of academic teaching and research, it was, in fact, a career of learning. Academic teaching and research were the vehicles used in the career of learning, not the primary objectives. Although academic teaching and research are often cast as joined yet divergent interests and pursuits, the two are inextricably intertwined in my retrospective analysis. My career of learning has been mutually dependent on both research and teaching. Certainly, both research and teaching have contributed to my learning. Perhaps more important, I have experienced teaching through research and research through teaching. These seeming contradictions can best be reconciled through retrospective analysis of experiences, my career of learning through teaching and research.

Learning through research is, perhaps, obvious; one undertakes research in an attempt to reconcile competing explanations of some phenomenon or to elaborate description of that phenomenon. Teaching, for me, also involves learning. It is an attempt to develop the understanding of others concerning some topic or issue. Subjects that are perfectly understood and about which there are no questions are rare and certainly require no teaching in the usual sense at the graduate level; learning the Taylor-Russell tables, statistical formulas, or even the formula for net present value provide examples. Other issues, such as learning how to improve employee performance through incentive compensation, have no certain and definite resolution and require examination of competing explanations from, for example, individual and social psychology. My goal of teaching at this level is to develop students' ability to employ multiple approaches in understanding issues that will never be resolved with certainty. As I assist students in this application of analysis, I also inevitably learn more about the topics of analysis as we jointly push beyond commonly accepted answers and understanding.

## Early Career Stumbling

I am not conscious of ever having selected a career of academic scholarship. Life as a student was fun, and I enjoyed learning. Study was less a matter of grades and competition than it was an excitement of learning something previously unknown by me. Something akin to the Socratic method was natural to me as a student. I tended to argue with assertions, whether experienced through reading, lecture, or laboratory experience. This arguing was fun and exciting and led me to unexpected realizations. Although I didn't realize it at the time, I was developing and elaborating my theories of whatever subject matter was under investigation. Those theories were constantly challenged, modified, and elaborated through confrontation with new ideas, observations, and competing theories.

One professor in particular influenced my mode of learning and inadvertently shaped my later approach to research and teaching. That professor taught classical microeconomic theory, my first introduction to economics. Students exposed to microeconomic theory, particularly as taught 40 years ago, were confronted with a tightly reasoned set of propositions based on explicit sets of assumptions. Given those assumptions and the laws of logic, the conclusions were inevitable and inescapable. Like many students, I found the conclusions of microeconomic theory contradicting my everyday experiences and observations. And I fought through argument with the professor. Everyday experiences and observations were not accepted by him in argument, however. Observations, he would assert, were momentary and likely to change or were a result of market imperfections. Rather than address current observations, we should focus on equilibrium conditions in a perfect market and, in consequence, address policy toward overcoming imperfections to hasten achieving the desired equilibrium. Instead, I was forced to master the theories presented and to attack them on their own grounds. As might be expected, I was unsuccessful in changing his construction of theory. I did, however, learn and master the theories presented. And I did learn how to work with theory and to use it in my own intellectual development.

As an undergraduate majoring in economics, I was expected to minor in another of the social sciences. Having taken a course in the history of philosophy, I was interested in more and successfully petitioned to minor in philosophy. I found the issues addressed in philosophy—the nature of humans, the nature of knowledge, the nature of good—intriguing and found the nature of change in answers to these issues over time to be exciting. Although economics and philosophy may appear to be quite different, I found them to be quite compatible and suited to the learning style I was unconsciously developing. Although both are concerned with vital issues of life, both approach these issues through abstract and conceptual reasoning. (Recall that Adam Smith was a professor of moral philosophy!) Study of the history of philosophy revealed the development of different schools of thought over time as one was found inadequate in response to various issues and was replaced with a different school of thought. The histories of economic thought and of philosophical thought display many parallels in the development and elaboration of concept and theory. I was learning how to think abstractly, to develop, challenge, and modify theory while learning the content of the course.

## On to Graduate Studies

Given the fun I experienced in learning through confronting new evidence and ideas, I was eager to continue learning in graduate studies and unready to make any career choice. Graduate study was unplanned and was an avoidance of career planning and choice. And my approach to graduate study continued as before, the seeking out of theories that might elaborate my conceptual view of the world. Graduate study was less a matter of learning new facts and evidence and more a matter of theory elaboration and development. The more I was exposed to theories from different disciplines, the more I sought integration of them. The confining of theories to disciplinary boundaries (e.g. micro- and macroeconomics, individual differences and social psychology, political science) frustrated me. Instead, I sought to confront these theories with each other and to seek out points of reinforcement and/or conflict. Elaborating the implications of different yet related theories was exciting and fun. In short, it was both research and learning at the same time.

One example relates to my rebellion against the conclusions of microeconomic theory concerning full employment in free markets and the effects of unionization on markets. Having experienced unemployment and the difficulties of finding a job and having worked in both unionized and non-unionized settings, I found the traditional conclusions irritating. Learning something about individual motivation from psychology, I was able to realize that the perfect market of microeconomics would never be realized. I was also able to explain, at least to myself, how collective bargaining, though a barrier to free market operation, might actually contribute to economic productivity.

Probably, the greatest influence on my development in graduate studies occurred through my experience as a research assistant, experience that was necessary as a means for support, although it provided significant professional development. That experience as a research assistant occurred at the Industrial Relations Center (IRC) of the University of Minnesota, then known as the home of "dust bowl empiricism." The guiding theme of the IRC at that time was "If you can't measure it, it doesn't exist." And that prevailing attitude provided a useful challenge to inclination to concept and theory elaboration. I learned that research is a combination of theoretical elaboration and empirical investigation and that both are necessary for the development of knowledge. Theory without a grounding in data is irrelevant, as are data without a grounding in theory. The empirical focus was exciting as an alternative or supplement to theory and concept. It also offered confirmation.

A large portion of research at that time was directed toward describing, through survey research, existing practice in industrial relations. Existing practice called for explanation—Why was it common, and what were the effects? One project on which I worked concerned the mobility of labor in the labor market. Theory assumptions of perfect knowledge and of costless mobility were clearly violated in our findings. Another issue that interested me for the MA thesis was the promotion of democratic participation of members in labor unions. I was unaware, then, of any relevant theory, and empirical examination of high- and low-participation local unions offered an avenue toward answers, as well as development of a conceptualization of participation in membership organizations.

Unintentionally, I had embarked on a career of scholarship through teaching and research all because I was pursuing a career of continued personal learning and development. And that combination of careers has continued since, although specific illustrations have varied over time.

## Teaching as Research and Learning

I entered an academic career as my means toward a career of continued learning. Teaching has been a vital contributor to that continued learning. Because most of that teaching has been at the graduate level and because illustrations are more readily at hand, I focus primarily on my graduate teaching. The same themes run through my undergraduate and postgraduate teaching experiences, but they are less apparent.

One theme has been a focus on analytic theory, rather than on description or presentation of so-called best practices. Graduate students preparing for professional careers in business and industry tend to seek "the answer" and want to know "how to do it." In response to that felt need, I typically assign a traditional text for them to read while I focus on presentation and application of theoretical models supporting and/or challenging the presentations of the text. I rationalize this to the class with the explanation that best practices vary over time and situations and that relevant theory will be their best guide when faced with these changes where best practices fail. Individual production incentives, for example, were quite appropriate when the individual worker controlled the pace of production but are inappropriate following a move to teamwork and interdependence among workers. Similarly, an increase in compensation to motivate mobility becomes less effective when there is an employed spouse or commitment to stability of child relationships in a school or community.

A second, related theme is an attempt to develop students' abilities to think and employ multiple theoretical models from multiple disciplines. It is rare, in my experience, that a single discipline can provide total and complete understanding of a phenomenon or issue, and use of multiple disciplinary lenses typically enhances understanding of the issue. An example is the focus of economics on monetary value (e.g., wages) with the rationale that this is, perhaps, the only outcome for which all would agree that "more is better." Analyses based on this presumption can be enhanced by incorporating views from psychology that some phenomena (e.g., temperature) have an optimal value for which both more and less are undesirable, and views from anthropology and social psychology concerning the common attribution of value to dominance and status. In short, more wages may be sacrificed for more status in motivating behavior.

A third implicit theme is a focus on a form of what might be termed a Socratic method of learning, whether conducted personally by arguing with oneself or in dialogue, and I have inevitably incorporated it into my teaching. I find my own learning advanced when I am alert to and seek out seeming conundrums and contradictions, and I attempt to provide similar stimuli to students. One example occurred as I was waiting at the Red Cross to donate blood. On the wall were plaques with names of 15-gallon donors. Examining these out of curiosity, I was struck with the fact that about 80% of the 50 to 60 names posted were male. Because females comprise roughly half the population, why were they not more equally represented among the donors? Potential explanations included motivation (males more responsive to whatever motivations are present) and opportunity (bloodmobiles at factories dominated by male employees). In any event, this puzzle exercises one's thinking and application of relevant theory. Another example is the absence of incentive compensation for production work and the heavy reliance on incentives such as stock options for executives, a total reversal of practice of 20 years ago.

This focus on anomalies and the use of multiple conceptual approaches has been aided by having matured in the field of study known as "industrial relations." That field began as an applied field seeking solutions for observed problems in practice. It was not a single, well-developed body of relevant theory, and scholars sought assistance from various related theories, particularly labor economics, industrial psychology, sociology, and political science. Each of these disciplines provides different sets of lenses for viewing and interpreting the world. These multiple lenses provide the arguments and contradictions that are part of the Socratic method of learning, and I have benefited from them. In consequence, I attempt to provide students with such lenses through mastery of the content of different theories and to encourage their use in the analysis of issues. For example, agency theory and human capital theory from economics, individual motivation theory, and social comparison theories from psychology all bear on issues of work motivation and performance. No one model or theory provides a total explanation of the phenomenon of interest, yet confronted one with another and combined in unique ways, they can improve understanding and control. One applied example is the work of a student interested in employment contract negotiations. Although models from economics and social psychology are fairly obvious references, the student found that models of gift exchange, reciprocity, trust, and discretion from anthropology enriched his thinking and led him into an improved model for his research.

Despite the various arguments for abandonment of core study and requirements in undergraduate and graduate education, I regret the loss of a requirement for some minimal breadth of study of different disciplines. Certainly, the breadth of disciplines I have experienced has contributed to both stimulation of interest and understanding. I attempt to promote students' use of multiple disciplinary lenses when I confront them with alternative explanations for some phenomenon and encourage them to develop their own insights into the phenomenon. In this process of confrontation and argument, students master the theories presented and then modify them and elaborate their own particular theoretical frameworks that they will take with them. It is my hope that they will carry the process of learning with them and continue this theory development through their careers.

It probably is obvious that this approach to teaching continues my own personal learning. As we compare theories and confront them with emerging experiences and observations, I also continue my personal elaboration of theory. An example concerns differentials in wage structures, long accepted as reflecting differentials in the difficulty of work. Confronted with some empirical research in sociology and working with interested students, I came to the conclusion that differentials are more reflective of status, particularly in reporting relationships, than of difficulty of work. And I also continue to learn from the often exciting discoveries made by students in their own learning experiences. For example, one favorite course ends with an examination in which about 10 issues or problems are presented for study several weeks in advance of the examination, the actual examination to be drawn from those questions. Students are encouraged to draw on the theoretical content of the course and to work in groups to analyze the issues. Many of the questions remain the same from year to year, and the answers improve from year to year. I learn and am challenged from these new and improved analyses. One question asked repeatedly concerns the perhaps tenfold increase in wages for men's barbers over the past 20 years despite any apparent lack of improved productivity; it still requires about 20 minutes for a basic haircut. Students draw on theories of marginal productivity, social comparison models of equity in the motivation of labor supply, models of consumer taste and value, and theories of human capital. Both the students and I thrill to new insights gained in the merger of relevant theories—the change in consumer taste in hairstyling as it affects marginal productivity value and alternative opportunities for employment in higher paid women's hairstyling as it affects employment opportunities for men's barbers, for example.

I find this approach to teaching closely related to research, both that of students and of my own. Research often is motivated by an apparent conundrum, some conflicting theoretical implications or some conflict between observation and theory. These conundrums invite continued study and research. A number of doctoral dissertations, as well as personal research projects of my own, had their genesis in issues discovered in teaching.

## Research as Teaching

Research, for me, is sparked by unanswered questions, issues that demand explanation, and contradictory explanations of some phenomenon. Research seeks some resolution, and that resolution is learning.

Not all research results in resolution of questions, issues, and contradictions, however. It is not uncommon for me to abandon, at least temporarily, a search for resolution that eludes me. One example was an inquiry into linkages between the constructs of motivation and satisfaction. Briefly, I reasoned that dissatisfaction serves to arouse, and I also distinguished between what I termed deprivational and aspirational dissatisfaction. *Deprivational dissatisfaction* relates to some comparison with some relatively fixed standard and can be overcome with satisfaction of needs. *Aspirational dissatisfaction,* I argued, can be controlled in terms of degree and intensity but likely is present constantly as one adjusts aspirations. Thus, aspirational dissatisfaction is a form of internal motivation and does not achieve equilibrium, as is possible with deprivational dissatisfaction. Early work found support for independent constructs of aspirational and deprivational dissatisfaction, but it became apparent that far more work would be required than I was prepared to commit at that time. The research process, however, always constitutes learning as I probe information and theories that are unfamiliar to me. Although the process often occasions frustration, it inevitably results in some change in my thinking and framework of theory. And, I find this learning fun. At minimum, my research efforts are teaching me as I learn.

Similarly, I view much of the work of students in class as research for them. They are confronted with issues and pushed to find resolutions. This research need not take the form of empirical measurement and analysis, but it is nonetheless research. Just as I do, the students learn the content of the course and how to use it in thinking about issues through their research. They are learning a research process as well that they can take with them into their future experiences.

Often, the most exciting learning through research I have experienced has been in the form of doctoral dissertation research. This research, of necessity, is more engrossing than the research encountered in the classroom. This dissertation research is made easier if students have been engaged as research assistant apprentices during their doctoral studies. They learn the craft of research by working with a supervisor and enter dissertation research at a level beyond those who have merely studied research in doctoral seminars. In either case, joint learning by both student and supervisor occurs as they jointly explore some unresolved issue and draw on often unfamiliar theory for new insights. Both experience the joy of new insights, as well as the frustration of following disappointing leads.

I have been fortunate to have doctoral students with a wide range of interests. The topics and issues that excite one hold no interest for another. In consequence, I have been able to research with these students issues as diverse as determinants of executive compensation, power and decision making within organizations, goal setting and performance, just noticeable differences in compensation, norms of pay equity, leadership impact of executives within organizations, internal labor market structures, the effects of dependence on negotiations, and the benefit and cost of employment downsizing. And the methods employed have been as diverse as laboratory experiments, survey research, field experiments, computer simulations, case studies, and archival analyses. The varied interests and approaches of these students have stimulated me to master the same issues with them. I have learned from this research as well as they have.

An advertisement in the *Wall Street Journal* (May 29, 1996, p. A2) quotes Albert Szent-Gyorgyi, a Nobel prize winner in 1937, to the effect that "research is to see what everybody else has seen, and to think what nobody else has thought." This insight expresses the close linkage between research and teaching, for students as well as myself. This ability to think what no one else has thought has been a clear goal in my teaching and research.

## General Observations

As is apparent, this chapter has been a retrospective analysis of a personal odyssey in search of learning. Much of the focus has been on the exercise and development of ability to think by using a variety of theories, models, and information. It seems to me that this is the function of, particularly, collegiate and graduate instruction. Although perhaps rarely enunciated, the primary task of the student is to learn how the instructor thinks. Although subject content will be examined, the implicit task of the student is to learn how the instructor uses this content or thinks about and with it. The inevitable question of the first class, "What will the examinations be like?" is the first attempt to learn how the instructor thinks. I alert students to this implicit task and also inform them that my task is to develop their own personal ways of thinking. I display my way of thinking in the arguments I pose and strive to help them find answers. When questioned for "my answer" to some issue under investigation, I remind them that their conclusions are more important; if I wish them to keep struggling with the issue, I postpone my answer until the last day of class, when they may press me for my answers to any question. Typically, by that time, they have resolved the issues and no longer seek my conclusions. Subject content can be learned through study of reading assignments, and no instructor need be required. That is of little value, however, in later experiences. Learning what to do with the subject content, how to think about it, provides the basis for going beyond that content. Ideally, students develop their own unique ways of thinking as they encounter various instructors with different mental frameworks and styles of thinking. They must master each and, in the process, identify what is useful for themselves. Yet, thinking in the abstract is a futile exercise. Mastery of subject content is essential for productive thinking. Either thinking skill or content knowledge is barren without incorporation of the other.

Throughout my career, I have been blessed with students capable of being interested, of being challenged, and of learning. Not all students fit this mold, but a sufficient number allow me to continue to learn, have fun, and enjoy the development of the students. In various ways, my teaching exemplifies what has become known as the phenomenon of self-fulfilling prophesy. I have come to expect students, particularly at the graduate level, to be interested in learning and to enjoy the thrill of mastering research that helps them understand problems around them and formulate responses to those problems. Over time, I acquired the reputation of being a demanding instructor, and most students knew what to expect when signing up for a course. I recall one student at the master's level announcing to me on the first day of class that he would earn the grade of A; he wanted to be known as having received an A from Mahoney. This task was challenging, given that he was near the end of his program and had yet to earn an A. Knowing his goal, I doubtless unknowingly challenged him more than would otherwise have been the case. And he earned a quite comfortable A, the only A in his program and from his most challenging course. Another student enrolled in the master's program, grew discouraged, and almost opted for withdrawal with a certificate of study but became excited about learning and wound up completing the Ph.D. requirements; he continues that learning today as a significant contributor to scholarship. Although the degree of fulfillment of my expectations varies from student to student, it is always exciting to participate in and observe the growth of each student.

## Conclusions

I began this examination as an exercise in recalling my experiences as they constituted a career. Looking back, it all makes sense. Yet, that sense is hardly something I might have foreseen 40 years ago and relied on in making a career choice. I doubtless would have weighted heavily extrinsic reward and reinforcement in making a rational and cognitive choice among occupations. Teaching and research are not commonly provided much in the way of extrinsic reinforcement. Furthermore, gratification in a career of scholarship typically is deferred. Certainly, it has been my experience that students only come to appreciate the learning I seek to provide in later years when they become aware of its potential. Doctoral students usually are around long enough to learn what an instructor has to offer well before completing their studies and to appreciate those contributions; master's students are far less likely to realize those contributions until after completion of their programs. I recall the first teaching award I received. The doctoral students argued with the master's students that their votes were always outnumbered by those of the master's students and that they wanted a more significant voice in selection of the award recipient. This was agreed to. In my case, master's students began to overcome their fear of my courses, enrolled in them, and I became the fortunate recipient of the award for a number of years.

The usual conceptualization of teaching and research as separate but joined endeavors in academic scholarship would have blinded me to what I now realize is an inevitable joining of them in a career of learning. The learning I thrill to and enjoy is not possible through teaching or research as a separate endeavor. And I have come to realize that the teaching I enjoy involves research; it stimulates and requires research. Similarly, the research I enjoy would be sterile without the accompaniment of teaching. For me, teaching and research are but different emphases or stages of the same process.

My analysis has revealed the role of intrinsic reinforcement in behavioral conditioning toward what can now be identified as a career. The one central theme that integrates my varied experiences into a career is that of learning. Although learning is not typically characterized as a career, it has provided the stimulus, reinforcement, and focus that characterize those experiences I call my career.

# 9 In Search of Myself in the Context of Russian and American Humanitarian Culture

NIKITA POKROVSKY

The suggestion to share my thoughts on the art of teaching, on research, and on their mutual interrelatedness took me by surprise. All my professional life has been devoted mainly to teaching and research. However, I have never before tried to think about the theory of my work. Everything seemed to come more or less naturally, and in my development I have obeyed an inner logic that, it is true, at times is also dictated by outside circumstances—exactly as it always happens in our lives. However that may be, I began to think and recall, and this chapter is the result. Here, then, are several realities of the past and present (and perhaps of the future) that will help us come to the material understanding that is so needed in these times.

## Intellectual Life in Russia

With the mind alone Russia cannot be understood; No ordinary yardstick spans her greatness; She stands alone, unique—In Russia one can only believe.

Fyodor Tyutchev (1866)[1]

Russians love to discuss general principles, theories, and suggestions and to build plans for the future, often impossible ones, creating a halo of reverence around them. This activity is its own self-justification. This is why we love to reflect on history.

Modern Russian humanitarian and scientific cultures began in the 18th century—in Peter I's reforms and in those of his successor, Catherine the Great. During this epoch, the first universities in Russia were opened—in St. Petersburg in 1726-1766 and in Moscow in 1755. The Russian scholarly culture formed under the influence of a galaxy of German scholars who had been invited to Russia in the 18th century; they brought their principles of university teaching and scientific research and strengthened them here. The main principles were (a) the cult of science and its acknowledgment as the highest social value, equal to the value of state administration, military service, and wealth; (b) the striving to develop basic research and theoretical science; and (c) a belief that the world can be transformed through science and on a rational basis, with an emphasis on the significance of the rational reconstruction of the natural and social worlds.

Even now, one may feel the breath of German academic culture on Moscow University. Without much exaggeration, I can assert that the curriculum of Moscow University and the style of encyclopedic teaching and the structural organization of the departments date back to those of German universities.

Nevertheless, the German influence was not the only factor in the development of an emerging mentality of modern Russia. At the same time, Russian Orthodoxy had just as mighty an authority over the minds of Russians. One of the three main branches of Christianity, Orthodoxy, implanted into the consciousness of Russians that which is habitually called *dukhovnost,* spirituality. In Russian spirituality, there is an unquestionable preeminence of an ideal and abstract moral tendency over all that is everyday, practical, and earthly. The Russian Orthodox theoretician or humanitarian always finds enormous delight and satisfaction in his or her contemplation of abstract truths, general principles, and ideals. In addition, he or she does not experience any particular incentive for being engaged in practical activity, especially commerce. At times, such a person is even afraid of it. That is why the Russian spiritual culture, it seems to me, can be called without much exaggeration a culture of thinking and contemplation, in contrast with the activity and practicality of Western culture and the Protestant work ethic.

This spiritual and moral abstractness and contemplativeness of Russian thinking has, today, an important aspect not adequately understood in the West. I am speaking about that wonderful feeling of anxiety that Russians feel for everything taking place in the world, in their country, in their city, an equal measure with what is taking place in their families and with themselves. The extreme hypertrophy of the spiritual-moral life was in radical opposition to everything material in the world. In many ways, even modern Russians, though quite progressive in the modes of daily life, admit that the concerns for others can be (and often are) superior to their own needs and problems.

Sobornost is a related moral and spiritual concept that comes from the depths of Russian national traditions. Linguistically, *sobornost* shares the root with the word *sobor,* which signifies a Russian Orthodox cathedral. In the cathedral, people get together and worship and maintain their communion with God. In other words, the sense of collectivity is essential for Orthodoxy, whereas individuality and self-reliance are far less important (Richmond, 1992, chap. 3).

The symbiosis of the German and Orthodox traditions determined the essence of Russian culture and national character. On the one hand, the Russian is a person who thinks in terms of the latest scientific achievements, having reached an extraordinarily high level of logical refinement and multidimensional functional thinking, implicitly believing in enlightenment and serving it. On the other hand, all this combines with faith in the common (not individual!) boon, a striving to devote oneself completely to the people, to society, and to family and to do this absolutely selflessly, without earning a single penny for it. Of course, these phenomena, especially in our day, do not lie on the surface of social life, and probably you will not find many people whose life totally or predominantly corresponds to these ideals. But these values are very noticeable and traceable in the semantic structure of Russian culture in the norms of behavior, in ethics and aesthetics, in works of art, and in humanitarian research—and, of course, in the practice of teaching.

Among my ancestors are representatives of the main traditions of Russian culture—namely, the German and Orthodox traditions. My forebears on my mother's side were German nobility who migrated to Russia at the end of the 18th century and naval officers of an old Russian family. The Russian family produced, during the 19th and the beginning of the 20th centuries, a galaxy of brilliant naval officers, including Nikolai Kachalov, the rear admiral and prominent engineer who founded the St. Petersburg Institute of Technology with principles quite progressive for those times and close to those of the modern Massachusetts Institute of Technology in Cambridge.

The German branch of my family presented Russia and, indeed, the whole world, with Alexander Blok (1880-1921), my grandmother's cousin, a poet-symbolist who was close in stature to Alexander Pushkin.

On my father's side, I inherited my surname of Pokrovsky, which was given only to those who were ordained priests. My great-grandfather had actually been a priest in the south of Russia, which quite strongly determined that respect for the Russian Orthodox traditions has always been cultivated in our family.

Paradoxically, the Bolsheviks and later the Communists, coming to power after 1917 and turning the whole social structure upside down, in their own peculiar manner and by the force of their ideological stand preserved the Russian investment in culture. In communist times, our intellectual traditions continued and developed in a kind of greenhouse (e.g., under special privileged conditions). But you may also describe it as a catacomb life.

It is certainly true that, after 1917, hundreds of thousands or even millions of Russian intelligentsia were executed or died in the GULAG camps or on the battlefields of World War II. Those who survived lived under the constant pressure of persecution if they violated certain codes of behavior. My grandmother, being of noble extraction and knowing several foreign languages, never reported to the authorities the extent of her education and never taught her children foreign languages. Command of a foreign language at that time was considered to be ideologically suspicious by the authorities. Nevertheless, she was arrested and spent 3 weeks in the terrible Lubianka KGB prison in Moscow, where she was brutally interrogated—the reason being my grandmother's participation in a home-based discussion club on theosophy, including the writings of Thomas Carlyle, Annie Bezant, and Helen Blavatskaia. My stepfather, Evgeny Kumankov, nowadays a leading Russian artist, was then an undergraduate student at the Moscow Institute of Cinematography. He was sent, in the winter of 1941, with 300 professors and students of that same institute, directly to the front line near Moscow. They had neither ammunition nor arms and no military training. No wonder almost all of them were shot in an open field by a small unit of Nazi tanks. My stepfather luckily was among the few survivors.

Nevertheless, over the years, those who managed either to cope with the authorities or to elaborate some sort of intellectual and moral niche enjoyed many privileges. First, in the eyes of the community and the state, the pursuit of culture—in any form—was highly appreciated. The unusually great pressure of centuries-old traditions could not be completely broken either by early capitalism or communism. As a result, scholars, people in the arts, scientists, and to a smaller degree, humanitarians, were allowed to do what was forbidden to others. This included comparative independence in expressing unofficial points of view, free use of one's personal time (including having an unfixed workday), relaxed social control, a greater access to Western values, and comparatively high guaranteed wages. Even such a classic tyrant as Stalin, who on the one hand destroyed hundreds of thousands of Russian intellectuals and on the other hand built huge universities, libraries, and museums, gave the professors very high wages and excellent free housing and surrounded the professions of scientist and professor with a halo of exclusiveness and public respect that was supported obediently by Soviet bureaucracy at all levels of the social structure.

In short, never, under any circumstances, had Russian humanitarian culture developed in an atmosphere of market relationships with their orientation toward producing market goods. This allowed Russian culture to preserve and multiply its immaterialism, its spirituality, and its worldwide anxiety. It gave rise to such great geniuses as Ivan Turgenev, Leo Tolstoy, Fyodor Dostoevsky, Anton Chekhov, Ivan Pavlov, Dmitry Mendeleyev, Pyotr Tchaikovsky, Dmitry Shostakovich, Marc Chagall, and Sergey Eisenstein. All this had a paramount influence on the formation of the perception and teaching of humanitarian subjects in Russian universities, if not for any other reason but that both students and faculty saw in their subjects primarily not a "profession" but a special, vital predestination of an ethical and spiritual nature—a mission to bring the Truth of Culture into this world. As for a practical application of humanitarian knowledge, that was considered to be secondary. That is why people used to say that, in Russia, "a poet should be more than a poet," meaning that poetry was a sort of prophetic and missionary creative role in the society. The same was also true for all other intellectual professions.

## Moscow University: The Decades of Stagnation

> Those born in eras of stagnation
> Cannot recall their chosen way.
> Children of Russia's terrible years.
> We can't forget a single day.
>
> *Alexander Blok (1914/1981, p. 247)*

In 1968, having finished secondary school in Moscow, I immediately entered the Philosophy Department of Moscow State University (now also called Moscow University or the University of Moscow). In Russia, there is no strict division between the humanities and social sciences. Sociology, economics, political science, and social psychology all are included in the so-called humanities. The closeness of humanitarian and social science disciplines does not create, at Russian universities, even in the basic teaching of undergraduate students, a rivalry between these academic disciplines. Social sciences and the humanities in Russia seem to rise from one root.

My entrance exams to Moscow State University coincided with the Soviet troops' invasion of Czechoslovakia. I still clearly remember how, over the big radio set standing in our Moscow apartment, the military news was relayed on the advance of the army troops over Czechoslovakia. The gloomy news usually ended with a short weather forecast: "All day today and tomorrow the weather in the European part of the Soviet Union and in the whole of Eastern Europe will be sunny and cloudless." Indeed, it was! The events in Czechoslovakia (as they were "modestly" called by the Soviet propaganda machine), in their turn, put an end to all expectations for a peaceful liberalization and democratization of Soviet socialism. The communist orthodoxy staked its claim on "the last and decisive fight" against the West, including the sphere of ideology, philosophy, and the arts. The mournful stagnation epoch of Leonid Brezhnev (also called the "Dream of Reason") gained strength, continuing to the end of the 1980s—the epoch of Mikhail Gorbachev and *perestroika*.

I now see that my most valued and golden years of self-education, personal growth, and entering life coincided exactly with the most inconsolable period of the agony of Soviet totalitarianism. The Philosophy Department of Moscow University presented an accurate reflection of the whole spiritual situation that had set in in the Soviet Union. The philosophy curriculum was permeated with orthodox Marxism in all its variations. And, like an oversalted brine, it began to give off residues. Marxist philosophy—or more correctly, ideology—was examined as an absolutely correct, perennial "truth of all truths," implying only its careful study, but not development. (True, an exception to the development of Marxism was made for the highest functionaries of the Communist Party and individual academicians of the Academy of Sciences.) These phenomena are important because they would re-create the atmosphere of teaching the humanities at Moscow University.

At that time, philosophical disciplines—such as history of Western philosophy or logics, which were not fully integrated into the framework of dogmatism and, by some miracle as well as by force of definite paradox, had been retained in the curriculum—interested many students, especially those who were not aspiring to a future career in the Communist Party. A division into communist ideology-oriented students (who, as a rule, come to Moscow State University from provincial cities) and academically oriented students (who, as a rule, were born in or were already living in Moscow) created not only theoretical but also personal friction within the university.

From a sociological point of view, this could be explained as follows: Students arriving from the provinces to Moscow University tried in every way possible to consolidate their position in the city so as to stay on after graduating from the university. There was but one way to do this: to make a career in the Communist Party structures. As for the students who already lived in Moscow, support of the orthodoxy was not so necessary. Of course, both sides had exceptions.

Deviations from correct Marxism very often ended in a student or professor being excluded from the university. My personal position was seriously endangered because, despite all my efforts, my roots in prerevolutionary Russia and my family ties, with the nobility of the past, were brought to the fore, and I soon found myself on a list of potential suspects who were under special control. Among the students were many secret informers who kept the special ideological division of the security service informed about undesirable conversations, suspicious statements, and other detrimental actions of students and faculty. Until very recently (and I hope not any longer), after 17 years of teaching, I knew that each of my classes contained usually two student informers who reported independently of each other to their boss about the contents of my teaching. And I never knew their names. How nice, indeed! All this, taken together, created an amazingly suffocating and threatening situation at the university. Only much later was I able to understand the utter catastrophe of that life. I was unable to realize then that I was practically treading a minefield, on which one awkward movement could have destroyed my future. The mentality of a Soviet academic was trained by life itself to scarcely trust anyone, to take into account that one's scholarly opponent or counterpart could play a double, if not a triple, role, to know that any purely academic discussion could be resolved by using purely nonacademic (organizational) means decisive to one's future. Such famous sociological concepts as "back-glance-casting," "dual thinking," and sophisticated "background understanding" were common among all levels at the university, although I personally never quite succeeded in learning those rules of the game.

Neither then nor later did I learn to integrate my academic interests and my statements with the secret and non-expressed demands of the community in which I worked. Even now, I find it hard to be diplomatic within the academic sphere and to include in my main academic function too many nonacademic variables. I consider this to be my positive trait, although many, I think, would not agree with me. I frequently and everywhere have occasion to hear that organizational wisdom and diplomatic refinement of the mind are just as necessary for a scholar and professor as for a minister of foreign affairs. I do not know. . . . Maybe it makes a lot of sense to others. But I think that, by not entering into this system of academic and university diplomacy, I have economized on my spiritual and emotional forces and have found and will still perhaps find a better use for them.

## Learning and Teaching in the Catacombs

Subjects that were not fully Marxist gave us a sufficiently wide circle for the observation of the academic situation in the world, or so it seemed at the time. Around these disciplines and the professors teaching them arose an informal association with absolutely no room for "politics." New books were kept constantly circulating on the history of philosophy, translations from Western sources and selections of the works of students and graduate students were published, and diverse conferences were held. Although not a total counterbalance to official Marxism and the pressure of the conservative administration, all this served as a sort of vent for those who were interested in the subject itself. Naturally, it was understood that, even at these progressive lectures, we could not talk of freedom of speech. The professors spoke the language of Aesop, at times saying one thing while having another in mind and only hinting at that other truth. For example, at the beginning of a lecture, they would laud Marx and Lenin for their outstanding critique of, say, Hegel. Then, a professor would say that, to understand the profoundness of Marx and Lenin, we would need to learn Hegel in detail. And 90% of the rest of the lecture would be devoted to Hegel without a single reference to Marxism. In this way, by introducing phony ideological teasers, professors used to save the main contents of their lectures for colloquiums.

The language of Aesop infused in the students the double-world characteristic of communism—truth as truth versus truth for official distribution. It is hard now, in post-*perestroika* conditions, to rid even comparatively young people of this constant back-glance casting. That is why I advise my foreign colleagues who are establishing contacts in our day with Russian scholars to always keep in mind that Russian background thinking comes, not from the nature of the Russian national character, but from these historical social conditions.

I remember well that our best professors—first of all Valentin Asmus, Alexei Losev, Yuri Melvil, Vladimir Bogomolov, Mirab Mamardashvily—taught us without giving us a handicap, as if we were their colleagues and not undergraduates. As students, our most important task was research—that is, looking for a new idea in one or another philosophical text or for a new approach to the interpretation of the intellectual heritage of a given philosopher. This work usually was of no pragmatic value. Our goal was to publish the results of the research in an academic journal or to make a report at a student conference. Here, I should note that, among "academically oriented" students, as distinct from the "communist ideology oriented" students, the prospects of getting a job after graduating from the university were never considered or discussed in practical terms. The future looked foggy but ensured because, in those years, the university conducted a so-called distribution of graduates—that is, giving guaranteed job positions to all its graduates without exception.

But even without touching on the practical question of the employment of the graduates, it is important to note that, as a whole, education in the humanities at Moscow State University had no hint of pragmatism. It stimulated, for many students, interest in the humanities disciplines for the sake of that interest only. It was countertraditional to raise the significance of the material factor in the sphere of spiritual and humanitarian activity of any sort. "Those who study the humanities are self-sufficient": That motto was never pronounced aloud but was always present among us. One can think about this important feature of our humanities education in two ways. On the one hand, this atmosphere inspired our perception of philosophy and everything related to it as a value in itself. On the other hand, we also took on a certain carelessness, a social naïveté, a defenselessness in the face of life's storms, of which we became well aware only during the Gorbachev *perestroika* years and especially afterward.

## Thomas Jefferson and Henry Thoreau
## As A Life Course Theme

> ... There is not a country on earth, where there is greater tranquillity; where the laws are milder, or better obeyed; where everyone is more attentive to his own business, or meddles less with that of others; where strangers are better received, more hospitably treated, and with a more sacred respect.
>
> Thomas Jefferson, *On America* (1944)

> I have lived for the last month with the sense of having suffered a vast and indefinite loss. I did not know at first what ailed. At last it occurred to me that what I had lost was a country.
>
> Henry David Thoreau (1854)

In the fall of 1970 (I well recall that day), Professor Igor Narsky delivered a lecture on Benjamin Franklin, Thomas Jefferson, and Thomas Paine. I cannot say what happened to me, but I immediately began searching for materials on the history of the American Enlightenment.

Thomas Jefferson drew me from the start. His astonishingly free and yet fundamental style of accounting in his own words, his extraordinary seriousness and philosophical mind—all this attracted me and suggested to me that, by studying Jefferson, I would be able to open up new horizons for myself. I began passionately to read everything I could find in our university library by Jefferson himself and what was written about him. Soon, my "Jeffersoniana" file had a good 200 cards in it, and by the end of the same year, my home-based archive contained two dozen voluminous folders, all filled with notes on Jefferson's writings and his biography.

Now, I rarely turn over the pages of my first essay on Jefferson. Despite all its simplicity and artlessness, it amazes me with its sort of inner sincerity and love for Jefferson. In the present day and at my present age, I understand very well that that sort of sincerity makes up the foundations of a genuine knowledge of the humanities. All kinds of scholarly baggage are mechanical. But sincerity can only be lost with the years; it will never be resurrected. Eventually, a paper of mine on Jefferson won first prize in a nationwide contest for student researchers. A paper on one of the founding fathers of American democracy, written by a frank and obviously apologetic source, received a first prize at a competition of essays in the humanities, taking place right in the middle of a totalitarian system? That was not such a paradox, given the privilege and status afforded the humanities at that time in Russia. By supporting my essay on Jefferson, in a roundabout way, some scholars and even officials expressed their opposition to the ruling principles of communist ideology.

My study of Jefferson, integrated with my own philosophical perceptions, led me to the idea that democracy is not so much a form of rule as it is a way of thinking, a certain structure of consciousness that does not demand as its prerequisite a particularly assiduous understanding of "philosophy" or "principles" of democracy. On the contrary, I thought, it is inherent in all normal people, one can say, from birth, and therefore it is almost intuitive (or self-evident, if we are to follow Jefferson's terminology). One has only to destroy the unnatural political and economic structure of totalitarianism, and almost the next morning, people following their intuition and their deeply imbedded democratic instinct will transfer to the rails of a new life. Enthusiasm for Jefferson's social philosophy lay on just such a possibility. Much later, I discovered the wonderful words of John Dewey, which it seemed to me, coincided exactly with my social and philosophical beliefs of that time. The great philosopher, "American Socrates," wrote that democracy "is not an alternative to other principles of social life. It is the idea of community life itself" (Dewey, 1927, p. 148).

I was not unique in my spontaneous and intuitive democratic aspirations among many of my colleagues, especially the young ones, and the representatives of the liberal Russian intelligentsia of the 1980s in general. In the meantime, the Soviet system, despite its obvious vices, seemed absolutely stable—like an Egyptian pyramid. Even in the boldest of dreams, no one except Andrei Amalrik and Zbigniew Brzezinski in the West could presume that the Soviet Union would hardly survive the 1980s. Simultaneously, an absolutely uncritical and purely Romantic perception of Western democracies was cultivated among the intelligentsia. No one among us ever pronounced the following words eloquently enough:

> Like communism, democracy is not even perfect in its ideation. It's a rough process, unfair sometimes even when it pretends to be fair (often the worst kind of injustice, that) but it's probably a good and necessary stage in human evolution, and one which it seems Russia needs to pass through. You learn a lot about yourself when you have (relative) freedom. Sometimes responsibility hurts and choices are painful. (in Pokrovsky, 1993, p. 82)[2]

Those words, with which I agree, belong to Arthur Rosenfeld, an American friend of mine, a scientist, and presently a man of letters.

Today, I understand the reason for my one-sidedness then. Not having any idea of legal culture and civil society, deprived of access to any forms of active administration of social processes, we hoped for the impulsive and unstructured burst of popular democratism because there was nothing else to count on. That is what I relied on intuitively, that is how all those who surrounded me thought, and that is what the intellectual atmosphere of Russian society was like—disposed toward progressive change. Need it be said that the years following Gorbachev's *perestroika* and especially Boris Yeltsin's post-*perestroika* substantially changed our view. Nowadays, Alexander Hamilton, with all his caution against sporadic-popular democracy and his skepticism against the quickly rising careers of the new rulers, at least in my eyes, seems to be as prophetic as Jefferson was, especially for Russia. At any rate, today I understand the contributors to the Federalist period much better and treat them with full respect.

From my early university years, I found my first scholarly and life course theme binding me strongly to the intellectual heritage of one of the best periods of American history and profoundly predetermining my future.[3] The more seriously I studied America, the more obviously I turned the results of my research toward my own society. My dialogue with my American alter ego constantly transformed my dialogue with my Russian alter ego. America served as a means of clarifying my attitude toward my own homeland. Following the historical streams of world culture, after the Age of Reason and Thomas Jefferson, I entered the Age of Romanticism. The reasons were not only historical and logical but also personal—maturing, acquiring more social soberness and a perception of the big complications of the surrounding social world.

The Romantic period in my research and corresponding teaching practice was connected with American transcendentalism, primarily with Henry David Thoreau. I met up with the Concord hermit and fell deeply in love with him. I am frequently asked why I was so interested then in Thoreau's ideas and devoted quite some time to them. I think this question is not so important because I do not value highly my personal contribution to Thoreauviana. But from a strictly sociological point of view, perhaps, it will be interesting to restore some pages of the past.

After I had won a definite success with my research on Thomas Jefferson, and wanting to continue studying the traditions of American social thought, I accidentally came across a dog-eared, ragged copy of Thoreau's *Walden, or Life in the Woods,* published in 1962 in Russian translation. In the margins of the library copy of *Walden* I had picked up were innumerable notes and resolutions made by students. The majority were messages of an irritated nature, in fierce criticism of Thoreau. That was not surprising because, in one night before the exam (it is always just only one night left before the Last Judgment), students had to cram the entire wealth of world literature of the 19th century. As Thoreau, with all his complications and paradoxes had fallen into their hands on the way to the exams, he became almost a curse for them. Even now, I feel sorry that I didn't exchange that copy of crucial misunderstanding with a clean one. What a marvelous exhibit item it would now be for the museum or even for my private book collection! Be that as it may, *Walden* not only fascinated me but also took over my soul. I began to read and reread it, trying to separate, as in prep school, the "needed" and "not needed" paragraphs in the book, but as a result I ended up realizing that they were all needed. Since then, Thoreau has became a permanent companion in my life. That is quite a pompous statement, but true, nevertheless.

The academic leadership of my graduate school department, however, was of the opinion that Thoreau was not a promising figure—not fully a philosopher, certainly an advocate of doubtful civil disobedience, a noncollectivist, having run off from society and much more. I was told to apply my efforts to John Dewey and pragmatism; he fully met the formal requirements of my department for being a "real philosopher." I started this work with mixed feelings and soon found out that Dewey was not exactly a philosopher whose style of thinking I liked. In those years, I was unable to fully understand all the depths of this thinker; he seemed to me too prosaic and simple in comparison with Jefferson and the Transcendentalists. (Now, I, of course, don't share my perception of Dewey of those times.)

The problem of the theme of my research work arose again after I entered my graduate program at Moscow State University. The sets of that new production and the cast were almost the same, but the principal actor was already different; by that time, I elaborated my own vision of things in philosophy, and it became more difficult to impose on me something I did not approve. I was about to advance my project on Thoreau but again clashed with the department. The academic council again assigned me the topic on Dewey—"The Ethics of John Dewey." Generally speaking, I liked Dewey a bit more at that time than 2 years before, but not enough to trade Thoreau for Dewey. Today, I am thankful to the department for their reasonable opposition to my project on Thoreau because that opposition forced me to read and reread Dewey's writings. After 2 years of struggle in the graduate program, I understood that I could not write anything sensible about Dewey's ethics. I read Thoreau constantly, however, and in ever-widening circles that included originals and commentaries. I continued stubbornly to demand returning to Thoreau. In the end, the department gave in and agreed "on Thoreau," believing that exclusion of a graduate student from the university would call forth more problems for the department than would diplomatic patience and a compromise with a different-thinking young academic.

At that point, I had before me half a winter, one summer, and half an autumn for the start and finish of my work. How often it happens that events take place in life, coinciding, piling up on each other and not always for the best. A series of all kinds of personal troubles so characteristic of young people and that later seem absolutely trivial swallowed my thoughts and feelings, pushing Thoreau and Dewey and even my beloved department to the background. In mid-summer of 1976, I, naturally, having lived through invariable disappointments and even "crises" (I insist on the quotes!), one beautiful morning became aware that only several months remained to the fateful end of my graduate studies, with its inevitable day of judgment for my sins of disobedience and neglect. And here again, *Walden* in an amazing manner became my healing doctor and comrade in misfortune. Starting to reread it from a graduate program angle of view, besides other things, I discovered Thoreau in Walden's recluse, a man with an astonishing complicated selection of "complexes" and, what is more important, an advisor, giving fully healthy and subtle recommendations on what to do "when things are bad." And it was particularly the advice I needed then. Work went on swimmingly. Everything I had accumulated during the years of my selfless love for Thoreau went into it: my home archive, voluminous notes, books. Here, Thoreau was able to inspire not only me but also a whole army of doctoral thesis writers.

After the semiofficial discussion of my thesis work within the circle of my professors and fellow graduate students, all unanimously acknowledged that the collective genius of the department had led me, a bad lot, onto the right road and that I, as an instrument of this genius, had demonstrated the prophetic wisdom of our professorship in designating Thoreau as the subject for my doctoral dissertation.

I did not object to such a formulation.

Much has happened in my life since those far-off days, in the lives of my colleagues and in the entire Russian academic community. My interest in Thoreau has never vanished. It would expand and swallow me entirely, which, as a rule, happened at the publication of one or another book dedicated to Thoreau or the Transcendentalists, or then would shrivel to the size of a narrow stream of night reading during insomnia and to a regular correspondence with American Thoreauvians. I want to speak particularly of the latter. In 1978, Thoreau (or more correctly, my modest efforts in the Thoreau studies) took me to the United States for the first time. That was when I was lucky to get to Concord, to Walden Pond, the Thoreau Lyceum, to meet the leaders of the Thoreau Society, of whom I would like to mention Walter Harding, and was even made a life member of this society as an award.

Later, I frequently went to America for research and teaching. At some point, the sphere of my professional work in social philosophy and theoretical sociology merged with the tenor of consulting for American commercial companies and corporations. With all this (amazing!), however, Thoreau and the Transcendentalists remained with me as primary scholarly specialization and field of expertise. More than that, when I muse over the balance of my successful and not so successful life projects and endeavors, be they in America or in my native parts, I unfailingly discover that everything really significant in my life to one or other extent has been connected with Thoreau or with those who keep his memory alive. If this connection does not exist, then a program either falls through or is forgotten or then falls into a "dead end." This is a personal secret that I share happily with you.

The attitude toward Thoreau cannot and must not be simple. You cannot praise him uncritically or turn him into a sacred martyr of philosophy. Thoreau does not yield to canonizing. At one time, he seemed to me to be an exceptional conductor in the labyrinth of American life and a genius archivist of American national consciousness. With time, however, I discovered that modern America does not necessarily submit to explanations from Thoreau's position. In my opinion, he belongs, for the most part, to an epoch that evaporated forever and that can today be of interest only without any pragmatic or political coloring. Is that good or bad? I think it's very good. Thoreau attracts you for himself, as an important fragment of the history of the human soul, whether the modern Americans live according to his principles or not.

Yet, Thoreau is not altogether useless from the point of view of everyday prose. On starting a dialogue with him, you begin to understand yourself much better, begin to pose questions to yourself and others, and this is a very effective way of doing something beneficial in the world. Finally, Thoreau teaches you not to judge others, not to accuse people of being unfaithful, but to build life with a humble alter ego and in concert with your own philosophy, not forcing it on anyone else. His whole life teaches this art of abstaining from shouting criticism at each other without reason and of preserving faithfulness to your idea under any circumstances. And, I think, no one, nowhere, will tire of these lessons.

I have tried to express my attitude to Thoreau and the Transcendentalists as best I can in my many articles and in four books and a collection of articles, as well as in a lecture course that I have delivered practically every year, beginning with 1977 (see Lawrence & Lee, 1984; Pokrovsky, 1983, 1986a, 1986b, 1989b, 1996a, 1996b; Thoreau, 1992). For all these years, Henry Thoreau has magnetized my students, and after every lecture they come up to me with questions on what they should do to become Thoreauvians. The latter is probably the most important thing I have attained as a result of my efforts in the history of American Transcendentalism.

My Enlightenment and Romantic periods ended with the Gorbachev years of *perestroika*. It goes without saying that I never planned anything consciously or adapted myself to the historical moment. It was simply that time itself, as Max Weber said, the "interest of the epoch," changed my perception of American culture. Jefferson and Thoreau, in different ways, opposed totalitarian ideology. When this ideology began to swiftly lose its position in Russia, much changed also in our perception of American humanitarian tradition.

## *Perestroika* at the University:
## Half-found and Half-lost Expectations

> If people define situations as real,
> they are real in their consequences.
>
> W. I. Thomas (*The Thomas Theorem*, 1936, p. 29)

Mikhail Gorbachev came into power in 1985. I well remember the sunny March afternoon when I found myself, owing to the force of circumstances, in the company of a prominent Soviet Party functionary who had just returned from the Kremlin, where half an hour before the Plenary Meeting of the Central Committee of the Communist Party had ended.

"Well, whom did you finally elect?" I rushed to ask with natural curiosity.

"Gorbachev!" he snapped with an air of complete perplexity, unable to control the expression of his face. And then he added, "That's the end to everything."

Indeed, Gorbachev's arrival marked—but did not predetermine— the advance of bankruptcy to some and the beginning of prospects for a rocketing career to others. In a more extensive view, however, it was the beginning of the end of one epoch and the accession of another. The Soviet Union was drifting slowly but inevitably into a period of all-embracing social revolution that even now [in the end of 1994] is far from complete. (I don't quite accept the relatively mild term *reforms*, which is often used to describe a modern period of Russian history. Russian society is radically changed, with all the multiple consequences of a real revolution.) The country, which had experienced a series of inner crises under the rule of a senile Soviet totalitarian bureaucracy, for the most part intuitively welcomed any alterations that had even the slightest tendency to change for the better. "It doesn't make any difference what or who," people reasoned. "Only not those stupid mugs of Party bosses, who can't pronounce three words in a row without making three grammatical mistakes." That is what the dominant mood was in society, although, of course, the palette of political forces and currents was more complicated. Gorbachev, however, talked very smoothly ("word for word"), without any notes, and made comparatively fewer grammatical mistakes. That's why he was liked by many at first. "That's no Brezhnev for you," people said, and they were quite right. In my own life, the year 1985 was notable, perhaps, for the reason that my book on Henry Thoreau and articles on the history of American philosophy, including those on Jefferson, received the highest national academic award conferred on young academics. This fact alone was curious because this prestigious state prize was given for my objective research on Jefferson and Thoreau, which by no means corresponds to the ideas of the official "correct" Marxist philosophy. Everything was incorrect with both Jefferson and Thoreau for Soviet ideology. And yet . . . the movement of new ideas and the appearance of strong, new tendencies in a way also told in the curious fact of my prize.

## *Perestroika* at the University Takes Off

How did our life at the university change? At the start, it didn't change at all, but at the beginning of 1986, the liberalization of the entire teaching process moved like an avalanche. Everything changed, at least on the surface. These years, the first of the Gorbachev *perestroika*, coincided with the years of my maturity in the teaching profession. And although I had begun to teach at the university in 1977, only toward the end of the 1980s did I gradually begin to feel that, perhaps for the first time, I could inform my students not only about the totality of historic ideas from the past but also about something coming from myself. Of course, I had always tried to express my point of view with the help of documents or texts. But before, I think, I had too much of Romanticism and not enough of the hard experience of life. Now, in the first Gorbachev perestroika years, life demanded more conceptual and constructive thinking. Now, my students wanted answers to the questions, What more can be done? and How should it be done?

## The Principles of My Teaching Method

Keeping in mind the fact that the subjects I teach demand many words and too little action, beginning from my very first class appearance, I try to instill more dynamics and action into our academic relations. But what sort of action can be in the history of philosophy or social theory? For me, this action means energetic research work, publications in professional periodicals, conferences, and the incorporation of new ideas into teaching programs.

### First Principle: Publish or Perish

To avoid that great sin in the humanities and social sciences—verbosity and verbal "froth" that are unintelligible—I compel all my students to transfer their ideas from talking and oral discussion to written work: to put down all their thoughts on paper, with the clear goal of publication. In our sphere of knowledge, in my opinion, nothing is more frightening than an energetic and ambitious talker who knows everything and knows nothing seriously. This is the AIDS of the humanities and social sciences. Not all my charges are easily taken in by my strategy, but those who survive will be rid for all time of the fear of facing a white sheet of paper. The need to publish at least one independent article is absolutely compulsory for my students before I sign the necessary papers that will give them a graduation diploma or an undergraduate degree.

Thus, a great load of organizational work lies on my shoulders. I have to edit my students' texts heavily, and often I even rewrite them from beginning to end. Then, I find a journal or other place in which their materials could be published. I'm able to do this in most cases; thanks to my own publications, I have definite contacts in the publishing world in Russia. I should also admit that publishers usually are very cooperative in publishing my students' works because, in Russia, everyone likes to help young folk and be a benefactor of young talented people.

### Second Principle: The Teacher-Student Interaction and Distance

I like my students very much and get pleasure out of my work with them. This productive association has a freshening effect on my private thinking. However, a disturbance of the distance between the professor and his or her students, in my opinion, can be problematic.

A certain category of professors in universities everywhere, to win popularity among the students, take on the role of voluntary confidante and confessor. With this, as these teachers affirm, the great educational mission of the university is being fulfilled, human relations are maintained, and psychotherapy in the form of endless heart-to-heart talks is realized. I do not hold to such a position.

In my opinion, upbringing, morals, and human relations are subsumed in learning and research work. All other aspects of teaching are secondary for me. All humanitarian and social science disciplines are so closely intertwined with the issues of professional ethics, human nature, and general ethics that the study of these disciplines is moral by its nature, both for the teacher and for the student. I scrutinize extradepartmental issues connected with my undergraduate and graduate students only if these touch on the professional growth and advancement of my students. For example, I concern myself with such issues as their publications, trips to conferences, technical support, and recommendations to continue studies abroad. It seems to me that a trip of an undergraduate or graduate student to a leading American university will have an incomparably bigger impact, including a moral one, on his or her future than a "soulful" talk about his or her family problems. (On my recommendations, many are today studying or receiving their Ph.D.s at the best American and Western European higher institutions of learning.)

It also seems to me that a rationally organized academic research process has an enormous moral potential; it is as if it normalizes both a collective and an individual consciousness. The same goes for the material problems of the students, I think. Instead of signing endless students' applications for material subsidies, which is a bit humiliating, I prefer to give them the opportunity to earn money by translating and writing abstracts of foreign publications, by interpreting into or from English at academic conferences, and by other means of like manner. I think research work, even in difficult economic times, can do much toward educating and especially does much for a person's self-education, be the person a professor or the youngest of undergraduates. But, of course, no one rule should become dogma. That is why the present principle does not exclude unexpected circumstances. One has to interfere at times in the life situation of a student. But, frankly speaking, I get incomparably less satisfaction out of it than reading an independent article, though still not perfect, by that same student.

### Third Principle: A Focus on Champions

I never make a forced selection of my students. I consider any volitional division into "capable" and "incapable" immoral. From the beginning of my academic relations with the students, however, I place the lath of my demands sufficiently high. Usually, at the first stage of our work together, several students leave. They leave themselves, without any coercion on my part. That's natural. But those who remain develop very soon into amazingly vivid, creative individuals. For me, there is no greater pleasure than to see the cognitive and professional growth of a young specialist. This is one of the most marvelous phenomena in the world. In this connection, my American colleagues (especially at teaching universities and colleges) often ask me, with some barely hidden discontent, "Is it democratic or right to educate primarily 'champions'?" My answer follows.

Educating leaders in the humanities and social sciences is a natural and inevitable process. Where can you rear champions if not in the major Russian university? Besides, I don't create a closed caste of elite young people. Everyone who wants to can take part in the competition. And even if a person doesn't win at the main "distance," he or she can continue the race, as the race is—endless. But I emphatically reject that category of undergraduate and graduate students who have not developed an interest in learning, who demand that we mollycoddle them and constantly explain the whys and wherefores of their need to study. Capriciousness and self-conceit seem to me to be the most obvious vices. In sorting out such a category of students (which is not, unfortunately, rare here), I am very strict, and even the dean of the humanities cannot persuade me to change my decision.

In short, if a student comes to me with the question, "What do you think I have to do in philosophy (sociology)?" I usually do not continue working with him or her. If, however, a student brings to our first encounter—no matter how well it has been prepared—a sketch of theses, notes made after reading an interesting article in a recent periodical, or cards from a personal bibliographical file and asks, "Which of these theses, in your opinion, is the most important and promising?" I start working with him or her immediately and at full strength. Or if a student, after a similar discussion and after hearing my opinion, acts as he or she thinks appropriate and sometimes against my recommendation, then that student has everything to become a champion and I give that student all my efforts.

Of course, at lectures, which I usually deliver to some 150 to 200 undergraduates, the talk is on a more average level and not particularly aimed at champions. But as soon as we move over to individual research work, everything becomes specialized to the maximum (my maximum!) and oriented to professional standards of publishers and experts. One more thing should be mentioned in this context. I never try to please my students or fawn over my students in any way. Yes, of course, I do whatever I can to make my lectures and class discussions truly attractive and interesting. But I never care about the number of students in my class. As a result, I always have a full class that continuously grows during the semester. The administration usually moves my class to a larger auditorium two or three times during a semester. But never, ever, do I go too far in making my teaching a sort of "candy bar" in which everything is oversweetened and packaged in bright wrapping. I constantly persuade my students to realize that the learning experience is a hard (sometimes painful) and time-consuming process before one can start thinking of oneself as a true professional. I also tell my students, in diverse ways, that their knowledge is and will be very limited and that there will always be plenty of room for expanding it. If you wish, you may call it a "Puritan approach" to teaching, as opposed to a widespread "entertaining or candy bar method," with its endless playing games with students and performing on the podium to keep the audience happy and pleased by all means.

In my opinion, the humanities and social sciences disciplines contain enough amusing aspects, methods of learning, and stimuli that grow from within the domain of science that they do not need outside gimmicks. I do not feed my students with candies—that is, artificially and simplified interpretations of the texts and concepts. In brief, teaching and learning are difficult jobs for both parties involved, and the students should realize that in full. Such is my unwritten social covenant with my students. And they buy it.

I rarely carry out joint research or write as a coauthor with my undergraduate and graduate students. A champion's approach rears definite individualism and the principle of self-reliance, so familiar to Americans through the efforts of Ralph Waldo Emerson. My students, both undergraduate and graduate, as a rule are vividly individualistic. Of course, self-reliance in teaching and research can be both positive and negative. But after so many years of leveling individuals under the communist regime, the main thing to do now is to give these vividly creative individuals the possibility to rise onto their two feet. I never dogmatize these rules of mine, and that is why I so easily violate them when the objective circumstances and the interests of students dictate it.

What do my students produce? The quarterly anthology *Current Materials in the History of Sociology* is fully translated by my undergraduate students into Russian from American sources under my general editorial guidance. We also publish excerpts from the original books and articles of G. H. Mead, Robert Park, Robert Merton, Pitirim Sorokin, and other classic American sociologists. Most remarkable is that, beginning with the translations, the editing, and the contacts in the printshop and ending with the circulation of the finished edition, the students do everything themselves. It is entirely their offspring. The principle of focusing on champions presumes the inclusion of students in active work of a research nature. Only the process of "making"—active, conscious, and creative—can create the foundation for attaining the heights of true science. Professional research work itself is the best tutor.

## Fourth Principle: Breadth of View

I think that a narrow, "technical" professionalization and desire to adhere only to a specific field of research will harm a scholar—both a young one and an already mature scholar. One can hear, at times, that the modern development of science simply leaves the person engaged in it no room for anything else. I doubt that immensely. If the inner urge is there to broaden one's own culture, one can always find both time and strength for it.

That wonderful American sociologist and social thinker Robert Merton ineffably encouraged me in these views. Beginning in 1990, I had frequent occasion to visit him in New York and to spend hours in discussion with him (Pokrovsky, 1991a). This living classic of world sociology supports a wide interpretation of both sociology and culture. He made the direct statement that sociology can and must accept as its study object almost everything connected with humankind and the social implication of their activity. Practically nothing in society could not interest the sociologist. To meet these demanding expectations, the sociologist has to possess a wide range of cultural knowledge and interests.

## Fifth Principle: From Curiosity to Sustained Inquisitiveness

The theme of developing a broad outlook on the world and one's place in it is closely interrelated with the ability to cultivate in oneself not an artificial but a genuine interest in the world of people. This means that, for students of the humanities and social science departments, in my opinion, it is far from enough just to possess a definite knowledge in one's sphere of expertise. The main thing that determines a scholar-humanist is a feeling of curiosity toward the world and every individual. At first, this interest is manifest in an unconscious and a nondifferentiating curiosity: "I'm only interested in knowing as much as possible about one or another person or social phenomenon." This primary feeling of curiosity and inquisitiveness cannot be taught; it must exist in a student from the very start (Berger, 1963, chaps. 2, 3). Gradually, the primary inquisitiveness instilled in a gifted student will pass into a fully registered phenomenon of interest in human reality. Here, perhaps, is where the teacher should interfere with all of his or her teaching skills and methods.

## Sixth Principle: The Professor's Personal Involvement in Research

Research should be a natural outcome and expression of the professor's self. Only with great difficulty can I recall a good professor who does not constantly publish his or her books and articles. To teach by someone else's books and textbooks, in the end, is not much of a joy. Similarly, I can hardly imagine a good professor who is not at the same time a good researcher, although some professors insist on being self-contained teachers or interpreters for students and not dedicated to writing and publishing. "Above all," they say, "someone should make teaching his or her main job!" I seriously doubt that such reasoning makes any sense.

## Comparing the Russian and American Educational Experience

Here in Russia, we strive to teach our undergraduates according to the highest professional standards without making any allowances for their youth. Many of our undergraduate students in the senior years at the university in their professional maturity are like the graduate students of Western universities. That is one side of the coin. The other side is that, in the graduate programs, a sharp slackening in the personal professional growth of the young scholars takes place. Something happens to them. According to existing traditions in Russian universities and especially at Moscow State University, our graduate studies are composed mainly of independent research programs, with minimum lecture attendance or consultations with academic advisors. I have repeatedly attempted to change this weak tradition in the domain of my responsibility and to transform it into one similar to that of the American doctoral programs, with their high level of departmental discipline, mandatory teaching (or research) assistantships, and class attendance. Hardly anything has come of my futile attempts. Naturally, strong talents will overcome this barrier, but the fallout of creative

potential is still very high. That's why, when I am asked what I dream
of as a scholar, I speak of my dream concretely: undergraduate programs according to the Russian standards, graduate programs according to the American.

A class of American students is basically very hospitable to a new
and, the more so, foreign professor. When I have taught in the United
States, I could feel how the collective spirit of the students strove to
help the teacher and to encourage him or her. Independently of how
well the students treat the teacher as a person, however, they are very
demanding toward him or her as a professor. Neither your former
academic awards and degrees nor your publications will give you a priori advantage or strengthened authority, even if you teach in a small
provincial college somewhere in the middle of Iowa. Every time, in
beginning a new course and even in every lecture, you have to prove
to the students that they didn't make a mistake in signing up for your
course, that they weren't wasting their time. That has logic.

My frequent academic trips to the United States have shaped a circle
of colleagues who are close to me in their perception of life and their
scholarly interests. Association with my American colleagues invariably enriches me not only in human relations but also professionally.
My entire library of Western social philosophy and social theory is
enriched with their old and just published books, texts of lectures, and
authors' copies of articles presented to me by my American friends. At
times, I receive whole boxes of books and textbooks that arouse my
fresh enthusiasm and some despondency on the part of my family,
who think, with some reason, of course, that our apartment is already
crowded with printed matter.

I keep to one rule about books: In my work with my students, I
display the new book arrivals and, naturally, give my students full freedom to make use of them. I seldom lose these books. We translate
articles and chapters into Russian and publish them here. We review
the new books and also publish those reviews. How happy my students
are, after having heard or read so much about one or other American
academic from me, that this scholar comes to my class during his or
her visit to Moscow, gives a lecture, and consults with them. After such
meetings, my students often establish direct contact with American
colleagues and begin to take part in their programs. I think that is
wonderful.

## The University After *Perestroika*

All these pictures of a happy university life after *perestroika* must not give my readers an idealized picture of what really is going on. All teaching and research, but especially theoretical sociology, take place in a world full of political, economic, and social currents and undercurrents. No doubt, in Russia, we are living in a time of upheaval—a revolution that totally transforms all social structures and institutions, including those of value orientations. Those who thought the departure from communism would be a painless, fast transition toward a liberal free-market society were obviously wrong or dishonest. Be that as it may, *perestroika* has brought to this country an unprecedented openness of public consciousness and liberalization of the entire educational process; there is no doubt about that. At the same time, our university is experiencing extreme material impoverishment of its departments. None of the faculty have their own office space, and we consult with our students in the corridors. Generally, no copy machines are available. There are few computers and not enough textbooks, and it is sometimes difficult to get a broken window in a lecture room replaced. Many of our lecture rooms look like the aftermath of a storming of armed hooligans. I'm not even including the wages of the professors. Moscow State University is swiftly losing its faculty, who either go to the private business sector or leave the country. A full professor at my university receives four times less than a bus driver and five times less than a receptionist, even without a 2-year college education, at a private enterprise.

It is also true that many students have lost the academic incentive to study. They perceive of their studies at the university as something of secondary importance as compared with their commercial businesses. This is not surprising; the entire Russian society and the mass media have fallen into some sort of uncontrollable and naive enthusiasm for private entrepreneurship, believing there are no real people in society except businesspeople. It is only natural that the students quickly catch on to this mood. Only much later will they learn that it is far from what it looks like on television and that it will be very difficult to catch up the lost time in the studies that they spent in the seemingly important and usually futile race for extraordinary material wealth.

It is also astonishing how fast the prestige of a professor can fall on the ladder of social stratification. Nowadays, our students, sometimes unconsciously, look at us with a feeling of superiority only because they make more money (e.g., doing street trade) per day than we do per month. They say very often aloud, "If you are so bright, why aren't you well off?" However, a new model image of a "true professor" has emerged in Russian society. To describe it briefly, a university professor has to be, first, entrepreneurial in everything he or she does. If he or she is also an acclaimed scholar, that's fine; if not, that's equally all right. But in any case, the professor has to be a wheeler-dealer in his or her academic and nonacademic activities. In other words, the values of a free market, in the most primitive way, got on the forefront of public interest and value scales. No doubt about it. The problem, however, is how long it will be this way and whether the traditional values of high learning and humanitarian culture will survive in such an atmosphere.

Although market values in higher education are already here, I see no evidence of markets for intellectual labor in Russia. Still, as for many years before, all faculty are strictly attached to their universities, and horizontal, vertical, or geographical mobility scarcely exists at all. There are rigid market values without free markets themselves. This is a very serious paradox of the current intellectual situation in Russia, including academia, that has undetectable consequences. Moscow University is being commercialized barbarously and literally in front of our eyes. Recently, for example, in our Sociology Department, in the midst of the lecture halls, a restaurant with loud music and alcoholic beverages was opened, running from 11:00 in the morning until late in the evening. The parking lot in front of our department building is filled with chic, expensive cars (which only a few of my American high-ranking corporate friends can afford) belonging to some of our students. I have never seen such stratification and polarization of the student body into the "super-rich" and "surviving" in any American university. It would simply be impossible there. I would not like to moralize on this, but I will make one final remark.

All this and much more that is taking place in university education and in the country as a whole are very alarming. The illusions raised during the first years of the liberalization and withdrawal from the socialist model vanished long ago, both in our country and with my more realistically minded American colleagues.

## Realities in Russia Today

With some bitterness, I recall 1989-1990, when I was working at the National Humanities Center in Research Triangle Park, North Carolina, and continually gave interviews or appeared in newspapers, over radio, and on television; the times were like that then. Americans wanted to know firsthand about what was happening in Russia. Then, greeting the fall of the Berlin Wall, the revolutions in Eastern Europe, and the *perestroika* in my own country, I could not but talk about the potentially dangerous and unpredictably fast destruction of the social structure in all those societies. Sociology teaches that not a single complicated and all-embracing transformation of these powerful structures can take place without arousing very negative and dysfunctional consequences into being as well. Unfortunately, those thoughts and warnings of mine were not heard by many. The world was wallowing in self-oblivion in the happiness of communism's downfall. In an interview given to a leading North Carolina newspaper in the early summer of 1990, when the euphoria had reached its climax, I said the following: "Now that the Perestroika and Glasnost have been set loose, deep uncertainty has set in. Everyone is very much irritated. The changes have stripped away much of the authority. . . . The country is falling apart, it is literally falling apart into a state of anarchy" (Pokrovsky, 1990, p. J5). I recall this and many other warnings I made, not because I want to be known for perspicuity, but because I have been trying to be— then and now—honest with my audience.

I have never wanted to be a cool and nonparticipatory, independent observer of the situation in my country. The days of the ultraconservative military coup in August 1991 I spent on the barricades of the White House, thinking that, at such critical moments of my life and history itself, I must say aloud what I thought (Pokrovsky, 1991b, p. 1). I believe that this gives me some right to be outspoken in social issues and the future in Russia. Progress of the Russian university education and the future of the Russian intelligentsia are, at present, in a period of great historical trial whose length is indefinable. If we cannot influence this process, then all talk about the perfection of teaching, about the moral world of the professor and the students, about the ties between research and classroom teaching could very quickly become senseless.

Freedom of the spirit and thought, brought to us so recently, demands from us not only uncritical admiration for it but also enormous responsibility, reasonableness, and a culture of social action. Otherwise, this freedom becomes highly destructive. Only the power of human reason, along with principles of humanitarian and humanistic logic and an all-penetrating inner consistency of all our deeds, can help us surpass the present crisis and the indefiniteness of our future.

We, in the end, can do something and are worth something in this life. This was said, in part, by that marvelous American sociologist William Thomas, who wrote, "If people define situations as real, they are real in their consequences." This instills hope in me.

## Notes

1. Fyodor Tyutchev (1803-1873) was one of the most acclaimed Russian poets of the 19th century; as a high-ranking diplomat, he spent most of his life in Germany.

2. I published excerpts from my correspondence with my American friends in the article "With Anger and Bitterness: Letters of the Sociologists of Two Countries" (1993).

3. Much later, I published the book *Early American Philosophy: Vol. I. Puritanism* (1989a), which I considered to be an introduction to the research on American Enlightenment, including Thomas Jefferson.

## References

Berger, P. (1963). *Invitation to sociology: A humanistic perspective.* Garden City, NY: Doubleday.

Blok, A. (1981). *Selected poems* (A. Miller, Trans.). Moscow: Progress Publishers. (Original work published 1914)

Dewey, J. (1927). *The public and its problems.* Denver: Alan Swallow.

Jefferson, T. (1944). To Mrs. Cosway, Oct. 12, 1786. In A. Koch & W. Peden (Eds.), *The life and selected writings of Thomas Jefferson* (pp. 400-401). New York: Modern Library.

Lawrence, J., & Lee, R. (1984). *The night Thoreau spent in jail* [Play] (N. Pokrovsky, Ed. and Trans.).

Pokrovsky, N. (1983). *Henry Thoreau* (in Russian). Moscow: Misl.

Pokrovsky, N. (Ed.). (1986a). *Henry Thoreau: Walden* (in Russian). Moscow: Belles Lettres.

Pokrovsky, N. (Ed.). (1986b). *Ralph Emerson: Essays* (in Russian). Moscow: Belles Lettres.

Pokrovsky, N. (1989a). *Early American philosophy: Vol. I. Puritanism.* Moscow: Vishaya Shkola.

Pokrovsky, N. (1989b). *Henry Thoreau* (in English). Moscow: Progress Publishers.

Pokrovsky, N. (1990, June 10). A Russian thoroughly mad about Thoreau. *News and Observer* (Raleigh, NC), p. J5.

Pokrovsky, N. (1991a). Early evening on morning heights: Subjective notes on Robert Merton. *Sociological Research, 5.*

Pokrovsky, N. (1991b, August 22). Thoreau scholar puts life on line: Democratic ideals dictate coup fight. *Telegram & Gazette* (Worcester, MA), p. 1.

Pokrovsky, N. (1992). *Henry Thoreau: Civil disobedience* (in Russian; World Without Violence Series). Moscow: Tula.

Pokrovsky, N. (1993). With anger and bitterness: Letters of the sociologists of two countries. *Sociological Research, 4.*

Pokrovsky, N. (1996a). *At the crossroads of loneliness and solitude: Henry Thoreau's philosophical visions* (in Russian). Moscow: Vishaia Schola.

Pokrovsky, N. (1996b). *Ralph Waldo Emerson: An intellectual biography* (in Russian). Concord, MA: Center for American Studies.

Richmond, Y. (1992). *From nyet to da: Understanding the Russians.* Yarmouth, ME: Intercultural Press.

Thomas, W. I. (1936). *Moments of thought in the nineteenth century.* Chicago: National Union.

Thoreau, H. D. (1854). *Slavery in Massachusetts.* Moscow: Khudodjestvennaya Literatura.

# III

## Finding Solutions
## in Practice

Each author in this book has something to say about the integration of teaching and research, and each has a story to tell about the life and practice of a teacher. In this section, we present the views of some of the authors on the craft of teaching itself. They share with us some of the hard-won lessons they have learned about the purpose of university teaching and describe techniques for making the learning experience meaningful to their students.

Beverly Cameron teaches economics to large classes (150 to 300 students) and sees her main role as teaching effective thinking skills. She describes the impetus to her teaching that came from discovering research on different learning styles. Applying this knowledge in her classes helped her identify why well-prepared students did poorly on her exams. "Once I understood the likely cause of the unsuccessful students' learning patterns, I wrote and suggested special problems that required students to see patterns and relationships between old and new situations. I also phrased my questions—in class as well as in my office—in ways that required students to make connections." Cameron talks also

157

about classroom control, self-renewal, and her growing role in developing and mentoring other faculty in their teaching performance.

Jeff Mello brings a decidedly applied orientation to his perspective on research and teaching. "True learning can only take place when a personalized experiential component is present." He chooses topics for his courses in terms of their significance to practical issues. This "not only makes material more relevant and holds students' interest but also makes it easier for me to plan for class." He discusses control in terms of finding a balance between allowing spontaneity and directing the agenda in the classroom. Like others in this section, Mello stresses the importance of being well organized. "In my teaching, nothing is random."

For Afsaneh Nahavandi, teaching is about "being provided and providing others with the means to grow and learn. It is about evolution." She discusses effective teaching in terms of thorough preparation, showing courtesy and respect, tolerance for others and valuing diversity, enthusiasm, flexibility, and a willingness to make mistakes. She has firm views on control: "Education is a commitment to learn, not an enforcement of rules." She also discusses ways to ensure self-renewal.

Pushkala Prasad expresses her frustration with students' disdain for organizational behavior courses and contrasts this with the excitement she has experienced as a researcher in this area. She identifies the problem of student disinterest as being a result of student ignorance of the contexts of organizational behavior topics when these are presented in class. She argues that we need to teach topics differently so that connections can be made between course material and its historical context. In particular, her objective is to help students see organized behavior as "one of the many managerial responses to a crisis of control" by focusing on critique and by finding ways for students "to experience the empowerment that comes from questioning 'expert' textual knowledge." Prasad describes some interesting and innovative techniques for accomplishing these aims.

Marcy Crary and Duncan Spelman provide a unique perspective on teaching as they discuss the challenges of working collaboratively in the classroom. They raise candidly many issues that surface when the composition of the teaching team comprises men and women and when it includes people of color. Their experiences while introducing and teaching a course on managing diversity in the workplace provide a rich case through which to examine the dynamics of collaboration in the classroom. They note, "At some points, the conflict we experienced in our teaching team about [different philosophies about diversity at work] was deep and painful. We certainly learned much from our explorations of the different philosophies, but not without struggle that shook the foundations of our relationship." They provide interpretations of what helps keep team teachers together effectively.

Donald Hambrick is a case teacher, though not a "purist." Like Mello and others in this section, he is a believer in "tangible application and experiential learning." He sees teaching in terms of relationships and, in particular, as a form of leadership. Teaching involves managing meaning: "A teacher must establish for himself or herself a vivid and compelling personal case for the material"; managing (getting and keeping) the attention of students; creating trust between teacher and students; and self-management. He is high on the synergies between teaching and research, and the chapter is replete with suggestions for enhancing the teaching experience.

Each author seems to be searching continually, through his or her practice, to stretch students and to help them grow. The authors want each student to be as excited about the material and the intellectual fields as they are. They want to light a fire under their students, to empower them, to see "lightbulbs go on" in students' minds, or to "light up" their eyes. They search for connections between theory and practice, between surface and more subtle aspects of issues, between the course material and the interests and preferences of the students, between teacher and student.

They bring passion to their techniques, and their love of teaching is unmistakable.

# 10 Learning to Teach

*An Ongoing Process*

BEVERLY J. CAMERON

## Who Am I? What Do I Do?
## What Do I Stand for as a Teacher?

Who am I? I've been working on the answer to that question for years. But I do know that, for me, life involves learning and change—a mix of the new and the routine and the courage to give up some of what is comfortable to try things that might allow me to grow as a person. I believe that although each person is unique, we all have a great deal to share with each other. Thus, I try to respect the individuality of people, as well as to learn from and give to them as I am able. For me, teaching taps into this core of who I am. It provides an exciting mix of learning, change, routine, newness, and sharing with and respecting the uniqueness of individuals.

It's easier to convey who I am by describing one of my more important roles in life—that of university teacher. As a teacher, I express my personal and professional values, my level of personal growth, my professional knowledge and activities, my life experiences, and my philosophy of education. I express a great deal of who I am when I teach, which is one reason I'm "hooked on teaching."

What do I do as a teacher? I try to follow the adage that an effective teacher acts not as "a sage on the stage" but as "a guide on the side." I can't make anyone learn, and external motivators such as grades have only limited effectiveness if a student doesn't care about or see the relevance of the course material. Therefore, when I teach economics, I try to tie the course concepts to students' lives, interests, and goals. When I'm successful, students see a reason to learn and use economic theory, and I become a guide to their learning. It's like lighting a fire in students' minds: Once the fire is started, it burns by itself, with only the periodic addition of fuel and some tending.

What do I stand for as a teacher? I'm a role model, an example of an economist, a university faculty member, a teacher, a professional woman, and a person with her own unique strengths and weaknesses. I share my enthusiasm for economics and my experiences. I model my professional knowledge, development, and mental patterns. I try to relate to the experiences and goals of my students and to work with them as a group and as individuals. In doing so, I share a large part of who I am and my personal and professional goals and dreams.

## My Perception of the Role of a University Education

My academic career has been greatly influenced by my view of what a university education should provide. Only within this larger perspective do many of the professional and personal decisions I have made form a rational whole. I have not followed the standard academic pattern and timing, and I do not fit into the standard academic career mold; but I do believe I've grown professionally and personally as a result.

My vision of what a university education should be was succinctly stated by Robert Hutchins, former president of the University of Chicago (1929-45): "It must be remembered that the purpose of education is not to fill minds of students with facts. . . . It is to teach them to think, if that is possible, and always to think for themselves." For me, a university education should teach individuals to be effective thinkers. This belief has strongly influenced my academic career.

Universities have many roles, traditionally viewed as teaching, research, and service. In carrying out these roles, institutions serve a variety of constituencies. But for each role and each constituency, I see the overriding goal as the teaching of effective thinking skills.

In its teaching role, the university must transmit much more than facts and acceptance of already-received knowledge. Facts and information can be memorized or looked up in the library, but how these facts and information are used, recombined, processed, analyzed, and synthesized allows the frontiers of knowledge to be pushed back and the human condition to be improved. Computers can store information and make it easily accessible, but the human mind is best at drawing unique inferences and making new connections.

Making inferences and connections is not easy to learn or to teach. Many students find it easier to memorize and accept what they are told or read, rather than to think about the information they receive. I believe, however, it is the role of the university teacher to model, explain, and require students to use thinking processes that analyze, synthesize, and evaluate information and ideas. When a teacher models, uses, and makes effective thinking an expectation, the chance is good that students will experience course material and a discipline as relevant, alive, and exciting. And students will see and use the strengths of that discipline to help solve some of their own and the world's problems.

In the university's research role, the teaching of thinking skills is equally important. Researchers who have been taught to be effective thinkers are better able to apply received knowledge, to analyze problems and results, to synthesize information from multiple experiments and situations, and to evaluate the meaning and relevance of results and hypotheses. Researchers who are effective thinkers are more likely to make valuable and relevant contributions in their fields and to draw inferences and insights that can lead to further contributions in a variety of fields. They are also more likely to pass on these important skills and viewpoints to their students and to the readers of their publications.

The university's service role provides the faculty with the opportunity for teaching effective thinking skills as role models. When a faculty member makes statements to the media, gives a luncheon address to a service club, or provides an opinion to a member of the public, the faculty member's words and the thought processes behind them serve as an example of a thinking process. Because faculty are often perceived as experts, the ways they draw conclusions, use facts, and think about things serve as models to the community at large. They are, in effect, teaching a thinking process.

Thus, a significant portion of an academic's role as teacher, researcher, and service giver involves teaching effective thinking skills. These are skills we must explicitly pass on to our students by being role models and by being clear about the process through which we solve problems and arrive at our opinions and conclusions. I see my role in the university as primarily a teacher.

## My Background

Arriving at this view of a university education and my role in that process didn't come overnight. My growth or evolution to this view was influenced by some special teachers I was fortunate enough to have known during my formal years as a student. (I say "my formal years as a student" because I consider myself a lifelong student.)

My undergraduate education took place at a large selective public university where I faced stiff academic competition. The emphasis at this institution was on research and attracting the best possible graduate students. Undergraduates were taught in classes as large as 300, and even "small" upper-level courses had enrollments of 40 to 80. Except in a few cases, the teachers who greatly influenced my ideas and ultimate career directions didn't even know me by name.

Two individuals in particular made a great impression on me. One was Dr. Daniel Fusfeld, who lectured on principles of economics to about 250 students. The other was Dr. William Neanan, who taught public finance to about 80 3rd- and 4th-year economics majors. I didn't know Fusfeld as a person, nor did he know me, but his enthusiasm for the material, the thinking process he modeled, and his general sense of concern for all 250 of us are still a gratifying memory to me. Neanan dealt with "smaller" classes, so I knew him, but not well. But again, his sense of humor, way of thinking about economics and life in general, and concern for us as individuals were clearly conveyed to me.

I earned a bachelor's degree in economics and, with it, a provisional secondary teaching certificate. The teaching certificate surprised even me because I had never wanted to be a teacher. I'd been taught at home that "those who can, do; those who can't, teach." So why did I get a teaching certificate? Perceived job security. My mother had suggested I'd always be able to get a job with a teaching certificate.

## My First Teaching Experiences

I graduated not really wanting to teach but having two strong role models for the teaching I would do. And sure enough, the teaching certificate was a job ticket. I taught junior high and substituted in a large urban high school while taking evening graduate courses in economics. In both schools, I quickly realized that, to keep order in the room, I had to relate to and intellectually engage my students. This was when I started to use the qualities Fusfeld and Neanan had exhibited. I displayed my genuine enthusiasm and interest in the material I was teaching; I attempted to explain my thought processes to my students; I looked for challenging assignments and activities; I tried to get the students actively involved in and responsible for the learning process; I tried to get students to explain how they had solved problems and reached conclusions; and I tried to get the students to think about the course material.

Most of all, I tried to show students and have them discover how course material was relevant to their lives, goals, and dreams. For example, I tied the concept of producer surplus to students' summer job interviews. I asked how employers might decide what wage to pay summer student help. How much would employers pay an individual with unique skills? I asked why employers might ask a prospective employee to state an expected wage before revealing how much they were willing to pay. It wasn't hard to see that students were interested in this economic concept. This theory could be used to put money in their pockets. I had the students' attention. They wanted to learn the theory of producer surplus and to apply it to their lives.

I loved watching students learn and apply course material to their lives and the real world. I saw a classroom full of lightbulbs clicking on. They were learning because they wanted to learn—because they were intrinsically motivated. I knew I had to try to present other concepts in an equally relevant manner. This wasn't (and still isn't) easy, but I was hooked on teaching.

I was (and still am) delighted and moved when a student made a connection between the ideas I'd taught and other parts of his or her life. I cared about many students as individuals, and I tried to challenge them to stretch themselves intellectually. In some moments, teaching was really fun!

My first taste of university teaching occurred when I was approached to teach a section of principles of economics for one year to fill an unexpected vacancy. This one-year job lasted for seven years and then became a "continuing" appointment as an instructor.

During that first year of university teaching, I "worked my tail off" preparing material. I learned firsthand that one doesn't really understand something until one can teach it; I rehearsed explanations and thought processes at home before class; I had beautifully outlined notes; I lived in fear that I'd fall off the elevated platform in the front of the room or that I'd be unable to get the overhead screen to stay down—or go up—when I needed it; I came to class early; and I spent hours answering students' questions. I gave teaching my all. I was hooked on teaching, and I believed that my efforts made a difference to many of my students.

### My Introduction to Life as an Academic

The part of my job that involved teaching was fun and rewarding. At departmental seminars, however, I frequently felt gaps in my ability to understand economics and to follow thought processes displayed by some of my colleagues. It often seemed to me that a few colleagues jumped from Step 1 to 3 to 5 as they explained their research. I needed the steps to proceed 1, 2, 3, 4, 5. Years later, I realized that some of my frustration resulted from my preferred learning style being quite different from those of most of my colleagues, but these experiences changed my teaching.

In my early years of university teaching, I was encouraged to know that the business school annually reserved a large number of spaces in my sections for their students. I knew that many business students enjoyed my classes, could follow my thinking processes, and did well in the course, but then so did other students who were in human ecology and other faculties. Later, when I read the learning styles literature, I discovered that my preferred style was the same as that of many people in business. I also learned that economists, by and large, were individuals with a quite different learning preference. Theoretical economists tend to "look at the whole forest," whereas the business faculty, myself included, are more inclined to "look at a few trees very carefully." It's the difference between preferring to see and looking for large patterns, relationships, possibilities, concepts, and the big picture and looking at the parts, details, practical applications, and realities. Or it's the difference between reading between the lines and reading exactly what is written. Disciplines have room for people with differing preferences, but when the majority of people in the field have one preference, the literature, research, presentation, and teaching styles tend to favor the dominant preference.

Discovering learning style differences was very freeing for me; it validated me as an individual. I was "different" from many of my immediate colleagues, and I realized that many of my students had preferences different from mine. This realization led me to examine my teaching style and to efforts to teach in ways that would appeal to a wide variety of learning preferences.

A particular incentive to adapt my teaching to a variety of learning styles came from a concern for students who worked very hard in my course but who never seemed to earn grades above a C or D. These students told me they knew the notes "cold," and they seemed to, but yet they were unable to use the theories or concepts in slightly different situations. The students were frustrated at the results of their efforts, and so was I. I thought that I was letting them down, that I wasn't teaching effectively, and I agonized over how to change my teaching so that all students could meet what I thought were reasonable and necessary course requirements.

With my new understanding of learning preferences, I realized that, frequently, hardworking, unsuccessful students memorized the text and my lecture material but had trouble seeing possibilities and patterns when the situation changed a bit. Because my tests generally asked students to apply and use course material in similar but new situations, students who memorized as opposed to understood the material had trouble. My tests required students to see patterns and relationships between theories and scenarios, rather than to memorize and "regurgitate" material from the text or lecture. Once I understood the likely cause of the unsuccessful students' learning patterns, I wrote and suggested special problems that required students to see patterns and relationships between old and new situations. I also phrased my questions—in class as well as in my office—in ways that required students to make connections. I added small-group work to my lectures to give students a few moments to think about a problem solution and then to compare their results with their neighbor's solution. I then modeled my own thinking process, trying to be very clear about why I followed the steps I did.

Because my learning preference is to see what is, to see details and facts, I had to make a special effort to present the "big picture" and to get students excited about the patterns and possibilities in economics. One way I did this was to present a conceptual diagram of each term's material on the first day of class. I displayed 12 concept boxes in sort of a "tree" to show how ideas were linked and to show the logical order of presentation and development. I repeatedly referred to the diagram as the term progressed to help remind students of where we had been and where we were going.

Another way I tried to address differing learning styles was to relate specific theories in the course to newspaper articles or current media concerns. A change in taxation policy, movements in the stock market, major industrial mergers, changes in the bank or foreign exchange rates, and so on can be seen both as relevant details and as important parts of a new economic trend, change in government policy, cure for high unemployment, warning of increased inflationary pressure, and so on. I tried to link details and facts to patterns and possibilities. Different parts of this process appealed to students with differing learning preferences and helped all students strengthen thinking and reasoning skills they might not prefer to use.

Knowledge of learning preferences opened up a new way of teaching for me. It was more work because I was often teaching contrary to my preference, but it was a personal and professional growth experience for me, and it seems to have helped a number of my students.

## Graduate Work in Higher Education

Frustrations, successes, and growing professional and self-knowledge led me to the realization that I had a very strong commitment to teaching and that my overall goal was to teach students to be effective thinkers. I worked as a workshop facilitator for University Teaching Services (UTS) to learn about, as well as to pass on, ideas about teaching.

I thought about teaching, read about teaching, and eventually decided to do graduate work in higher education. So, at age 44, I returned to the university that granted me a BA and became a full-time graduate student. My graduate work focused on how best to teach students to become effective thinkers. When it came time to write a thesis, my students became "research subjects."

My thesis research involved teaching effective thinking skills and measuring the results of these efforts in large lecture-based principles of economics courses. I used small-group work to hone students' thinking skills in one lecture class but not in the other; included active learning exercises in both lectures; measured students' motivation to learn and how relevant they thought the course material was to their lives; asked students to group course concepts and compared their groupings to mine at the start of the term and at the end; and compared the results from my classes with those from students in three control classes with colleagues who used traditional lecture methods. I ran countless regressions, wrote for what seemed like an endless period of time, defended my thesis, and rejoiced that I could return to my students, armed with greater knowledge, research experience, and the results of my own growth that occurred during this process.

My research conclusions were that explicit efforts on the part of the lecturer to (a) teach a process of effective thinking, (b) use active learning activities in lectures, and (c) require problem sets that explicitly implement and use effective thinking skills positively influenced the development of students' effective thinking skills. Small-group work, as used in this research, did not produce a statistically significant increase in skill development. As a result, I've continued to be explicit about effective thinking skill development in my classes and to include special problem sets and active learning exercises in my courses.

### Work as a Faculty Developer

After finishing my doctoral work, my commitment to university teaching took a wider and more public turn when I assumed the half-time position of director of UTS. Like many people who start out in faculty development, I didn't really know "how" to be a faculty developer, but I was committed to the idea of enhancing the climate for teaching and learning. So, with enthusiasm and the idea that the goal of a university should be to teach students how to become effective thinkers, I started to build and revitalize UTS.

## A Slow Process of Maturation as a Teacher

My commitment to excellence in teaching and efforts to enhance the teaching and learning environment developed from good (and bad) experiences I had as a student, a desire to help students learn and develop as thinkers and as individuals, a wish to be the best that I could be as a teacher/scholar, and a personal quest for wholeness as a person. As a result of my own growth, I have become more willing to give of myself.

In more professional terms, I have benefited from some very good mentoring. My first attempts at faculty development work involved working with Dr. Bob Headly, a senior professor. I co-facilitated two workshops on lecturing and explaining skills with Bob, but 9 months into our relationship he was diagnosed with advanced lung cancer. Three months later he died. We'd scheduled one more workshop before his diagnosis, but it became clear that he would not be able to work again. Sitting in his living room, connected to oxygen tubes, he convinced me that I had the skills and was ready to lead a successful workshop on my own. As it turned out, he was right; I was ready to work on my own. Bob not only nurtured my development as a professional but also believed in me. Sooner than either one of us had anticipated, he helped me cut the mentee-mentor ties so that I could work confidently on my own.

Drs. Joan Stark and Bill McKeachie at the University of Michigan also provided me with valuable mentoring when I returned to graduate school. Being an older student and an experienced faculty member, I wasn't a typical graduate student, and in that way I'm sure I was a challenge to mentor. Both Joan and Bill did a great job of treating me as a colleague and a friend while guiding me through the inevitable insecurities and doubts of course work and writing a thesis.

As a result of this positive mentoring, I am ready to become a mentor, at least in some areas. I've had informal mentoring relationships with a number of junior colleagues over the years, but starting this fall I've been assigned by my dean as a mentor for a new faculty member. My mentee is in a different discipline, but I'm sure I can pass on some of the wisdom, patience, advice, respect, and encouragement I have so generously received from my mentors.

I've also learned that, for me, teaching involves love—*love* being defined as helping another person grow to become the most that he or she can become as a person. In my experience, all very good teachers have been able to give their students love. Certainly, the great teachers I have had gave me self-confidence, acceptance, respect, and part of themselves when they showed me how they thought and how they approached their discipline. I believe that these things can only be given through love.

I've been motivated by frequent one-on-one teaching relationships with my students and by sharing the excitement of learning and thinking. But whatever the motivation, it became clear to me over the years that the desire to be involved with the learning and teaching process was what made my academic career important and rewarding for me.

## A 3M Teaching Fellowship

In 1991, I was selected as a 3M Teaching Fellow. This award, sponsored by 3M Canada and the Society for Teaching and Learning in Higher Education (STLHE), is given each year to 10 Canadian college and university faculty. The criteria for the fellowship involve excellence in undergraduate classroom teaching and a demonstrated commitment to leadership in teaching and learning in higher education.

The 3M Fellowship starts with three hosted days at a beautiful resort in the hills of Quebec. For me, the best part of this time was meeting other Fellows and sharing hopes, frustrations, dreams, concerns, and efforts as teacher scholars and human beings. The 10 Fellows selected in 1991 came from a wide variety of disciplines and backgrounds: chemistry, veterinary medicine, psychology, communications, biology, Greek, management, physics, and English. During our time together, we shared the highs and the lows of being teachers, talked about personal and professional plans, related what had worked for us in the classroom and what hadn't, and discussed what we'd given up personally and professionally to devote so much time and energy to teaching. The time we shared together at Chateau Montebello in Quebec was very special. Despite the differences in our disciplines, we sensed immediately that, in this group, we were with "our own kind." Now, when we meet at conferences, we greet each other with hugs and the special enthusiasm that comes from seeing a special friend. Our common visions, career paths, and commitments have bonded us as a group and as individuals.

## Comments on Teaching

### Issues of Control and Authority

My teaching experiences have generally been with classes of 150 to 300 students, so control has been an issue at times. I can remember joking with a colleague who taught equally large classes, "It would be all over if they (the students) ever turned on us." Looking out at 150 to 300 faces, some of whom are not terribly motivated to be in class, can be an awe-inspiring situation.

Even now, I remember walking into the first university class I taught some 25 years ago. Seeing the hall half-filled with students, I thought that if I just took a seat, no one would know who was supposed to teach the class. For a few seconds, the idea of abdicating the authority of the front of the room seemed very appealing.

On other occasions, I've had to confront two or three students who sit—usually in the back—in large classes and continually whisper. For me, this is an issue of control. (I'm at a disadvantage when I don't know everyone's name, and I've never been able to learn even half the names in my large classes.) I usually start by looking at the talkers and asking them to respect others sitting around them who want to listen. At times, I have had to directly confront individuals after class to ask them not to talk or to sit separately, and on one occasion I had to ask a student to leave the classroom. I never enjoy these situations in large classes because, at some level, I worry about actually having control. I exercise control out of respect for all the students, however, especially the ones who came to learn.

Generally, I've dealt with issues of control by trying to make the class and material as interesting and relevant to students as I can, by respecting students as individuals, by actively involving students in the learning process, by helping them see how course material is relevant to their own lives, and at times by resorting to my position of authority. Attendance is never a requirement in my classes; I expect students to attend my classes because they are open to learning and willing to think about the course material, and I tell them so. I still tend to react personally, however, when someone leaves the room in one of my large classes.

I address respect for the learning process by frequently referring to Bloom's (1956) cognitive taxonomy of thinking skills: knowledge (or recall), comprehension, application, analysis, synthesis, and evaluation. I believe that if students know what learning and effective thinking involve, if they see me explicitly model these skills, and if I am explicit about the skills I expect students to demonstrate during class and on assignments and examinations, it's more likely that these expectations will be met. I believe that being explicit about the thinking and learning process allows students to appreciate the value of the process taking place in the classroom.

### My Keys to Effective Teaching

I've been struck, over the years, at how difficult it is to explicitly explain the steps I follow in problem solving or effective thinking. When my son was 4 years old and wanted me to teach him to ride a bicycle, I had trouble remembering exactly how, as a rider, I balanced the bike, exactly where I put my hands and feet to get started, exactly how I managed to get and keep my balance, and so on. I'd ridden a bicycle for so many years that I "just did it." Now, I had to explain the process step by step, and it was difficult! With the help of a 7-year-old neighbor who still remembered clearly how he learned to ride a bike, our son managed to become a competent cyclist, but the experience made me reflect on my teaching. I've used some economic tools so many times that I now find it hard to explain step by step exactly how I reached a particular conclusion. But being able to explain the steps explicitly is often what good teaching is about. So, I spend a great deal of time deciding how to explain a concept or an idea to a student who is hearing it for the first time. The key for me is to try to remember what it was like when I heard the idea for the first time. I try to put myself in the student's position, and I believe it improves my teaching.

## My Limits as a Teacher Scholar

My limits as a teacher scholar are probably closely tied to several things: (a) my ability to grow as a person, (b) the mental limitations I put on my own career, and (c) my physical energy level. The process of personal growth has opened many possibilities and given me the self-confidence to pursue a supposedly unrewarding (nonstandard) academic career path. I believe that growth has made me a better teacher and colleague by helping me be less self-centered and more other-centered and by reducing the mental limitations I place on myself. There are fewer things that I tell myself I "can't do." I have also grown in my ability to assess potential projects in the light of my overall professional and personal goals and to make decisions on the basis of my own criteria, as opposed to what I think is "expected" of me. Growing hasn't been an easy process, and I still have a long way to go. However, I think I'm on the life path that will bring me both personal and professional fulfillment and allow me to make a worthwhile contribution to the lives of many other people.

I also have limits as a teacher, based on my own mental preferences and patterns. I continually work to present the big picture, relationships, and patterns, but it is not likely to ever be my strength. As a result, students who prefer to see the big picture first may find me less inspiring as a teacher. Knowing my own preferences, however, will help me be conscious of my limitations and allow me to teach in ways that address the needs of all my students.

Another limitation is the amount of physical energy I have. My answer has been to try to work smarter rather than longer. Sometimes I accomplish this; sometimes I don't.

## My Future as a Teacher Scholar?

In many ways, I think I am just beginning to hit my stride as a teacher scholar and a leader in higher education. My career has a definite focus that it didn't have earlier. When I started, I thought I had to fit the standard academic mold of researcher, teacher, and service giver/administrator. Now, I know that the standard mold does not fit my interests or talents. Successes in the area of teaching have validated a much heavier emphasis on the teacher scholar role.

The strength to carve out my own niche has come partly from the pain of struggling to conform to a mold that didn't fit. It's difficult to determine what motivates individuals to grow, change, and find their own place. From many talks with other 3M Fellows, however, my professional and personal growth and my career path are similar to theirs. It would seem that the process of struggling to find a niche can lead to wholeness in both professional and personal life.

I hope to continue to grow as a person and as a teacher. I hope to continue to expend a great deal of energy to make teaching the collegial, rewarding, and exciting activity I believe it can be. I'll continue to look for opportunities to add to faculty development activities at my own institution and, where possible, at other institutions. I'll continue to espouse the view that the goal of a university education should be to teach effective thinking skills and to listen when colleagues espouse their goals. I want to be part of a community of teaching scholars where there are as many "molds" as there are individuals.

## Concerns With Personal Renewal

I view teaching as the giving of myself, as the giving of love, so personal renewal is an inevitable issue. I have been concerned with "burnout" at several times during my career, and I've dealt with it in a number of ways. Some remedies have been career-long solutions; others have been tailored to the time and situation.

The career-long solutions involve never teaching summer school for fear that I won't be "fresh" and "recharged" in the fall. I am concerned that the basic material I teach will become too familiar to me and that I'll be tempted to go into "automatic pilot" in the classroom. It's also best if I have to refresh myself before each class so that the material has a "newness" and an excitement for me. If I'm relearning and reprocessing before a class, I think I can better convey the excitement that comes from the ideas, concepts, tools, processes, and skills I use in class. Coming to the course material fresh helps me see the material the way I saw it for the first time and, I hope, present and explain it in a manner that most benefits my students.

I try to keep the material interesting and relevant to myself and students by applying economic theory to the real world to as great an extent as possible. I bring in current newspaper articles, refer to events or concerns on campus, and use examples that relate to the age group of the majority of my students. (Admittedly, this gets harder as the age gap widens, but I work at it.) My students appreciate seeing the theory being applied, and applications give me a chance to model effective thinking skills by using course material.

I also make efforts to talk with colleagues who enjoy and are stimulated by their teaching. We talk of teaching responsibilities, not teaching "loads"; we share teaching ideas; and we use (appropriate) humor to diffuse some of our concerns and to keep us excited about teaching. Many other 3M Fellows have been especially valuable as e-mail correspondents for discussions on teaching. With colleagues who are committed teachers, I can be frank, open, and honest about my concerns, problems, and joys. I think these colleagues will understand the context and meaning of what I say.

On a more personal level, I try hard to make time for exercise and for interests far removed from my profession. I spend time with my family, I cook, I'm on the board of trustees of a nonacademic institution, I belong to an orchid-growers group, I ride a horse, I spend time with my dogs, and I cultivate friends outside the academic world. I try to give my life a balance so that I can approach my academic job refreshed.

As with many people in personally and emotionally draining careers, my efforts to keep myself fresh and renewed are a constant challenge. Some years, months, and days, I feel that I'm successful and have the optimal amount of energy to give my students and my research the best I'm capable of giving. Other times, I'm not so sure, and that bothers me. I like to know that I can do a very good job or not do it at all. The time may come in my academic career when I feel that I'm not able to give at a level I think is acceptable. When this happens, I hope to have the courage to move on to a new career and stage in my life.

## Comments for Young Academics Who Aspire to Be Excellent Teacher Scholars

Most academics are under pressure to conform to the system and to fit the standard academic mold their institution espouses. My advice on this would be to conform and fit into that mold only to the extent that it doesn't constrain you from being the best teacher scholar you can become. If your love is teaching, if that is where you get the most personal fulfillment, if that is where you think you can make the greatest contribution, then become a teaching scholar. Allow some or all of your research to be in the area of teaching and learning within your discipline. If you check, you will probably find at least two or three teaching-related refereed journals in your discipline or general journals that will accept your classroom research. Publishing in discipline-based teaching journals allows you to focus on teaching as well as on scholarship in your discipline.

I also urge young academics to start collecting material for a teaching dossier (or portfolio) as soon as they start their careers in the same way they collect information for their research and service dossier. Not only does a teaching dossier document the wide range of teaching achievements and efforts of most teacher scholars, but it also helps the preparer focus on future directions for his or her career. For instance, writing a brief teaching philosophy for my own dossier proved invaluable because it made me think again about what I attempt to accomplish when I teach. If I'd clearly articulated my teaching philosophy at the start of my career, I may have been a better teacher, the frustrations may have been fewer for me and my students, and most important, my students may have learned more and become more effective thinkers.

If your first love as an academic is research, make a commitment to research and to teaching others to become good researchers. Try to pass on your skills, your excitement, your sense of commitment, your enthusiasm, and your ability to think effectively about research. Document your formal research efforts and your efforts as a teaching researcher.

A final comment to young academics is to give as much of yourself to your teaching and to your students as you can without burning yourself out. I truly believe that in giving you also receive and that both the giving and the receiving will make your career more rewarding.

It is also important to take time for yourself for renewal and recharging. Try to associate with colleagues who share your goals even if this means seeking out national conferences such as the Society for Teaching and Learning in Higher Education (STLHE) and the Organizational Behavior Teaching Conference (OBTC). You need to take care of yourself in order to grow as a person and to give your best as a teaching scholar.

# Conclusion

My career as a teacher scholar has and continues to be both person-ally and professionally rewarding and challenging. I am still learning and growing, and I consider both to be lifelong processes. I hope I will continue to have the strength and confidence to set my own goals and to work toward those goals even though it may seem at times that I am swimming against the flow of expectations in my institution.

# Reference

Bloom, B. S. (Ed.). (1956). *Taxonomy of educational objectives: Handbook I. Cognitive domain.* New York: Longmans, Green.

# 11 Teaching in the Real World

JEFF MELLO

You really had no weaknesses, so to speak. Your grades and references were impeccable . . . and you really impressed all of us in the interviews. You come across as really intelligent and articulate. The applicant we chose, though, has been out of school for a couple of years and has a little bit of experience. We're really sorry . . . it was a very tough decision and in no way reflects upon you or your qualifications. . . .

Not again!?! Here it was, my proverbial 16th apology. It was 1981, and I had just graduated from one of the more esteemed undergraduate business programs in the country at Boston University. After being an underachiever in secondary school, I had decided to really apply myself in college to (a) ensure a great job upon graduation and (b) make my parents proud. At least I succeeded in the latter. My transcript looked like a huge scarlet letter. I was ranked in the top 2% of my class, was named to three major honor societies, and had worked my way through school, working two jobs each summer and one during the school year to pay for my education. I couldn't land a job, though, not without some postcollege full-time work experience. At times, I was incensed: "How can you get that experience they all want if none of them are willing to give it to you?"

In the months after I graduated, I looked back at my undergraduate career. I realized that I had retained very little from it relative to the subjects I'd studied. I had certainly matured personally and further developed a variety of intellectual skills, but what could I actually offer an employer? I could demonstrate quite well that I knew how to get good grades (and, one might assume, to take tests and write course papers), but could I actually do anything to make myself employable? At that juncture in my life, I realized the importance of education that was oriented toward the real world and real problems that organizations faced. I realized that grades meant little if they weren't backed up by an understanding of real-world issues that organizations faced and relevant (read: marketable) experience.

These realizations were soon reinforced in an amusing way, although I didn't find it amusing at the time. Four months after I graduated, I was at a party and happened to meet someone who worked for the firm that had the position I had coveted the most during my interviewing. (After a series of five interviews that whittled the applicant pool down to two finalists, I ended up being the runner-up for a job I would have killed for.) On further conversation, I determined that this person I was speaking with was the individual who'd beaten me out for the job! When I quizzed him regarding his qualifications, I found that he had barely graduated from college (having twice been on academic probation) and had finished with a C average! He had, however, attended a university with a cooperative education program that had provided him with 2 years of work experience en route to achieving his bachelor's degree in 5 years. I entertained the thought of revenge by putting cyanide in his drink but realized that that would be immature (besides, I'd probably get caught). I did, however, have the last laugh when, nearly 10 years later, he entered an MBA program. Guess who taught the first course in his program!

This early career experience has had a profound effect on me professionally. I came to believe it is impossible to underestimate the importance of management education that is applied, practical, and operational. When I returned to school to pursue an MBA on a full-time basis, I worked three part-time jobs simultaneously and took the majority of my courses with students who were attending part-time in the evening to gain more real-world perspectives and networking advantages. My academic career has been spent exclusively in what many of my colleagues would refer to as nontraditional institutions. This experience includes 8 years at the aforementioned cooperative education university that requires a 5-year baccalaureate program, offers a cooperative education MBA program, and requires cooperative education in its JD program; and several years at a large urban university, housed in the downtown business district, that enrolls over 70% of its students as part-time graduate students. With these rich, rewarding, and challenging experiences under my belt, I don't think I would fare well or be happy in a more traditional academic environment. This is not to devalue such institutions or to imply that teaching in these institutions is necessarily an easy task. It's just that the experiences I have had have affected my personal ideology in a way that makes me teach a bit differently from the traditional norm and have higher expectations for students mastering practical and operational applications of theoretical concepts.

## Some Personal Background and Commentary

Probably one of the unique facets of my background involves the fact that I was a teacher long before becoming an academic per se. I think this fact was critical to my being able to develop fully as a teacher before being "programmed," as I find academics so often are. In academic careers, teaching is too often viewed as a necessary evil to be avoided as much as possible. Academics generally do not gain professional status or recognition through teaching; they gain it through their publications and networks developed through professional, research-based associations in their disciplines. Institutional reward systems further downplay the importance of teaching by granting "release time" from what are supposed to be, in many institutions, the professor's primary duties. Research is rewarded; teaching isn't. Tenure and promotion committees look heavily at publication records and letters of support from colleagues in the academy. Teaching not only is ignored in these instances but also is devalued because a release from teaching is the common reward for research productivity for most academics.

Doctoral programs generally don't instruct students in the importance or value of teaching. Although some may provide students with teaching assistantships, performance in the classroom is rarely measured, and degree requirements have no component to ensure that teaching abilities have been developed. This, of course, is in stark contrast to measuring the development of research competence. The problem becomes one of teaching being a necessary evil in academic circles; it isn't taught or discussed in doctoral programs or reinforced in employment. Hence, the overall culture of the academy doesn't train teachers. Unless one has developed as a teacher prior to beginning a full-fledged academic career, the chance is good that one may never become a truly effective teacher or enjoy the teaching experience itself.

The nontraditional nature of my academic background has probably been an important component in my success as a teacher. On entering a full-time MBA program at a large private university in the Northeast, I was awarded a teaching assistantship in an undergraduate management course. I had virtually no professional work experience and was only 1 year out of a traditional undergraduate business program. The main criterion in my being selected for the position was the grades I had received as an undergraduate. I was not interviewed or screened for this position in any way and received no training prior to my initial teaching assignment. The institution was apparently of the mind-set that if I could master the material well enough to have received good grades in it, then I must have the ability to effectively teach it. I have subsequently found this mentality to permeate the fabric of most academic institutions. During the 2 years in which I instructed 20 sections of this undergraduate course, I never had a classroom visitation or concrete evaluation of my performance. The mentality seemed to be that if no students complained, then everything must be proceeding smoothly. No one had any idea what I was or was not doing in the classroom . . . just as long as there were no problems.

Interestingly enough, this initial teaching experience forced me to reevaluate my career direction. I enjoyed teaching immensely and decided to abort my original career plans to work in the advertising industry in favor of working in higher education. On receiving my MBA, the institution from which I graduated offered me a part-time teaching position. In retrospect, I was a warm body in the right place at the right time. I didn't have a job and was hired less than 24 hours before the first class meeting to teach two sections of a course I had absolutely no background in or familiarity with. I was provided with a departmental syllabus and a text and was basically wished good luck. I was quite fortunate, however, in that I was one of six faculty members (the other five were full-time) teaching a total of 12 sections of the course and the department head held weekly "teaching group" meetings where we would share and discuss issues, pedagogies, evaluation techniques, and course content. These exchanges with colleagues were critical to my development as a teacher, especially given the circumstances under which I had been hired. To this day, I strongly believe in and advocate teaching groups around multiple-section courses. They not only keep teachers fresh and allow new cases, exercises, assignments, and teaching strategies to be shared but also help provide more consistency of coverage and pedagogy across multiple-section courses.

After teaching for 2 years on a part-time basis (despite the fact that my teaching load was heavier than all the full-time faculty members), I was offered a full-time nontenure-track lecturer position. Throughout my first 2 years, my teaching evaluations had been stellar, and in one of the few instances in my life in which I have seen effective teaching rewarded, I was subsequently given an unprecedented full-time assignment without a terminal degree or any study toward it. It was clearly stipulated to me that my sole responsibilities were to teach and teach effectively. There were no research or service expectations. The fact that my teaching evaluations were to determine whether my 1-year contract would be renewed gave me the motivation to perform at a high level as a teacher.

After 3 years of teaching full-time, I decided, for three reasons, that it was time to enter a doctoral program. First, I had a natural curiosity concerning many of the unanswered questions relative to what I was teaching. Second, I realized that I would never advance in this career without a terminal degree. Third, the inequities between what I was paid and what tenure-track colleagues who held a terminal degree but were less effective in the classroom than I and didn't do any research were paid were staggering. For the next 3 years, I pursued my Ph.D. on a full-time basis while also teaching 44 to 48 credits per year (11 or 12 classes). I am certain that, during my entire tenure in my doctoral program, I did not hear teaching mentioned a single time. During this time, my teaching effectiveness suffered only slightly. My student evaluations were off just a small statistically insignificant amount. The real damage, however, was to my enthusiasm and energy. Teaching became a real chore. For 8 consecutive years, I had taught 44 to 48 credits per year. This involved 32 consecutive academic terms (all 12 months per year) without a break. As a teacher, I was effectively burned out. During this experience, I learned one of the most important lessons of being an effective teacher: It's important to take some time off. Even if it just involves teaching during the fall and spring semesters and not teaching during the summer, a break is critical to maintaining performance, enthusiasm, and energy. It also allows one to rethink and/or reframe what one is doing in the classroom and to do additional reading to a far greater extent than is possible while classes are in session.

## How I Teach

In selecting course topics and teaching strategies and in the delivery of material, one overriding theme frames the learning environment I attempt to create. This theme involves asking myself, What is the real-world significance of what I'm teaching? Before even venturing into the classroom or devising a lesson plan, I need to justify why the topic is being covered. This rationale not only makes material more relevant and holds students' interest but also makes it easier for me to plan for class. A sense of why the topic is so important makes the appropriate pedagogy much more obvious to a teacher. In determining whether a topic has real-world significance, it is important to determine whether what is being taught can be operationalized. Theory for theory's sake alone provides little value to students unless they see a link to practice. This vision can be a challenge with traditional undergraduates, who may have very limited practical work experience from which to draw.

An institution at which I formerly taught requires all undergraduate business students to take organization theory as a core curriculum requirement. Students traditionally have never been crazy about the course, nor have faculty members had much interest in teaching it. This apathy (at best) or contempt (at worst) can be traced to the highly theoretical nature of the course and the fact that students could see no direct relevance of course concepts. My approach to the course involved letting students see the real-world applicability of theoretical concepts by putting them in the real world itself. In small groups, students were required to go out in the field and analyze a large complex organization, using every course concept to understand the validity of the theoretical concepts by applying them to real organizational problems. Furthermore, in discussing course concepts in class, liberal references were made to the institution in which the students were enrolled and, hence, had firsthand experience with.

A major factor in my success as a teacher has been questioning the relevance and applicability of all course concepts. Class lectures/discussions always focus on specifics, rather than on abstractions. Doing this effectively can be difficult because it generally requires the professor to do endless reading of the popular business press and/or to develop an extremely significant network of practitioner contacts. Although this requirement can be difficult and time-consuming, it need not have to be. Many faculty members fail to realize or tap into one of the vastest sources of practical knowledge available—namely, the students seated in their classroom. This may be less true for classes consisting exclusively of traditional full-time undergraduates, but the majority of business school classes contain students with a good deal of practical work experience. Given the fact that institutions, particularly business schools, are enrolling more and more nontraditional and part-time students who work, tremendous opportunities exist for discussing applications of theoretical concepts. In many instances, I present a theoretical concept and then ask students to consider, within the context of their experience, whether the concept is relevant and can help them in understanding some organizational issues or process or whether the concept is just theory for theory's sake.

This process has allowed me to build a wealth of examples that I can present to subsequent classes when seeking their input. It also gets students much more actively involved in their own learning (rather than passively via more conventional pedagogies). To do this successfully, a teacher has to realize the critical fact that, in an optimal classroom environment, the flow of learning from teacher to student is only one flow. Learning flows from student to student and even (gasp!) from students to teacher. Faculty members who rely on a very hierarchical type of classroom environment and feel a need to remain somewhat aloof and distant from students will miss out on an important opportunity to enhance both their students' learning and their own learning. This is particularly true of the management disciplines. I fashion my role in the classroom more as a coach than a controller and more as a facilitator than a manager per se. Again, it is important for faculty members to realize that they can learn as much (if not more) from their students as their students can from them, given the richness of student experiences. It is important, however, to not totally relinquish to students the "real-world expertise" component of the learning process. Students enjoy hearing about the real-world work experiences of their teachers, both hands-on and through consulting. Mention of these experiences can model behavior for student participation and also can validate the real-world expertise and connections of the professors.

Whereas this approach is particularly well suited for students with practical work experience, traditional undergraduates often lack the experiences and frames of reference necessary to successfully employ such a pedagogy. Cases, simulations, and field research projects (e.g., the one described above) can assist in the learning process with these more traditional students. It is important to realize, however, the limitations of pedagogical tools such as cases and simulations. Although they may isolate some of the important learning concepts, they invariably fail to convey the personal emotional intensity of situations. This is of particular importance in courses in managing human behavior/human resources. Students have commented on and I have observed the fact that it can be difficult in a role play to muster the emotional intensity of situations because students aren't actually experiencing and feeling what the characters are. In performing small-group experiential survival exercises, students have often commented that the warm, well-lit, well-ventilated classroom hardly simulates the conditions of a plane crash in the Arctic or an unexpected landing on the moon.

True learning can only take place when a personalized experiential component is present. Organizations consist of people and groups of people, and the only way for students to really prepare themselves to be more effective organizational participants is to gain a more first-person perspective of themselves relative to interpersonal and organizational phenomena. Even undergraduate freshmen have life experiences on which they can draw meaningful data about themselves. All have some interaction with organizations, including part-time jobs in high school, extracurricular activities, sports teams, peer and social groups, their formal schooling organizations, and even their families. To truly learn about the management disciplines, students need to learn about themselves, and learning more about oneself is a lifelong process. Toward this end, I balance real-world work experiences with real-world life experiences in my teaching because the two are mutually dependent on and affect each other. Experiential exercises are the base of introspective writing assignments in which I help students see and understand themselves, organizational life, and the interface between the two more clearly.[1]

Achieving these outcomes involves some break with traditional types of classroom environments. This break does involve some risk for the teacher. The process involves *relinquishing control* of the class and classroom and much more *active management* of the class. An environment in which the teacher retains total control will not facilitate the nature of depth of participation described above. Relinquishing control, however, requires the teacher to be alert, focused, and concentrating for the duration of the class. A teacher cannot come in on "automatic pilot" to this type of class: She or he needs to be active in managing a process that can and often will unfold in ways that were not anticipated. The teacher needs to be able to respond to spontaneity and be spontaneous yet also remain cognizant of the learning objectives. To me, effectively balancing this tension between allowing spontaneity and controlling direction is what distinguishes success in the classroom.[2] Effective teaching involves leaving the classroom tired because of the mental and physical energy expended, not tired because of the repetitive and, hence, boring nature of a "canned" presentation. The former state is exhilarating; the latter is depressing.

Whereas the above discussion highlights the major philosophy I hold of teaching, I also employ a few additional techniques that, I believe, assist in my overall effectiveness. First, I integrate other disciplines into my teaching regularly and frequently. Management education has and continues to be criticized for its departmentalization and narrow focus within courses. Teaching about organizations provides the most fertile opportunity for cross-pollination. Budgetary restraints on human resource programs, typical conflict between departments responsible for responsiveness (marketing) versus those responsible for efficiency (manufacturing), behavioral issues in accounting, and operational constraints on product variety are a minute sample of such discipline integration. Students respond quite favorably when material from other disciplines is integrated within a newer topical area, rather than just repeated. (How many times is Maslow's hierarchy of needs repeated in the curriculum?)

Textbooks have been the traditional backbone of classroom education, but few teachers are ever genuinely excited about the texts they use, nor do they generally even really read them. Although I do use texts in some courses, I rely much more heavily on outside readings. I also sometimes use readings packets in lieu of a text; they generally consist of articles from the practitioner business literature, former students' papers (presented anonymously, of course), and my own writings, both those written for publication and those written specifically to illustrate course concepts. The only way to truly customize a course to meet teaching objectives is to seek out materials that assist with those objectives, rather than to use a generic textbook geared toward more generic objectives. This is not to say that texts, in general, are bad or unnecessary. I propose that my effectiveness in the classroom can, in part, be attributed to the fact that I don't feel locked into using a text or having it as the main reading. The objectives of a course determine the appropriate instructional material and pedagogy. More often than not, this involves students doing field-based research as well.

One personal trait has assisted me very much in my teaching. Despite the fact that I am detail-averse and have no tolerance for precision, I am impeccably well organized. In my teaching, *nothing* is random. There is always a logical progression from one topic to the next. As a student, my worst classroom experiences involved teachers who weren't organized, who had no real sense of what they were trying to get across, and basically who were unprepared for class. To reiterate the above theme, topics should all be connected in that they have direct relevance to management practice. Organization then merely involves providing the appropriate transition or link between topics. A very easy way to do this is to spend the first 5 minutes of class recapping the previous session and then bridging the "lesson learned" to the new topic.

One aspect of my teaching that students consistently comment on in their course evaluations is that I know all of my students' names by the fourth session at latest. This generally involves 100 students per academic term and is clearly a tremendous amount of work. From the first day, I never call on a student without using his or her name. If I haven't learned it yet, I ask the student to tell me, and then I repeat it aloud. Students seem to think that learning their names shows the teacher cares about them as individuals. I find it promotes a friendlier, more open, participative class.

## Teaching and Other Duties

Teaching involves many challenges, but clearly one of the greatest challenges to being an effective teacher involves balancing teaching with other duties. Depending on the institution, "teachers" are often called on to be productive, if not prolific, researchers, members of sometimes exclusive professional networks, outstanding "organizational citizens" who support their institution through committee work, and/or holders of a joint teaching/administrative position. The critical issue becomes balancing teaching with other time-consuming obligations without letting either suffer. Although many may argue that time pressures prohibit excellence in multiple areas, that need not be the case.

Faculty members need to confront two critical issues relative to these multiple responsibilities. The first issue involves making an honest assessment of strengths, weaknesses, personal and professional preferences, and career goals. Many academics have no interest in publishing, for example, whereas others avoid teaching as they would avoid root canals. Despite this, the person who has no interest in scholarly research still accepts a position at a research university, and the person who has no genuine love for teaching accepts a position at a teaching institution that offers virtually no release time or research support.[3]

Once a person has determined her or his personal and professional goals, the second issue, that of finding an appropriate institution, becomes much easier. Many different types of academic institutions have different missions and seek different types of individuals. A faculty member or prospective faculty member can greatly minimize any potential role conflict or personal conflict (and associated stress) by simply looking at an institution's mission and reward structure and finding the appropriate "fit" with personal and professional goals. All of us have seen examples, some of which might include ourselves, of inappropriate fit between a faculty member and an institution. There is no "standard" for an institution of higher education and, hence, no absolute standard for academic positions within these institutions. One way to minimize the potential conflict between teaching and other duties is to more judiciously select an institutional affiliation.

Despite the fact that different institutions have different requirements for faculty members, a good number of us end up at institutions that expect teaching excellence with simultaneous "achievement" in other areas. Although time spent in such other areas certainly takes time away from teaching, one can engage in research and service activities that *directly support* teaching. Teaching and research, for example, need not be mutually exclusive. Teaching materials constantly are in need of updating, and research can be conducted to support this. A synergy can be developed when teaching assignments are clearly within the areas of a teacher's intellectual interest. For example, my own research in employment law[4] constantly uncovers the latest court cases and decisions that I can and do bring into the classroom. The newness of these cases generally makes them unavailable to the class via any other means. A distinction does need to be made, however, between theoretical and practical/applied research. The critical point here is that teaching assignments can involve significant, publishable research opportunities simply in the carrying out of teaching responsibilities.[5]

Similarly, "service" and/or administrative assignments need not take away from teaching. It is critical to realize that the vast majority of service assignments directly support teaching. As an example, I served on a curriculum committee that allowed me to make significant input relative to overhauling a course I taught. Being able to "mold" the curriculum in this regard helped me pass through needed changes in courses I taught and so allowed me to teach more effectively. Similarly, when once faced with a large number of students who needed outside academic assistance because of poor secondary school preparation, I championed the formation of a committee to develop an academic assistance center that significantly reduced the amount of time I had to spend after class with remedial students. It also put these students in the hands of professionals who were better trained than I to assist them with their fundamental deficiencies. It is critical to remember that service assignments need not take away from teaching. Judicious selection of such assignments can be a vehicle by which teaching effectiveness can be dramatically enhanced.

In sum, there need be no inherent conflict between teaching and other academic responsibilities. Faculty members do have choices relative to the types of institutions they become affiliated with and the responsibilities of their positions. In addition to meshing personal and professional goals at the time of employment, it is critical to also keep an eye toward the future. I have seen colleagues accept positions in teaching institutions to avoid research and publication responsibilities and later find their employment opportunities limited when trying to relocate geographically with a spouse because of their restricted marketability. In time, most faculty members can and do find the optimal balance between teaching and other duties, a balance that keeps them motivated and effective as teachers, as well as current and marketable as scholars, practitioners, and consultants.

## Identity

When wearing the many hats that these different roles of teacher, researcher, committee member, consultant, and so on require, it is critical for the academic to maintain her or his sense of identity. Identity involves (a) a sense of self, both personal and professional, (b) the development of appropriate relationships vis-à-vis others (e.g., colleagues, mentors, supervisors), and (c) realizing the limits of one's "reach."

### Sense of Self

A sense of personal self, to me, means having an understanding of who one is as a "whole person" and how one's career meshes with other dimensions of one's life. For me, this involves autonomy and independence. Growing up as an only child with a very small extended family (including all first and second cousins; in a 20-year period, I was the only person born in the family!), I was forced to be independent and self-sufficient. As a child, I often played board games as multiple players simultaneously. I usually chose individual over team sports, playing tennis in high school and being a skier, cyclist, and competitive long-distance runner for the past 19 years. Although as an academic I do have a strong network of teaching and research associates, many of whom are close personal friends, the bottom line is that both teaching and research are still highly independent activities for me. Consider that, unless a person is team teaching, she or he walks into the classroom alone. Although many academics do coauthor research, there is still always a first, principal author. To date, I have neither coauthored nor copresented any research nor team-taught a class, although I would welcome any opportunities to do so. The autonomy and independence in my career reflect my own self-identity and personal background.

As an academic, the sense of purpose I receive from my work provides me with a great deal of pride. When I am afforded the opportunity to hear about how what we've discussed in class in a previous session has helped a student be more effective in her or his current job, I feel a tremendous sense of satisfaction. When students who have graduated contact me several years later and tell me they've applied some course material to their jobs or, more commonly, want assistance with or reference to material to help them solve a problem, I feel that I'm making an important contribution to society and upholding what

I consider to be my ongoing professional obligations to my students. I may not change the course of the world or go down in history for finding a cure for AIDS or bringing about world peace, but I do gain a tremendous sense of the importance of what I do by knowing that I help students in their careers and life pursuits and in making their organizations more effective.

## Relationships

Despite the fact that academic work is largely autonomous, a strong sense of one's identity relative to others in the academy is critical to one's success. To a large extent, academic work does involve a hierarchy or "pecking order." Politics can and often does run rampant in professional associations. Networking can be frenetic as junior faculty members attempt to make contact and then gain sponsorship or mentorship of those in power. This sense of identity involves making personal decisions relative to the extent that one will need to be a part of such networks and the extent to which one's identity will be molded by these conventional expectations.

When I decided to enter an interdisciplinary doctoral program outside a business school, several friends and colleagues who had done so in their own careers advised me against it. They warned that it was very difficult to break into the established circles of the academy without a highly regarded, well-connected mentor/sponsor to facilitate entry. I realized, however, that the types of teaching and research I wanted to do and the type of institution I wanted to work in were nontraditional; I thought it important to be true to both my interests and my self-sufficiency by blazing my own trails. I think my subsequent study and career direction have allowed me to break from established research agendas and pedagogies and to promote greater change within management education. My paradigm is very much my own. Although deciding not to let others dictate what I *should* be doing and not to follow the "business as usual" mandate has been and continues to be a very risky strategy, it has allowed me the opportunity to be more innovative and to pursue the mission of improving management education much more than would be possible otherwise.

The strong bias I have against producing theoretical research for academic discourse rather than practical application is probably evident. This has not blocked, but rather has emancipated, my progress as a teacher and scholar. I have chosen to pursue my career through an alternative track, one that is more personally significant and meaningful for me and for those involved in the cutting edge of management practice. An overabundance of scholars are performing heavily theoretical research. I prefer to critique management practice from a real-world perspective, rather than a scientific one.

Regardless of whether one pursues an academic career through conventional or nonconventional means, another area of identity relative to others needs to be addressed—that of power and control. Because of the increasingly large number of well-qualified academics, faculty members need to consider the means to acquire some power and control over their careers. The critical way to achieve this is through developing some distinctive competence and/or experience. A basic premise of economics is that the value of a commodity will increase if no replacement or substitute is available. Having an institution dependent on you for some area of expertise (e.g., teaching a specific curriculum area, unique technical skills) allows you to increase your authority and sphere of influence. Careful management of relationships with colleagues and superiors and appropriate self-marketing can assist you in developing and maintaining a sphere of expertise.

### Limitations of Reach

A final area to be addressed in establishing and maintaining an identity involves realizing the boundaries of one's ability to influence. To a large extent, many academics find very little limitation to their reach. Academic titles and status tend to bring respect and privilege and help open doors that might otherwise be closed. I have found that, in many instances, the fact that I hold a Ph.D. and am a university professor has invited others to seek and value my opinion in many areas that are clearly outside my areas of expertise. Students, particularly those with high authoritarian personalities, may respect and believe anything you say (and repeat it verbatim on an exam).[6]

Our profession is generally accorded a great deal of respect, but with this privilege comes the danger of abuse. It is important, as part of one's identity, to be fully cognizant of one's area of expertise and to use this influence wisely and fairly. I have seen faculty members fabricate answers to questions in order to maintain their sense of "respect" and "dignity." Such behavior can easily serve to undermine one's credibility.

Credibility is important in our profession. I build it on a foundation of trust and openness. If I don't have the answer to a question, I admit it and am not afraid to pose such questions to the class to try to reach some conclusion collaboratively. Part of being a credible teacher involves an awareness of the credibility that exists within the class. The single most important lesson teachers in the management disciplines need to learn and fully believe in is that they can learn from their students.

Relative to my identity, the vision I have for myself for the future is to improve my own teaching by staying involved in the cutting-edge areas of the discipline from a practical rather than theoretical perspective. I intend to improve my teaching by integrating my consulting with real organizations on real problems and publishing this research in operational terms for practitioners. It is critical for me to gain and maintain a synergy between other academic and professional responsibilities and teaching. Much as when I prepare courses and individual class sessions by asking myself, What is the real-world significance of what I'm teaching? I approach nonteaching responsibilities by questioning their significance for my teaching and for my students. As organizations and the environments in which they operate continue to change and evolve at an accelerating pace, the commitment I have to my "holy grail" of promoting new and better ways to teach in the management disciplines is strengthened.

## Reflection

### On Teaching

One of the most critical aspects of teaching in the management disciplines involves the fact that the "state of the art" is not static. Innovative management education is dynamic and responsive to changing business conditions and larger social environments. The proliferation of a variety of nontraditional institutions, degree programs, course offerings, and pedagogies is testament to this fact. Effective teaching needs to be anticipatory and foresightful, as well as designed to facilitate lifelong learning in students. Effective teaching requires faculty members to know themselves well relative to their own strengths, weaknesses, goals, and interpersonal styles and to find the career path in which they'll be most effective. Many roads can be taken in an academic career, and not everyone has the ability and commitment to excel as a teacher.

Effective teaching is exciting, rewarding, and also very draining. Maintaining effectiveness in the classroom requires a tremendous amount of time and energy, often expended without the direct support of administration. As a result, identified means of renewal are critical to continued teaching effectiveness. Inordinately heavy teaching/work loads clearly inhibit teaching effectiveness by limiting one's ability to keep fresh, relevant, and informed as a teacher. Even with heavy academic responsibilities, however, a faculty member can still seek out opportunities for renewal. Organizations such as the Organizational Behavior Teaching Society not only sponsor international, national, and regional conferences but also publish teaching-oriented journals. The networking opportunities provided by such professional, teaching-oriented groups can provide a significant sense of renewal, as well as a supportive network of like-minded colleagues. The aforementioned teaching groups within a department or school can also be of tremendous value in making teaching more timely, relevant, creative, and less onerous. Students who have jobs can also be a critical source of renewal through updated knowledge about what real organizations are actually doing in practice.

Effective teachers in the future will realize the importance of bringing the real world into the classroom and that they as teachers can learn a substantial amount from their students, particularly those students who are employed. They can use this expertise to remain current in the evolving needs of students and organizations and on the cutting edge of management practice. Much has been written about the boundaryless organization. Perhaps it is time to apply that paradigm to the classroom, as well and to fully integrate the real world into the classroom setting. In doing this, teachers need to see themselves more as facilitators of learning, than as directors of it. A critical outcome of effective teaching is self-motivated students.

The irony of teaching effectiveness is that most institutions want it but few reward it. As management education becomes less of maintaining the status quo and requires more innovation and creativity on the part of those delivering it, the challenge for institutions will be to change their reward systems. Currently, the rewards for effective teaching are largely intrinsic; few institutions really measure or acknowledge teaching effectiveness in any systematic way. Most of those who excel at teaching find the main rewards to be senses of personal satisfaction and pride. With management education now at a crossroad, creative, innovative, and effective teaching will be the lifeblood of an institution. Any institution that fails to value or reward teaching risks being left behind and becoming obsolete as we approach the 21st century.

## On Myself

In retrospect, it is relatively easy for me to see why an academic career made and continues to make sense for me despite the fact that I accidentally fell into it. The main reason probably concerns the fact that I view an academic career as *entrepreneurism without risks*. For someone like myself who is fiercely independent and fairly creative yet often has problems dealing with traditional hierarchical structures, entrepreneurism is advantageous. The autonomy of entrepreneurism, however, comes at a steep price because it requires tremendous personal risks, both financially and personally.

To me, an academic career provides maximum autonomy nearly analogous to entrepreneurism without the inherent risks of entrepreneurial endeavors. Although I have the "security" of working for someone else, hence requiring no large financial risk or outlay, I see myself as a sort of independent contractor. I "own" all that I create (e.g., published research, course design, pedagogy) and provide that to the university for a price. My "creations" are portable and can go with me from one institution to another. Unlike other highly trained autonomous professionals, such as physicians and attorneys, I don't have to worry about a geographically contained client base. I can take my "business" virtually anywhere in the world to a client base that the employing academic institution will provide me. Of all possible careers, an academic career probably offers the greatest combination of personal ownership of output coupled with portability of one's trade. I feel damned lucky to have fallen into this profession and realize that success as a teacher does have an incredible reward . . . though let's just not spread the word around too much.

# Notes

1. One example of this is having students write about a specific strategy for managing their boss after reading the classic article of the same title. A follow-up writing assignment has them report on and evaluate their strategy.

2. There is no "magic" way to achieve this balance. It is an acquired skill that one develops over time, much like acquiring skills for case teaching. I find two cognitive processes critical to achieving this balance: (a) listening actively and (b) keeping focused on learning objectives.

3. The reasons why people make these decisions are intriguing. Relative to the former decision, the status or allure of a well-known research institution may be a motivating factor from two perspectives. First, doctoral programs are concerned with their reputations. Program directors, dissertation chairs, advisors/mentors, and so on might push students toward higher-profile institutions regardless of potential fit to maintain or enhance the integrity of their program. Second, peer competition among graduate doctoral students might cause them to try to "outplace" each other, much like high school seniors applying to colleges. In addition, there seems to be more evidence of ease of movement from research to teaching institutions than vice versa.

The motivating factors behind the latter decision are less obvious but may be related more to geographic location, family obligations, and perceptions of marketability. Nonetheless, the high incidence of academics not staying with their first employer is often attributed to an inappropriate fit.

4. My primary areas of research involve employment law and social issues affecting organizations. Both are highly practical operational areas for organizations and not only allow me to publish on relevant, cutting-edge, evolving areas of management practice but also provide me the means to integrate into my teaching the latest breaking developments in these areas. As a result, my classroom presentations and discussions always remain one step ahead of the text and readings.

5. Respected and widely read publications such as the *Journal of Management Education* provide outlets for the dissemination of innovative approaches to teaching. Similarly, a class critique of popular management theory could be developed into a publishable paper in both pedagogical and theoretical journals.

6. One humorous anecdote illustrates this well. When I discuss personality traits while teaching organizational behavior, I describe to students the trait of dogmatism by telling them, "I know this is going to sound a bit strange, but I'll explain this after you write it down. The personality trait of *dogmatism* refers to one's love or affinity for canines, just as the term sounds." (The term actually refers to the rigidity of one's personal belief system.) I repeat this again while maintaining a straight face (with much difficulty) and proceed to watch an average of 75% to 80% of the class write this in their notebooks. I then use this as an example to illustrate the just-discussed trait of authoritarianism.

# 12 Teaching From the Heart

AFSANEH NAHAVANDI

Writing this chapter made me think, an event that has become all too rare in my current life as parent-spouse-administrator-teacher-researcher (listed in order of time importance). The thinking led me to realize that although teaching is often considered to be separate from the rest of those wonderful and important roles, what connects all the roles is the give-and-take of learning and teaching. In each of my current roles, I am learning from others and teaching them at the same time. So, teaching (as a two-way street) is, for me, central to being human. It is about being provided and providing others with the means to grow and learn. It is about evolution.

In addition to teaching and growing being at the core of much of my life, I get a great deal of satisfaction in having as much power as is traditionally ascribed to a professor and choosing not to use it and not to become entrapped by it. I also find much pleasure in being with others and in having the opportunity to affect their lives. Having been born in pre-Khomeini Iran, the value of education was tangible. People changed their lives through education. On the one hand, all that happened that was positive in the country happened because of education.

197

On the other hand, lack of education was the root of many of the problems. After the revolution, many of us walked away with our lives and only one asset: our education. Growing up in such an environment has made education a cornerstone of my activities. Learning, formally through institutions or informally through life experiences, was and continues to be key to growth and success.

## Integration of Teaching and Scholarship

I have always been confused about the debates over the integration of teaching and research. I just don't seem to get it! The debates continue to have little meaning for me, and the solutions confuse me. I have never seen the two as separate or mutually exclusive. Teaching is teaching others and learning. Research is learning and teaching others. When I teach, I communicate my own and other people's research philosophies, findings, and methods. When I am involved in research, I write, collect data, and communicate with my colleagues; I am therefore learning and teaching. Where is the separation? Teaching and learning are inseparable; so are teaching and research. Why do we need to integrate them?

As I keep trying to understand the debate, I suspect my confusion may stem from the fact that the research I do makes "integration" easy. I am interested in leadership and culture. Both topics are broad enough to be continuously integrated into OB courses. Perhaps I am unable to see the "integration problem," however, because both my teaching and my scholarship are continuous processes. I think about research ideas and examples when I read the morning paper or a magazine or a novel. I look for confirmation or disconfirmation of my hypotheses while storing away examples for my teaching. I am not a hyperactive (well, maybe), work-consumed (definitely not) person. It is just that all of my activities are part of a whole. Some very fluid boundaries exist among my different roles and activities, and occasionally they conflict. However, all that I do, of which teaching and research are only two parts, coexist in my mind. They all interact to form the whole that is me.

I suspect that being married to a business professor who works at the same institution helps with this sense of wholeness. Time spent at home is not clearly compartmentalized, but then neither is time at work. We often work on manuscripts together at home and are regularly interrupted by our children or the thought of our children. At work, my personal life always seeps in either in the form of a telephone call or in having to coordinate professional and personal activities. Teaching and research undergo much of the same processes. I engage in them simultaneously. What may appear to some to be a difficult and fragmented schedule feels for me like all of the activities are connected. A major reason for my involvement and love of my "job" is that I am not pushed to form separate compartments. I can talk about my family and my latest research project in my classes and relate them easily to some of the concepts I teach. I can relate my professional life to my children and my family and think about my own leadership skills and the skills I am helping develop in my daughters. I can practice what I preach, and I preach what I practice. Where is the separation?

Another reason for the sense of wholeness may be the topic of leadership and the way I approach it. I have always found the traditional debates and fragmented approach to leadership somewhat trite. The differences among the various theories and concepts, which I teach in great detail, look more like different angles of the same problem, rather than different problems. I have started talking about leadership in very broad ways. For example, rather than seeing leadership as a special process that is separate from managing others (à la Abraham Zaleznik, 1990), I talk about leadership as the process of helping others get things done—perhaps bringing about change in one's department, setting goals with one's subordinates, organizing a group of student government volunteers, or even getting one's children to wear season-appropriate clothing in the morning (one of my biggest leadership/parental daily challenges in the Arizona heat!). With this approach, leadership permeates all aspects of my life and my students' lives. Leadership is not something we study in others; it is something we develop in ourselves and in others continuously. While we are discussing the daily challenges of leading others, the theories become helpful and applicable. Teaching in this manner further reinforces the integration of research and teaching.

## Vision of My Contribution

I do not know whether my research has had an impact and has changed the world; however, I suspect that even though the impact was good enough to get me tenure and to win me some recognition among my colleagues, my research has not yet changed the world. I do know, however, that my interest and enthusiasm for what I do has affected others. I see my contribution in teaching and in having encouraged others to think, to question assumptions, and to consider the possibilities. The process of teaching and the interaction with my students in and out of class is just as important to me as the content of the courses. A majority of my MBA and undergraduate students play as many different roles in life as I do. They are students, parents, managers, spouses. The way I play my roles serves as a model for them. The language I use, how I deal with conflict, and how open-minded I appear all are absorbed and are part of the teaching and learning process. Therefore, the content of my teaching or research is just as relevant as the context in which it takes place.

I also see the cultural background that I bring to class as one of my major contributions. I am Iranian by birth. I spent my childhood in Iran while going to a French school, where I interacted with the children of diplomats from many countries. I came to the United States for my undergraduate and graduate studies. I have never fully felt a part of the Iranian, the French, or the U.S. culture. I am, by definition, what sociologists call a "marginal" person. This marginality, however, has allowed me insight into all three cultures and into many others. By being closely involved with, but not fully part of any culture, and growing up never seeing them as truly separate, I have learned to see them as a whole rather than as separate parts.

This integration of cultures and learning to live with their differences, while still remaining whole, is a recurring theme in my courses. I provide students with many personal examples. I challenge their views of culture differences and force them to rethink many of their assumptions about culture. For example, as soon as they think that a concept we covered (e.g., goal setting) is well defined, I introduce the issue of culture, sometimes in very simple ways: "If you were Iranian and expected your boss to know all the answers, how would you react if your boss sat down with you and asked you for your goals and negotiated them with you? How do we need to reconsider our theories and practices of goal setting when we cross-cultural borders?" Because of my background, such cultural discourse is an integral part of class and a very personal contribution to my students' learning.

## Being an Effective Teacher:
## What I Try to Achieve in My Classes

The key to being an effective teacher, for me, is not whether my students have learned a large set of materials or understood a particular theory. Although that is important, it is not the focus. Rather, the focus is on lighting up my students' eyes and on getting them confused so that they start questioning their own and other people's assumptions. The content of the courses is often just the vehicle to do those things. For example, I would like my students to understand Fiedler's contingency model and to know its limitations and how to use it. But more than that, I would like them to become aware of their own assumptions about leadership and their consequences. What do they expect leaders to do for them? What kind of leader can they be and why? How does their culture affect their ideals for leadership? How does their culture restrict them? Through the presentation of concepts and theories, these issues are discussed. The focus is always personal. I do not believe that we learn anything unless we can relate to it on a personal level. One of my mentors, Irv Altman, used to tell his graduate students that the choice of a research line is often related to something very personal. Although it may not always be obvious to ourselves or to others, according to him, our research questions often revolve around something that is at the core of who we are. My interpretation of his statement has been to try to personalize much of what I teach for my students. I try to establish a personal connection to self, family, community, and organization.

Teaching OB and leadership (the two courses I usually teach) is a unique opportunity not only to teach content but also to model the paradigms that are central to my approach. I teach content and I model philosophy. The sacred principles for me are relatively simple, and I consider them to be the core of good leadership and good management as well as good teaching (see Table 12.1).

### Being Prepared

I wish I could say that I have never gone to class feeling unprepared. Like most of us, I have. The sense of being unprepared is less common as I have more experience, and I can always use something from previous

**Table 12.1** Effective Teaching Behaviors and Impact on Students

| My Behaviors | Impact on and Message to Students |
| --- | --- |
| Being prepared | Responsibility and competence |
| Being courteous and respectful | Respect and tolerance of others |
| Being tolerant and valuing diversity | Tolerance of others and openness to ideas; ability to integrate diverging points of view |
| Showing enthusiasm | Love of learning; relevance and importance of material |
| Being flexible | Openness to change; desire to experiment |
| Making mistakes | Focus on learning rather than blame |

lectures or workshops to fit the topic of the day. So, even when I am not well prepared, I "pull it off." The best, most exciting, most challenging, most spontaneous learning experiences for me and for my students, however, have come when I was thoroughly prepared. The ideal situation for me is to know my lectures, cases, exercises, and articles inside out and to have them almost memorized so that I need no notes (I get there a few times every semester with a lot of effort). The magic of being prepared is that I can either leave all the preparations behind or draw from them at will. The thorough preparation gives me the confidence I need to be creative and improvise as needed to challenge my students and involve them in the topic.

My preparation also sends a very strong and clear message to my students. If I do it, they have to do it. I can only expect them to do what I do. Being prepared means that I am fulfilling a big part of my responsibility to my class; expecting them to do the same is, therefore, reasonable and appropriate. As they expect me to come to class prepared and energetic, I expect them to do the same. I am often much harder on myself than I am on them. Whereas I grade and return papers, exams, and other assignments within 5 to 10 days, I am very flexible with the deadlines for the students (more about this in a later section). The image of competence and of being in control of my time and schedule is one I try to establish early. I also have another side, however, that I share openly with my students: I let them know that I have had a terrible week and have not had all the time I needed or wanted to get everything together. Because we all follow the same academic calendar, my busy weeks often coincide with the students'. I use my very human inability to always be on top of all my work as a mechanism to allow students to be flexible. Although I strive to be always prepared, at times I am not; the same consideration is given to my students (more about this later).

## Being Courteous and Respectful

Few if any theories of management and leadership (at least not those we find in our best journals) deal with the need to be courteous and respectful. Too many managers achieve financial success for their corporations without even a shred of those characteristics! As courtesy and respect are key to my view of management and to my personal philosophy, however, they are expected in the classroom. As is the case with preparation, I consider modeling the behavior key to conveying it to the students. In all the good-natured humor and teasing in the classroom and in listening to sometimes endless comments from students, there is never an intentional put-down or lack of respect. Opinions are expressed, and disagreements are strongly encouraged. Courtesy toward others and respect for their points of view are required. Violations of that rule are handled with much humor and courtesy. If students interrupt one another inappropriately or are less than civil, I remind them about our rules and find some humor in the situation. If a student uses off-color language with which I am not comfortable and that does not belong in a professional environment, I either ignore both it and the student and deal with the issue outside class, or if I know the student well, I may joke about the comment and, without embarrassing the student, send the message that this should not happen again.

Aside from being a desired outcome for my classes, courtesy and respect are also key processes that allow for the exchange of information. Without the knowledge that I can express a thought without facing hostility and disrespect, I cannot challenge my students. Without the same knowledge, the students cannot explore the boundaries of their assumptions and thinking and therefore cannot learn and grow. The cost of this strategy is the great deal of time spent in class on discussion and having to sometimes listen to points of view that are outrageous! Within an atmosphere of civility, however, the latter are probed, analyzed, and shaped.

## Being Tolerant and Valuing Diversity

Along with courtesy and respect comes an implicit and often explicit requirement to be tolerant of others' points of views. Our students have to learn to value diversity (maybe a cliché, but true). Watching the training videos, reading the seminal articles and books, performing the various exercises, and discussing the insightful cases are all useless if students do not see diversity valued and encouraged in the classroom. For those of us who do not have culturally or ethnically diverse classrooms, the message can still be conveyed by valuing intellectual diversity. The modeling of those values through the treatment of students is key to internalization of the message.

Once again, being from outside the mainstream U.S. culture allows me to talk about many of my personal experiences. I often good-naturedly confront my students with the stereotypes they have of Iranians and provide them with an opportunity to "safely" discuss diversity. I also share with them many of my cultural stereotypes of my home country's neighbors. Other opportunities for nonthreatening discussion of diversity and tolerance arise in discussions of the students' functional areas or majors. The points of view of finance, accounting, and engineering majors are widely different from those of management, psychology, or philosophy majors. My task in class is to reconcile those differences, pointing to the insufficiencies in each while affirming their validity. Demonstrating how highly diverse points of view can coexist and be integrated supplements the academic message students receive about the value of diversity.

## Showing Enthusiasm

I like what I do. I enjoy the process of teaching, and for the most part, I enjoy the content I teach. Although there are more than a few topics I would rather not cover, I manage to find an interesting twist in almost anything. The process of learning about a new area is always interesting to me and keeps up my enthusiasm. I have a lot of fun in class. The enthusiasm is often contagious. The 7:30 a.m. students may have a difficult time moving around the classroom to perform the role plays, but my bouncing around the class forces them to wake up and get moving. Additionally, why should students get interested and excited about learning something if I convey my boredom with the topic? Most of us like teaching electives because we are interested in the topic. Students also enjoy those classes partly because of the instructor's enthusiasm and interest. Although I also enjoy teaching electives, much of that same excitement and energy goes into teaching my required courses.

I look with anticipation to almost every class session. Whether I am going to try a new exercise and cannot wait to see the students' reactions, or I have simply improved a previously presented lecture and hope to get better student reaction, the events in the classroom are exciting. The interaction with the students is often stimulating (unless I am returning exams!), and I look forward to learning something new from them. Faced with my excitement about the class and the material, students find it very difficult not to respond accordingly.

### Being Flexible

My college is in the never-ending process of setting its mission and goals, and most of the discussions we have in our faculty meetings, in one way or another, come back to the issue of teaching our students to be flexible. So many of us seem to think flexibility is key to success in the uncertain and sometimes chaotic world our students face. Many of us complain about how rigid and rule-bound our students are. We report instances of temper tantrums if the syllabus is changed or if the format of exams is altered, or of serious anxiety attacks if one part of an assignment is altered. How many of us are flexible with our format, deadlines, and content? Many colleagues believe that allowing flexibility in deadlines or personalizing assignments based on student needs, for example, breeds irresponsibility and leads to inequity. They therefore stand their ground against any student requests for change. Partly because I think such unyielding protection of standardization and uniformity models inflexibility, and partly because I was the type of student who invariably wanted to do something different from what was required in the assignments, I err to the other side. I allow tremendous flexibility in many aspects of my courses.

To provide some common ground and to address some students' need for structure, however, my syllabus has all the makings of a legal contract. It describes all the goals I want to achieve. The assignments are clearly stated. Deadlines are printed in bold letters. Several appendices describe the format and content of each assignment. The criteria for evaluation of papers and presentation are stated and explained. The "contract" provides a base of operations for all of us. It provides the framework. Some students abide by it as if it were a religious document, and I respect and reward them for that; it is, after all, a contract. This contract sets the ground rules that then allow us to move freely. I spend some time at the beginning of every semester discussing the syllabus. I explain its contractual nature; it's my commitment to my students. I then inform them that I am totally open to any change. If they want to stick with the contract, so will I. If they want to digress from it, I am game.

As a result, I routinely change many elements of the syllabus on the basis of student requests and class discussions. Deadlines become flexible, and exam formats are negotiable at any point during the semester. I entertain any rational and equitable proposal for changes in the course content and the number, type, and content of cases, exercises, and lectures. They are all open for rational debate and discussion. I am flexible in everything but the topic of my course. I will teach OB if that is the course, and key issues will be covered in one way or another, sooner or later, but the flexibility to "go with the flow" is key to the success of the course and, I believe, a crucial step in teaching students to also be flexible.

For example, I use the standard mix of essay and multiple-choice individual exams to test my undergraduates. In the fall of 1993, someone in my undergraduate OB class asked why we do not do group exams. The idea was particularly interesting to me because I had just been to several workshops on cooperative learning. What happened in the next few classes was pure improvisation. We spent close to three class sessions discussing the possible format and process of group exams. We had lengthy discussions about protecting high individual performers from freeloaders. We discussed the responsibility of team members, allocation of rewards in groups, the limits of the teams' power for getting all members to contribute equally, the time constraints students faced that made meeting difficult, along with issues of communication and leadership. While we were debating all of these issues, one by one, I put aside my notes on different aspects of teams and group dynamics. Most of the issues were being covered in discussion. If we started straying, I would nudge them back on course by asking questions and throwing a challenge. There was tremendous interest and involvement. Different groups of students were presenting various proposals and defending them. Several presented research data to support their position. After we reached a consensus on the format for group exams, all I had to do was summarize the issues we had discussed and point to the correspondence with the text and reading material. The applicability of what could have been dry material was immediately obvious. The new format led to a lot of work for me and doubled the students' work because they ended up taking both an individual and a group exam (based on their choice). It also led to a much higher grade distribution in that class (grade inflation or learning?). The experiment, however, modeled the benefits of flexibility while providing a spontaneous learning experience.

## Making Mistakes

Although I don't think I fit the image of the stereotypical "absentminded professor," I make a lot of mistakes. I have tried, but I have not yet had a syllabus that does not have at least one mistake in it (like scheduling a class on Thanksgiving Day!). I seldom manage to number my exam questions correctly. I tell my students to check my addition skills for correcting exams and inform them that I am prone to making errors and very willing to correct them. These sometimes not-so-small errors provide an opportunity to poke fun at the "Prof," which even my working adult part-time MBA students enjoy tremendously. They bring a sense of perspective to the class and demonstrate not only that it is all right to make errors but also that there is always a chance to recover. If I want to encourage students to learn from their mistakes, I have to provide the same opportunity for them in the classroom. Within limits, students have to be given a chance to correct their mistakes. Part of learning to be flexible is learning that we are not infallible. Students also need to move beyond blaming themselves or me and to focus on correcting and learning from their mistakes. I offer to read one draft of each paper, and students can rewrite their papers once if they are not satisfied with their grades. I occasionally return a paper without a grade when it is unsatisfactory and work with the student on a rewrite. The opportunity to try to succeed is not based solely on a mastery learning concept; it is also based on the chance to correct mistakes and to learn from them.

The elements that I believe make me an effective teacher are all rooted in providing a supportive and nonthreatening yet challenging environment. If students have to face a competitive and fierce world outside the classroom, they can at least feel safe and focus on development and growth inside the class.

## What Got Me Started and What Keeps Me Going

I learned how to teach and how to learn from good and bad teachers. One of my favorite Iranian proverbs suggests that one learns to be polite from rude people. For me, this has meant that a learning opportunity is found in everything. Positive role models are great, but I have learned just as much from observing teachers who were incapable of communicating with their students. I have, however, learned a lot from a few excellent teachers. Marty Chemers, my Ph.D. advisor, for example, taught me the value of a supportive and nurturing environment and the need for thorough preparation. I learned that his wonderfully witty and relaxed style was the result of hours of preparation. From my husband and colleague, Ali Malekzadeh (who also happens to be a great teacher), I continue to learn how to give students clear and specific messages. From some other colleagues, I have learned to stand my ground when needed and to curb my tendency to be too flexible, a lesson I have trouble remembering. I need so little structure that I forget that other people may need more than I. I have seen wide-eyed, horrified students staring at me from the back of the class as I was discussing whether we should have exams in the course. Many of my students have difficulty with such flexibility. Some will also take advantage of it and stray from the learning goals. My more structured colleagues, through discussion and advice, help me stay convinced that one student's proposal to not take the final exam or another student's regular absence may not be legitimate.

What I am always looking for is the impact the teaching/research has on me. I am always trying to assess whether I can duplicate or avoid such impact through my own behavior. Another source of learning has been the teaching conferences and journals. They often provide me with techniques, but I am not a "joiner," and I have very limited time to seek out such opportunities. I also spend a great deal of time personalizing the exercises. They have to fit with my style and the format of my courses. I therefore learn from all that is around me. To be good at what I do, I have to find enjoyment in the task and the process. If teaching were just a part of my job, that is just what it would be. I could improve my technique, be better organized, correct my mistakes, and build on my strengths. What makes my teaching effective beyond all these is the joy and excitement that is communicated to students.

## Power and Control

I am not in the police business. I have no interest in controlling my students. Because I am not teaching young children or adolescents, I assume, maybe incorrectly, that I am dealing with adults. They—or their parents—are paying the tuition to be in my classes. They have therefore made a choice to be there. If they choose to be absent, to cheat, and not to learn, it is their problem, not mine! Learning is the students' choice and responsibility. My choice and responsibility are to be prepared and to teach. I do not believe that I can make 20-some-year-old students (or often much older, in the case of both my undergraduate and MBA students) learn by controlling them. The students have to make a choice and a commitment to be active participants in the learning experience. If they do not make that choice, it is their loss!

I give exams and use all the traditional means of testing, but with more experience, I am moving more toward cooperative and mastery learning. Exams are more and more taken as groups. I encourage my students to talk with each other (cheat?), to teach each other, and to learn from each other. In the very rare instances where I have encountered "cheating" (plagiarism has most often been the case), I have used the university and college policies appropriately. In addition to focusing on students' personal choices and responsibilities, however, the types of activities and testing that are taking shape in my classes render cheating meaningless. For example, as I emphasize teamwork and co-operation, it appears incongruous to me to, on the one hand, encourage such activities in some setting and preach the value of teamwork in achieving better results, and then, on the other hand, tell my students not to cooperate on assignments. This incongruence sends conflicting messages to students and does not help in the internalization of the concepts that are taught.

Education is a commitment to learn, not an enforcement of rules. I am often aware that students have not completed all the assigned readings. I do not do their work for them or make them feel guilty about it; I simply continue to assume that they have done their assignments and let them take responsibility for their choices and actions. Poor work is not accepted, and poor quality has clear consequences. I also give a chance to correct it. If a student wants to rework something, I let him or her do so within the limits of my time and resources. If a student chooses poor work, he or she has to accept the consequences of that choice. The role of the professor has traditionally been one of power and control—as has the role of parent and boss. As I present new and sometimes radically different views of the latter roles, my view of the role of teacher has to change as well.

A book by Peter Block (1993) has helped me crystalize my thoughts. The case for separation of the role of boss from that of parent is one issue that Block presents well. I feel very strongly about such separation, as I do not see my role as a teacher to be a parent for my students. My role is to provide direction and to clarify the rules of engagement that would allow the class to function (e.g., respect for others, dealing with disruptions). I also provide the overall learning objectives often dictated by curricular needs with which students agree by virtue of enrolling in the class. What students want to obtain from the class is entirely their choice. If they stay, they implicitly agree to the general framework and to the rules of the class. That is given; I do not control it or enforce it. Other students in the class often do. They depend on their team members to be ready. They ask the talkative person in the last row to be quiet. I deal only with extreme and outrageous behaviors, of which I have faced very few. We are there to learn. I choose to do my part and more; whether they do theirs is their choice.

## Renewal

Sources of renewal have been difficult to find. I burn out very easily. I put a lot of energy into every class session and need to replenish somewhere. My simplest short-term strategy has been to avoid teaching for part of the year (usually during summers) at all costs. I simply need the rest. Another aspect of renewal is my need to learn or relearn how to teach. Beyond what I learn in class from my students, I need to grow and evolve. I know what I need to do. I need to hook up with my colleagues, visit them, attend meetings, and read about teaching and learning. The reality of my life—with two children, a spouse, a part-time administrative position as director of the MBA program, in addition to a three-course teaching load, an active research agenda, and heavy service responsibilities in a developing institution—is that I simply cannot find the time to undertake activities to renew myself!

In the meantime, I have found some things that have helped me:

1. I take one semester off from teaching each year.
2. I vary my preparations. I do not teach the same class more than two semesters in a row.
3. I change the textbooks I use at least every 2 years.
4. I change at least 10% to 20% of my course materials every time I teach.

These relatively short-term, simple activities allow me to keep the content and the process of teaching fresh. Taking summers off allows for rest and refocus. The summers are spent on writing—the only time when I do create compartments and my life becomes the whole without one of its elements. Teaching is left out entirely; I box it off so that I can have the pleasure of rediscovering it in the fall with enthusiasm and energy.

## Conclusion

Writing this chapter has been one of the most pleasurable yet difficult parts of the past few months. It has involved much introspection and a search for reasons for the causes of my behaviors and approach to teaching. I always thought that most of what I do and how I do is guided by some basic principles, but beyond some general ideas, I never thought much about what those principles were. My behaviors and approach seem to work with my students. They like the course and like me, and on occasion, they even say they learned something that helped them with their lives and careers. Beyond facilitating my students' growth, my teaching is part of my personal fulfillment as well; I enjoy it thoroughly. My teaching comes from the heart and warms my heart.

I consider myself lucky and privileged to be trusted with part of the education of the people who have the opportunity to shape the future. Almost every day, I leave my classes feeling energized. On my way back to my office, I remind myself that what just happened in the classroom is one of the primary reasons I chose this profession.

## References

Block, P. (1993). *Stewardship: Choosing service over self-interest.* San Francisco: Berret-Koehler.

Zaleznik, A. (1990). The leadership gap. *Academy of Management Executive, 4*(1), 7-22.

# 13 Between Text and Context

## RESTORING CONNECTIONS
## IN THE OB CLASSROOM

PUSHKALA PRASAD

In the summer of 1987, a close friend in graduate school and I began jointly preparing to teach our first classes in undergraduate organizational behavior (OB) at the University of Massachusetts. When I look back on those months of early preparation, my overwhelming memory is one of intense frustration and sharp disappointment—with the standardization and uniformity of the OB textbooks, with the rigidity of the traditional curriculum, and with the seeming lack of relevance of the subject matter to the "real" world of work and organizations. Added to this was the collective wisdom of the teaching assistants, who informed us that most students despised OB as being "fuzzy wuzzy" and a bit of a "blow-off" course.

This sense of immense frustration also sharply contrasted with my early encounter with another sphere of academic life: scholarship. At that time, I was part of a close and committed group of graduate students at UMass-Amherst who were exploring many exciting avenues in research and scholarship. I remember the sense of constant intellectual excitement and exhilaration that pervaded our seminars, our office discussions, and our lunchtime conversations. For me, one of the most powerful intellectual currents informing our visions of organizations at that time was *critical theory*. Critical theory seemed to offer enormous possibilities for management education to be more relevant. I was particularly attracted to the philosophy of Habermas, Gramsci, and Marcuse, as well as the organizational applications of their thinking proposed by Benson (1977), Frost (1980), Steffy and Grimes (1986), and others. Above all, I was attracted by critical theory's explicit commitment to emancipation and its relentless questioning of our taken-for-granted assumptions about life, work, and the human condition.

I also wanted quite desperately to transfer some of this intellectual excitement I was experiencing in graduate school to my undergraduate OB classroom. When I searched more closely to pinpoint the source of my frustration with OB teaching practices, it seemed mainly to stem from the *disembodied* nature of the OB curriculum and classroom. It seemed to me that much of management education was highly fragmented. Courses were taught with little attention paid to their interconnections. Even the most interesting courses remained relatively disjointed experiences for both students and professors, having no contextual embeddedness or connection. As a result, students frequently "shopped" for the "easy" and most entertaining courses regardless of the value or relevance of these courses to them.

For me, it became important to restore some sense of *connection* between research and teaching, between myself and my students, between the classroom and the world of work, and between student life experiences and organizational learning. From that point onward, my experience of teaching OB has been an endless and both rewarding and frustrating attempt to restore some of these connections. In this chapter, I share a few of these personal experiments and experiences.

## Connecting OB to Managerial Practice:
## Historicizing the Curriculum

To many of us in academe, our research endeavors not only absorb much of our attention but also define our identities and sense of selves.

That this crucial element of our lives is kept separate from our classroom experiences is as wasteful as it is unfortunate. For me, the most significant and yet difficult part of the teaching experience has been the integration of these two vital areas of my life.

How can one do this? The source of much of my intellectual excitement came from critical theory's questioning of given texts and assumed knowledge. Yet, for the most part, dissemination of OB is conducted without much questioning of its nature and objectives. Why do we engage in the practice of OB? When did OB become an important element of the business school curriculum? What/whose interests does OB serve (in research, teaching, and consultancy)? These not only are vital questions for us as teachers to explore but also are questions that help students connect the OB classroom to industrial work, life experiences, and the agendas of business schools.

Above all, my exposure to critical theory underscored the need to *historicize* the development and practice of OB with my students. Therefore, in my very first class session, I began to engage my students in a historical exploration of the rise of OB in U.S. industry. Typically, I ask my students to reflect on the nature of work in preindustrial societies and to list commonly held occupations in the 18th and early 19th centuries. My students usually arrive at a list that includes blacksmiths, carpenters, tailors, glassblowers, shoemakers, and so on. We then jointly explore the central features of these occupations, which include control over individual work, time and production, physical proximity to family life, the apprentice system, and the supply of goods to local markets. Overall, I help students recognize the dominance of the *craft* system in preindustrial work and appreciate its consequences for the way work was organized and structured for the individual.

Next, I facilitate a discussion on the rise of industrialization that was also accompanied by the deterioration of craftwork and the institutionalization of scientific management. In doing so, I have always relied on a number of historical readings, including the work of Daniel Nelson (1975), Rick Edwards (1979), Judith Merkle (1980), and Frank Fischer (1984). Students very quickly appreciate (a) the dramatic way in which industrialization reduced the autonomy of the crafters and (b) the resistance that followed in the form of output restriction, sabotage, absenteeism, and worker militancy. The time was ripe for the findings of the Hawthorne Studies, with their emphasis on social needs, personal growth, group norms, and informal organization. As I also point out to my students, the genesis of OB can be located in this effort to help forepersons smooth over the transition from craft to industrial work. Later on, OB also came to be used in managerial and administrative situations.

This critical historicization is important for a number of reasons. At a very functional level, students understand the early significance of OB and its continued use in management education. At a more critical level, they also begin to appreciate it as one of the many managerial responses to a crisis of control in the shop floor. OB is no longer seen as a set of simplistic and commonsense propositions about human behavior, but more as a set of strategies to reassert managerial control over the workplace.

## Connecting the Text to the Context: Critiquing OB as "Received" Knowledge

Given my theoretical bent, it also became crucial to work with students in understanding the OB "text." In my experience, most students are not greatly excited by the standard OB texts. Students (with a few exceptions) tend to find the texts ponderous, obvious, and needlessly expensive. One option that I seriously considered was not to use any text at all but to only use different readings. After much discussion with many colleagues, however, I decided not to do this. It seemed to many of us that the OB text was, in many ways, a *representative sample of contemporary managerial discourse.* It was therefore important that students encounter the text, but not in an unquestioning fashion.

Above all, I wanted students to experience the empowerment that comes from questioning "expert" textual knowledge while recognizing the significance of that text within its institutional context. I also found that instilling an ongoing critique of textual wisdom in the classroom is not an easy task. Typically, management students are not used to the employment of such critique and are sometimes made uncomfortable by it. Working closely, my close friend and colleague Mike Cavanaugh and I developed an accessible framework (Cavanaugh & Prasad, 1990) that facilitated textual critique while remaining a reasonably relevant process to most of our students. We adapted a simple and familiar framework—the Johari window (Luft, 1963)—as an analytic tool to facilitate a critique of received knowledge.

| THE OPEN TEXT<br><br>Conventional wisdom and<br>espoused theories | THE BLIND TEXT<br><br>Interdisciplinary perspective and<br>visions of management theories |
|---|---|
| THE HIDDEN TEXT<br><br>Unacknowledged beliefs<br>and values in the text | THE DARK TEXT<br><br>The unknown |

Figure 13.1 The Johari Window as an Analytic Tool for Understanding the Text

The Johari window is an intuitively appealing framework that enhances self-understanding through self-knowledge and awareness of others' perceptions of the self. The model broadly details the existence of an "open" self (that aspect of ourselves that is freely expressed and shared); a "hidden" self (that aspect of ourselves that we either consciously or unconsciously choose to conceal from others); a "blind" or unseen self (that aspect of ourselves that we are blind to but is seen by others); and a "dark" self (those aspects of ourselves that are equally unknown to ourselves as well as to others). The model also assumes that both the blind and hidden areas can actually be reduced through self-disclosure and feedback, thereby resulting in a more informed and open experience of the self.

Early in the semester, we would introduce the Johari window to the students by using any one of a number of interpersonal exercises. The central learning provided by the window lies in the notion that the open and expressed part of any phenomenon is only one aspect of it. We stressed the idea that, like people, texts, organizations, and so on also have open, hidden, blind, and dark sides to them. As managers, employees, and executives, we need to become adept at reading the various *subtexts* that underlie everyday life. As a beginning, we used the four quadrants of the Johari window as a metaphor to understand the OB text itself. Figure 13.1 illustrates our analytic extension of the window.

In session after session, we returned to this framework, trying to understand the OB text's interpretation of such topics as leadership, motivation, and group processes from these four diverse angles. Needless to say, although students were initially cautious in employing this framework, they very quickly became quite comfortable with it and soon surprised us with the insights they generated. Thus, quite apart from taking motivation and leadership theories at their face value (open text), students unearthed both the hidden and blind sides to these theories. To illustrate, they saw motivation theories as being systematically *blind* to different work contexts and, therefore, largely unaware of the monotonous rigidity of the assembly line, the demeaning nature of certain forms of manual labor, and the increasing fragmentation of clerical and administrative work. Our students also suggested that motivation theories are blind to instances of excessive motivation such as workaholism and therefore fail to derive insights from it regarding the significance of work to people.

Similarly, students have suggested that leadership theories are largely blind to realities of power and political influence and are usually situated within managerial contexts too narrow to be really relevant. Much of such discussion then spurs students to locate readings, such as Robert Jackall's (1988) work on managers and Barbara Garson's (1972) work on a variety of routine work situations, that can offer greater insights into organizations.

Why are we so committed to engaging in a systematic critique of the text? First, such a critique helps students appreciate sources of knowledge outside those encountered in standard texts, manuals, and documents. Second, such a critique actually makes the OB text seem more interesting because it is transformed into a social and cultural artifact rooted in its own values and ideologies and blind to insights from other cultural texts. The text itself becomes like a layered puzzle that students can intellectually engage, rather than treat as a passive document. And third, the art of critique is actually very exciting, provided it does not remain solely destructive, but can then be used to construct new visions of organizations and management. The next exercise discusses how such a critique is possible.

## Connecting Life Values to Career:
## The Obituary Exercise

Another way of making critique more relevant is to restore connections between student lifestyle preferences and values and career planning. As I continued to teach undergraduate OB, I found that one of the most anticipated classes was the one on career planning. Students looked forward to this session because they hoped it would help them in making important career decisions and in strategizing for the future.

Over the years, however, I also found that despite the variety of career models employed in the texts and the range of exercises I used, my classes in career planning frequently failed to live up to my own and my students' expectations. For the most part, I experienced difficulty in injecting a *meaningful* quality into the discussion and planning of careers. I speculated that one reason for this was the dry and detached discussion of careers in the texts that was lacking in relevance to juniors and seniors with scant organizational work experience. I tried using some popular career exercises, including a variety of skill inventories, lifeline exercises, and career goal-setting exercises, with little success.

Although all of the above activities have their merits, in my experience, students were relatively uncertain about specific career choices and were mainly looking for ways to clarify for themselves how they would like to spend the rest of their lives. In other words, the exercises often assume that students already know what kind of career they want to pursue and only need help in planning ways to succeed. In reality, my students seemed to want to use the classroom to *explore* their own and others' visions of careers and to discuss the relevance of personal relationships and value systems to careers.

Additionally, I found that I was not entirely alone in feeling frustrated with the treatment of careers in the OB textbooks. In a powerful and evocative article, Harris and Brown (1990) critique the discussion of careers in OB texts as being overly simplistic and optimistic and for failing to take into consideration ordinary and everyday personal concerns in the planning of careers. I began to think that a way was needed to connect students' own personal values and lifestyle preferences to their conception and planning of careers. Primarily, I saw the need for students to reflect on the kind of lives they wanted to lead, to be exposed to a range of career possibilities, and to explore some common contemporary career dilemmas. I also thought that some reflection and discussion of how the notion of careers is shaped in our cultures was important.

The implementation of these goals, however, was far harder to accomplish. I then had an aha! experience when I encountered an exercise, devised by Sid Simon (1982), that had students write up their own epitaphs as a way of value clarification. It occurred to me that I could do the same by having students write their own obituaries and further link these values to career choices. I spent weeks debating whether this exercise would be feasible in a class of aspiring young management majors, and it was not without trepidation that I introduced the exercise. Before doing the actual exercise, I had students read the chapter on careers in the text, as well as Harris and Brown's (1990) article. In the course of a preliminary classroom discussion, we also covered diverse issues, including career stages, Holland's model of career orientations, and the impact of personal values and relationships on career decisions.

I then handed out index cards and asked each student to note down his or her first choice of career in one corner. I then asked each student to invent his or her own *fantasy obituary* and to write it down on the card. I typically would emphasize that the students were completely free to decide what went into their obituaries. The main point was that each student's obituary needed to approximate as closely as possible one that the student would want written about him or her. It therefore needed to reflect his or her aspirations, achievements, and desired lifestyle. I usually also shared my own fantasy obituary with the class. The most interesting step that followed was analyzing our obituaries in terms of unearthing the values and self-images embedded in them. With the help of certain guidelines, students extracted the subtext of values and lifestyle preferences contained in each other's obituary. They were then able to ascertain whether their initial career choices were compatible with these values and preferences. They were also encouraged to locate other career options that were more in keeping with their preferences.

Quite unexpectedly, I also found that the exercise raised some common dilemmas regarding the accommodation of family life and personal interests with the demands of career. Even more interesting, students often raised this as a gender issue; that is, both men and women in the class often suggested that female students have unrealistic expectations of having successful careers and fulfilling family lives. Inevitably, this idea usually turned into a lively discussion around some common career dilemmas, with students exploring ways of dealing with them. I found this one of those rare moments when students made sustained efforts to make connections between life and work and between the text and context. Students themselves, when confronted with a common career dilemma, were led into discussions about "mommy tracks," hard choices, limitations of flextime, and the design of work around family issues. To me, it is most powerful that, through an analysis of obituaries, students can begin to reflect on and discuss one of the most central organizational issues today: the clash between work and family pressures. Because most of my students have rarely paid much attention to these issues, the act of analyzing their obituaries compels them to envision the *process* of living a life at work and at home and gets them to connect the notion of career to their everyday and personal lives.

When I first used this exercise, I would stop at the individual level of analysis. But I soon found that students were very curious about each other's obituary and wanted to have a sense of their classmates' values and career orientations as well. With the students' permission, I began to copy the obituaries produced in class and to circulate them as a handout. The obituaries stimulated considerable discussion and debate, which I thought could be structured into a more macro-level discussion of careers. To do so, I asked the students (in groups) to examine the obituaries for common themes and non-themes (what is missing from the obituaries).

In all my classes, some themes surfaced again and again:

- Narrow conceptions of careers. Each semester, students have commented on the narrow range of careers found in the obituaries. Careers are invariably seen as taking place solely within large corporations (Fortune 500 and multinational companies figure regularly) and are usually confined to senior executive and top managerial positions. When confronted with such a uniformity of vision in the obituaries, students are actually struck by the lack of variety and the lack of interest in such areas as public administration and individual entrepreneurship.
- Images of materialism. One striking shared value found in the obituaries is that of materialism. When confronted with a whole set of student obituaries, my classes have often been taken aback by the emphasis on the possession of money, real estate, and luxury items such as yachts, antique cars, and clothes. Interestingly, students often mention how they have never thought of themselves as being particularly materialistic. This has often provoked an interesting discussion on the impact of such a dominant value system on the way our organizational reward systems are structured.
- Images of "climbing." Side by side, students have also commented on the focus on "climbing" the organization. The obituaries often reflect a strong preoccupation with reaching the top and almost seem to equate career with climbing. Success becomes mostly defined in terms of ascent within the corporate hierarchy.
- Values of hard work and perseverance. Another common value often discussed by students is that of hard work and perseverance. Most obituaries either

explicitly or implicitly suggest that the success of the writer stems directly from hard work and perseverance in the face of adversity. This view also ties into Harris and Brown's (1990) discussion on the persistence of the Horatio Alger myth in North American society and its influence on how we envision our own and others' career paths.

Students often found it much harder to pinpoint non-themes in the obituaries. Mostly, they tended to arrive at this list on the basis of the content of the obituaries that were somewhat different from the rest. I particularly remember one young man whose obituary described his achievements in building and establishing a basketball team for students with disabilities, and one young woman whose ambitions centered around developing consciousness around environmental concerns and issues of global poverty. Students have commented that the obituaries mostly lack an emphasis on self-actualization. One remark that has stayed with me was that, for the most part, the obituaries stopped at the esteem level of Maslow's hierarchy. Another non-theme mentioned frequently is the failure to leave any kind of legacy for one's community or humanity. And finally, students have often been struck by the preoccupation with career to the near exclusion of everything else. This failure to think and plan for a more balanced life can also alert students to how they should be thinking of living and planning their careers within their notions of the "good life" and restore some sense of context to the whole exercise.

Above all, I have tried to get students to understand that the notion of career itself is both socially and culturally constructed. Our images of career are substantially influenced by the culture in which we live. These images provide us with some sort of *cultural script* that we then proceed to act out without much reflection. Career choices and plans are then played out almost automatically, and many lifestyle choices are not taken into account. If nothing else, the exercise grounds a discussion and planning of careers in students' personal value systems while locating it within a cultural and social context.

I have shared here some of my favorite experiences in undergraduate OB teaching that were also substantially influenced by my theoretical orientations. These experiences were special for me because they demanded that my students and I connect our readings, models, and so on to our worlds of work, home, and family. They were not always eagerly received by all students. Some students questioned whether thinking along these lines was of any use to business majors. Others pointed out that habits of questioning the text were often actively discouraged in other management classes, as well as within many work situations. Yet, many students welcomed the opportunity to reflect on these issues. The central issue here for me remains: What is OB teaching all about? At the end of several semesters of teaching, although it can include many things, it primarily remains an opportunity for my students and me to explore and connect the lessons of the text to personal experience and the world of work.

## References

Benson, J. K. (1977). Organizations: A dialectical view. *Administrative Science Quarterly, 22,* 1-21.

Cavanaugh, J. M., & Prasad, P. (1990). Beyond text: Making the implicit explicit in the OB classroom. *Organizational Behavior Teaching Review, 14,* 102-108.

Edwards, R. C. (1979). *Contested terrain: The transformation of the workplace in the twentieth century.* New York: Basic Books.

Fischer, F. (1984). Ideology and organization theory. In F. Fischer & C. Sirianni (Eds.), *Critical studies in organization and bureaucracy* (pp. 172-190). Philadelphia: Temple University Press.

Frost, P. (1980). Toward a radical framework for practicing organization science. *Academy of Management Review, 5,* 501-508.

Garson, B. (1972). *All the livelong day.* New York: Penguin.

Harris, C., & Brown, W. (1990). Careers in context: Multiple perspectives on working lives. *Organizational Behavior Teaching Review, 14,* 15-27.

Luft, J. (1963). *Group processes: An introduction to group dynamics.* Mountain View, CA: Mayfield.

Merkle, J. A. (1980). *Management and ideology: The legacy of the International Scientific Management Movement.* Berkeley, CA: University of California Press.

Nelson, D. (1975). *Managers and workers: Origins of the new factory system in the United States, 1880-1920.* Madison: University of Wisconsin Press.

Simon, S. (1982). *Value clarification.* Amherst: University of Massachusetts Press.

# 14 Anatomy of a Colleagueship

## COLLABORATIONS IN AND
## OUT OF THE CLASSROOM

MARCY CRARY
DUNCAN SPELMAN

This chapter represents a collective reflection, an attempt to step back and describe 14 years of our colleagueship in and out of the classroom. We describe how our partnership developed, what we value in it, the challenges we have experienced within it, and what we think helps keep it together. We use the language of *we* in the telling of the story of our colleagueship but attempt to include our individual voices from time to time (perhaps to remind the reader that we are not as much of a "unit" as the *we*'s would appear to make us).

## How the Partnership Developed

Our relationship as teachers together grew out of our relationship as co-presenters and co-authors. Soon after ending up at Bentley College together, we began doing scholarly work—a case, presentations at professional meetings, and articles for a variety of publications. We experienced early success in these endeavors, receiving acceptances and feedback from colleagues that our work was valuable. Undoubtedly, this success deepened the relationship and encouraged further collaboration. Although we shared a graduate school background, we had not worked together prior to coming to Bentley.

As co-presenters and co-authors, our relationship has been complementary. Our working styles are quite different: We usually describe this to ourselves in terms of Marcy being a diverger and Duncan being a converger. Marcy thrives on the exploration of possibilities and on viewing an issue from many perspectives. Duncan's inclination is to sort the complexity and to name conclusions. Usually, these contrasting approaches have served us very well in our scholarly work, Marcy's openness allowing us to be creative, Duncan's focus moving us to completion. The dynamic of becoming stuck in our disagreements seems to have happened less in connection with presentations and writing than in our teaching. This is probably because the interdependency in research is less intense and less frequent.

We are in our 5th year as two members of a four-person teaching team, offering both undergraduate and graduate courses in managing diversity in the workplace. The team meets with our students once a week for class and also meets once a week to plan and debrief the class sessions.

The other two members of the team have full-time job responsibilities beyond their faculty role for this course, one being an administrator on campus and the other being an entrepreneur. At times, either or both are able to attend team meetings. As a result, we often believe ourselves to have greater ownership and responsibility for the course. We have more time to devote to strategizing about the course, and teaching is more central to our professional identities. Our both being white and the other faculty being of color can add another layer of complexity of our connection to each other. Defining ourselves as primary course organizers, we struggle to be mindful of who is assuming what responsibility in and out of the classroom, without playing into our own or students' gender and/or racial stereotypes.

Outside the team meetings, the two of us are likely to talk about the course, daily or more, by telephone or in person, to check everything from logistical details ("Did you reserve the video machine?") to design specifics ("How shall we word this white privilege assignment?") to fundamental discussions of what and how we are teaching ("What is our teaching objective for this session?" "Are we putting the students of color at risk in order to 'educate' white students?").

We navigate through rhythms of closeness/distance and connection/disconnection from each other in the transition from class planning sessions (particularly when we are doing them as a twosome) to working with the rest of the team and students in the classroom. Our *relationship* is figural during the intimacy and intensity of our discussions in preparation for the class. These interactions are often characterized by deep connection and synergy and by struggle and impasse. We often feed off each other very effectively in our course planning, suggesting new approaches, offering new perspectives, and building on each other's ideas. We often can unstick each other from a design dilemma. And yet, we often get very stuck.

For example, we seem to reach and understand the students in quite different ways. In the best times, we complement each other well. In the worst times, we get in each other's way. Marcy thinks Duncan talks too much. Duncan thinks Marcy doesn't talk enough. Marcy's top priority is an opportunity for the students to speak. Duncan wants a balance between class input and comments from the faculty members who bring greater experience on these issues.

These differences regarding what should be emphasized in the course process can hang us up. Each of us is very capable of struggling to win the argument, apart from the merits of either side. We often are unwilling to concede a point, and if we do, the conflict will often resurface later.

The time spent in the classroom can, at times, create a sense of distance between the two of us. If the class design doesn't run as well as we thought it would, we can respond quite differently to where to go in the moment. Differences in our styles (in addition to the styles of our teammates) can complicate the decision about how to manage the emergent dynamics in the class. But these very differences have also fueled many lively dialogues between us over the years.

### Variations on the Theme

One professional variation of our relationship is our role as leaders of an organizational change effort related to diversity at Bentley. The college is undertaking an initiative focused on making the institution more diverse, more welcoming of its diversity, and more able to use the resources of its diversity. We have been central to the initiation and implementation of this effort. In collaboration with an external consultant (who is a mutual friend from graduate school) and one other member of the teaching team, we have been the primary strategy-making group.

As the initiative has unfolded, our roles have become increasingly different, and as a result, our overall relationship has become more complex. The principal source of the difference in roles appears to be time. Marcy is on a part-time schedule at the college. Duncan works on the initiative almost full time. Consequently, Duncan is involved on a day-to-day level, is visible on campus in connection with the diversity work, and participates in most activities related to it. Marcy's participation is limited to leading the faculty development "action team," membership on the collegewide steering committee, and involvement in strategy discussions when she is available.

The professional variations of our relationship are blended with several personal variations. We are friends. We know about each other's life. We share our thoughts and feelings about much that is important to us. Very often, these friendship connections occur as intertwining threads with our professional work together. We ask how the other is. We talk about what's going on. We go off on long personal tangents in the midst of our professional work. Our telephone conversations and meetings in Marcy's office can almost as easily focus on personal issues as on the "work" at hand.

A particularly significant component of our personal bond is that we are parents. Marcy has a stepdaughter and a stepson in their 20s and a 6-year-old daughter. Duncan has a 16-year-old daughter. We often share our parenting dilemmas, heartaches, and celebrations. Again, these discussions are interwoven with our professional conversations.

We are also friends within a group of friends. We get together "socially" with our spouses and usually with the mutual friend from graduate school who is working as consultant to Bentley's diversity initiative. These gatherings are, most often, dinner at one of our homes. For two summers, we have rented houses for the same week on a nearby vacation island, including our children (and assorted friends) in the social grouping.

These interactions are characterized by depth of connection and conversation. In few other friendships do we talk so personally about what is significant for us. Our relationship seems an important center to this larger group, complemented more recently by the multiple and reinforcing connections with our consultant friend. An interesting variant in this manifestation of our relationship is that Marcy easily assumes the hostess role, taking responsibility for managing the social situation. This role presents a contrast to some of the professional interactions in which Duncan is more up front.

## The Value of Our Friendship

Our relationship connects the pieces of our lives. For each of us, it integrates different aspects of ourselves, allowing us to feel less fragmented in our work setting. During our conversation for the writing of this chapter, we said the following:

DS:  One thing I get from the relationship is that I don't feel alone here. I think I'm able to be a person in my work life rather than just a "professional." It's because you're here and we have the relationship we have that I feel I'm able to be much more of myself at Bentley than a lot of people are able to be in their professional lives. I think that they feel much more alone in general, that they have to be in roles, and that the roles are fairly rigidly defined. I think that our relationship allows me to be much broader.

MC:  A significant part of our relationship for me right now is how it acts as a bridge in my transition from home to work. When I come to work and come in and talk about things going on at home with my family or whatever, you have context knowledge for listening and commenting on my experiences. This helps me make the psychological transition from home to work. I don't always have to work at putting aside feelings, concerns that I'm walking in the door with.

This bridging has also been very important to me as I have cut back to a part-time role here at Bentley. It's very easy to become isolated in one's work as a professor here at Bentley. Our shared work within the diversity initiative itself has kept me connected into work at Bentley that feels very important.

## Challenges to the Relationship

A relationship as multifaceted and central as ours inevitably presents challenges and conflicts. We would not have continued to reap the benefits described above had we not developed some understanding of what threatens our relationship. We have noticed five elements that seem to have a particularly powerful effect on the nature and strength of the challenges we face: (a) the intensity and complexity of our interdependence, (b) the audiences we address, (c) differences in our official roles, (d) the "heat" in the content of our work, and (e) gender dynamics.

### Interdependence

Over the life of our relationship, we have steadily increased our interdependence. In doing so, we have also increased the challenges we must deal with. A particularly powerful example of how deeply our interdependence confronts us with new tests was our decision to teach together as part of a four-person teaching team.

In the fall of 1990, we introduced the management elective Managing Diversity in the Workplace. The development and first teaching team included the two of us plus Earl Avery, Special Assistant to the President and Equal Opportunity Officer at Bentley College; and Barbara Walker, then International Manager for Valuing Diversity at Digital Equipment Corporation. We had never been quite this interdependent before. We were faced with weekly, sometimes daily, decisions about how the course would be taught. We now each had a legitimate voice in what would happen in the other's teaching. And other players added to the complexity.

In this process, overt conflicts in philosophy, primarily between Barbara and Duncan, created tensions between Duncan and Marcy. In discussing the philosophy of the course, Duncan and Barbara represented what appeared at the time to be two opposing perspectives on how one should do "diversity work." Marcy felt very much in the middle of the conflict between Barbara and Duncan and their relative "positions." She felt responsible to Barbara, having worked to bring her into this project, and was concerned that the conflicts between Barbara and Duncan might jeopardize what felt like a very rich, developing friendship with Barbara. She was also attracted to Barbara's philosophy, but not to the exclusion of Duncan's. Duncan, who liked Barbara personally, felt very torn by their disagreements about how to do the work and was also deeply concerned that he might be losing Marcy as an ally.

It felt as if we might be deciding to join different tribes; this seemed to challenge the very foundation of our collaboration. The challenge seemed to be to keep our relationship intact and, at the same time, to do justice to our different positions and perspectives. The challenge of teaching together would have been significant enough without the deep philosophical complications and personal dynamics involving other people!

### Audiences

As we have collaborated, we have performed before various audiences. Early on, our work was for our professional colleagues, either in writing or in conference presentations. Although the stakes there felt high, the performances were occasional and short-lived. When we began teaching together, the stress increased because we were performing weekly for an entire semester.

Today, our most demanding audience faces us in our work on Bentley's diversity initiative. As change agents attempting to lead an organizational development effort in our own institution, we face our immediate colleagues (both faculty and staff) on an ongoing basis with the message that the status quo is flawed. And the issues we raise in this effort—racism, sexism, ethnocentrism, and heterosexism—feel deeply personal. Some colleagues question why we want to explore personal belief systems in a professional setting. Sometimes, the stakes seem very high indeed. Questions of what to say when and to whom have become much more complicated and loaded than ever before.

### Roles

Before the diversity initiative, our formal roles had always been equal—as faculty members, as co-authors, as teachers. In the diversity initiative, our roles are not equal. Because Duncan is full time and Marcy is part time, Duncan has a considerably more central and visible role in the change effort than Marcy does.

The difference in roles has created tension between us. We consider: Is Marcy being as supportive of Duncan as she could be, given his very visible and vulnerable position? Is Duncan including and consulting with Marcy as much as he should be? The tension is exaggerated by our differences in philosophy regarding how the organizational change effort should be pursued.

We have the following reflections on the dynamics related to our different roles:

MC: I am positioned as an outsider on the inside of the diversity strategy team. I think my marginal position on the strategy team can drive both Duncan and me crazy. It gives me the freedom (and feeling of license) to step back and critique a design that Duncan feels more investment in as the full-time internal consultant. My diverger self also loves to indulge in thinking about all the possibilities in a design session, which makes it very difficult for Duncan when he is feeling the need and responsibility for converging.

DS: I struggle with how much to consult with Marcy on the diversity initiative. I want her knowledge and her perspective, but it sometimes feels frustrating to have to reconstruct history she has missed. I don't want her to feel excluded, and I appreciate her company, but I also don't want to take advantage of her, given that the college is only paying her part time. And it feels funny to be in a decision-making role about this—for me to be deciding when she's in or out. I try to give the choice to her, but I'm afraid I don't always do that very well.

## Content of Our Work

The nature of the work we do represents another source of challenge. Work on "diversity" issues in a management context is hot in two senses. First, it is the focus of much attention as more organizations take on diversity work, more consultants claim the expertise to deal with it, and more people write about it. Second, it is hot because it is controversial and emotional. All of the usual turmoil that surrounds any major movement for change is exaggerated by the personal, moral, even religious overlay that can accompany diversity issues. Because of its heat and its relative newness, the field is characterized by strong differences of opinion about what should be done. These differences sometimes inject themselves into our relationship as we work together on diversity issues.

We sometimes experience each other as representatives of conflicting philosophies about diversity work, disciples of different religions.
The philosophical conflict within our teaching team mirrors a significant conflict in the diversity field. The "valuing differences" approach
contributed to the team by Barbara Walker, and the "managing diversity" strategy brought by Duncan from work he was doing with Elsie Y.
Cross and Associates, a Philadelphia-based consulting firm, differ in
significant ways. The differences between them revolve around which
group identities are given the most attention and the extent to which
oppression is kept as a figural issue in the work.

The valuing differences approach stresses the importance of exploring difference dynamics that occur in relation to all kinds of differences—the "traditional" diversity issues of race and gender but also
any other difference that is important in a given situation, whether it
be function, learning style, smoker/nonsmoker, or some other difference.
Furthermore, this approach emphasizes the importance of addressing
the experiences of being discriminated against that all people have had.

The managing diversity perspective suggests it is crucial to focus
work on a few key issues—usually racism and sexism—because of their
powerful impact on organizational life, their distinctive histories in
U.S. society, and the possibility of diluting diversity efforts by dealing
with too many issues simultaneously. This approach expects that learning
about these issues will make people and organizations more able and
interested in dealing with other key differences. The managing diversity philosophy also emphasizes the significance of oppression and
power dynamics in diversity work, believing it crucial to understand
the very different experiences of those in powerful and powerless groups.

At some points, the conflict we experienced in our teaching team
about these issues was deep and painful. We certainly learned much
from our explorations of the different philosophies, but not without
struggle that shook the foundations of our relationship. The legacy of
this struggle sometimes plays itself out in dysfunctional ways. Because
we had such significant "valuing differences" versus "managing diversity" battles, we seem to fall easily into interpreting current disagreements as another skirmish in that war. Duncan assumes Marcy is back
into that valuing differences stuff again, and Marcy sees Duncan too
fixed in his managing diversity stance. Our tendency to do this gains
strength from the ongoing tensions in the field between these and other

philosophies. The dysfunctional aspect of this dynamic is that we easily distort the other's position, exaggerate the significance of our disagreement, and dig in to defend.

Our areas of agreement about how to address diversity issues are much greater than our areas of disagreement, and our agreement has increased over time. We have both come to appreciate the contributions of valuing differences and managing diversity (as well as other perspectives). Today, our disagreements are usually much more about how much emphasis to place on something, rather than about whether it should be considered at all.

And yet, we can still find ourselves seemingly defending polarized positions. We tend to believe that the other is a true believer in a narrow philosophy that needs to be resisted. When we can get beyond the polarization, we realize that we imagined the other's position to be more extreme, more exclusive of our own than was actually the case. Our disagreements and discussions about what should be emphasized are functional and developmental because we learn and relearn not to fall into the trap of defending against a threat that doesn't exist.

## Gender Dynamics

At times, this challenge of gender dynamics feels like the most complicated of all and the most difficult to put into words. We have found that the very act of "seeing" and "naming" an interaction between us as being gender linked can cause tension between us. We've noticed that our more difficult "gender times" are germinated out of situations that seem to have the following ingredients:

- We are "in public" in some kind of shared leadership role with a class or in a workshop, so whatever we're doing we have an audience for it and we are feeling the press of being "online."
- Something happens in the situation that triggers at least one of us to interpret our interactions as being gender based.
- At least one of us is concerned that we, in the moment, not collude with traditional sex roles and/or be interpreted as doing such, but we are not sure whether we should make this issue public.
- Simultaneously, we have three or four other process issues to be managed on the table, so the tension builds about what should be made figural in our work at the moment.

An example of one of these situations is a class session on gender socialization; it began with some "housework."

Duncan was up front informing the class that we had decided to reshuffle the membership of the dialogue groups because of a diversity concern—even though the groups had already had one meeting. We had spent significant time thinking through this decision and had decided we would inform the class of our decision and give them the rationale for it. Unexpectedly, one female student voiced her concern about the change and asked whether the class could vote on it. Duncan responded by saying he was personally not willing to have a vote on this and by stating he thought it was our responsibility to make this kind of decision.

DS:   When our teaching team had discussed this issue in preparation for class, we had considered what process made most sense for addressing our concerns about the membership of the dialogue groups. On the basis of previous unsuccessful experiences with involving students in decisions about course management issues, I had recommended against opening this up to the class. My history was that some students welcomed the opportunity to participate but that many others resented class time being spent in that way. I thought we had agreed as a team to *present* our decision, rather than open the issue up to class discussion.

Duncan looked at Earl and Marcy for their responses (the fourth teacher was not at that session). Earl did not respond at first, and Marcy was unsure of what to do at the moment. She turned to the group and said, "This is an interesting moment!"

MC:   I was struck with how autocratic Duncan was being in presenting his stance to the group. His style seemed to heighten the power differential between the students and the instructors. I wondered why we couldn't take time to talk about their voting on this issue. I felt torn. I wanted to support Duncan because he was hanging out there, but at the same time I hesitated to cut the group off from the decision making in such a unilateral fashion.

Later in the class session, Duncan asked the students to think of a gender socialization message they had received that they rationally disbelieved but were influenced by anyhow. He provided an example from his own experience. He said he was socialized to believe that women could not make the hard decisions. Even though he knows this is not what he rationally accepts, when faced with a problem in a gender-mixed task group, he is very likely to move into making the decision himself, taking up the space. It would then be hard for a woman present to come into the process herself. After Duncan finished his example, Pat, one of the students, put up her hand and said, "Duncan, I don't want to put you on spot, but wasn't that just what happened here?"

After class, we had a discussion about the session, recognizing that it had been complicated and tense. Marcy admitted she had winked at Pat after Duncan had given his example, because Pat had looked at her as if saying, "Are you seeing the connection?" Duncan was angry when he heard Marcy had done this. And Marcy was angry that Duncan was overreacting to the significance of the wink.

Within the next few weeks, we wrote up a description of this "case" and talked over our different emotional responses to it, feeling seeped in gender dynamics and interpretations as we did so. We presented this "case" at one of Marcy's practicum sessions at the Clinical Development Institute, working with the perspectives of other members of the practicum to sort out our different experiences of the event. As we told our "sides" of the experience to each other, both of us were struck with the ambiguity and complexity of this classroom interaction. Although we recognize the importance of tracking our gender dynamics, we also realize that we must attend to how these dynamics interact with other factors.

The act of putting on a gender lens to look at our relationship heightens our awareness of our differences. Marcy is apt to spend more time considering whether or not something is gender related, perhaps because of her nondominant gender status. But we are both wary of oversimplifying the issues by interpreting a struggle that goes on between us as purely a gender issue.

With increased interdependency in our roles over the last few years, we can see that we have sometimes established our division of labor by using traditional sex roles as our template. This is not something we were necessarily conscious of at the time, but looking back we can see the effects of our gender socialization and gender cultures at work. We struggle to stay awake to these dynamics because we have seen how stultifying the old gender templates can be. But they do have powerful tugs on us.

MC:  At times, I feel as if I'm asking Duncan to be president so that I only have to be vice president. Being part time, I find myself avoiding roles where I have to be the person who is front and center on a regular basis. I also hate the anxiety that comes with being asked to be the one in charge—particularly when emotionally laden issues are on the table. Duncan always seems comfortable being the lead person, so it feels very easy to set ourselves up in this pattern.

Over the last year or so, I have begun to feel stifled by this "role arrangement." At times, I see myself as being too dependent on Duncan and wonder about the costs of our role patterns for us both. I wonder about its effect on my self-esteem and on my ongoing ability to exercise my own voice and style of leadership.

Our role designs at times seem too collusive with larger gender role patterns in our culture. It was shocking to have a student write in her journal for the course that she realized she had been looking at our team and making the assumption that Duncan was really the one in charge and that the other three of us were, in effect, his assistants. This put a bee in my bonnet and made me realize that I had better get my act together—not just for my own self-esteem but also for the purpose of being an effective role model to other women.

Having a more clearly differentiated role in the faculty development action team for the diversity initiative does seem to reflect a different role pattern than in our other joint adventures. Having to rely more on my own resources and working interdependently with other folks feels refreshing.

DS:  I experience a variety of reactions to the roles we play in relation to each other—and the related gender dynamics. Sometimes, I don't even notice that I'm up front and Marcy is in a supporting position. Other times, I am very aware of it and want her to move forward because it feels lonely and scary up there. Occasionally, I'll feel like somebody's got to step up, even take control of a situation, and it seems I have to be the one.

These variations evoke complicated emotions because I want to avoid falling into old and dysfunctional gender dynamics in which I, as the man, would take a dominant role; and yet I don't want to hang back when the situation requires a response. I'm particularly concerned that I not be a white man who is silent or passive about diversity issues. That could too easily maintain my privilege or function as resistance.

Another ongoing struggle that seems to have a gender component is our differences in boundary management—that is, orientations toward self-disclosure, inclusiveness, and control. We often find ourselves at different ends of the continuum on these dimensions. Marcy is generally more at ease with self-disclosure, often is concerned with the inclusion of others, and likes to share control of an event with others. Duncan is more selective about when and with whom he may share his backstage feelings or thoughts and is more apt to stay focused on the need to maintain credibility in his leadership role in a tightly networked institution. He is more apt to be aware of the risks of being too open with others, such as the risk of being seen as "touchy-feely" or the potential for information to be used by others in harmful ways.

Each of us has concerns about how the other manages her or his boundaries. For example, Duncan may see Marcy's disclosures as "airing one's dirty laundry," whereas Marcy may see Duncan's cautiousness about disclosing as a barrier to connecting with others.

We seem to have different interpretations of the risks involved and wonder how much this is related to the different "injunctions" of our respective gender cultures. One hypothesis we have been exploring is that we are, in effect, shaping our behaviors with different audiences and roles "in mind"—even when we are meeting in the same room, with the same people. Duncan's concerns about how others will see and evaluate his self-disclosures may be linked to the notion that men shouldn't make mistakes or look weak. Marcy may see herself as less accountable to the male culture in the room and feel freer to be a deviant.

## What Holds It Together?

Stepping back from this relationship for the purposes of this chapter, we found ourselves asking, What holds this relationship together? Sharing a common professional development experience and similar values and understandings about the management of relationships seems to be key to meeting the challenges we face.

### Our "Case" Experience

One critical underpinning of our connection with each other is the fact that we both did our doctoral work in the Organizational Behavior

Department at Case Western Reserve University. Although we were 2 years apart in the department and did not work together there, we see ourselves as having come from the same tribe, with a particular set of values and worldviews about how people should work together—about the importance of understanding and respecting the integrity of each person's ways of making sense of the world, about the significance of personal development in the context of one's professional development, about how one designs effective learning environments, about the power of action-research, and about how one goes about the management of organizational/system change. This common heritage leads us to be interested in similar projects and gives us shared orientations as teachers, writers, researchers, and practitioners. Each of us also had strong personal/professional relationships with fellow students and faculty at Case, and we use these experiences as models for the design of our own colleagueships. In sum, the emotional bottom line of this shared past is that we feel as if "we're family."

### Similar Values

We realize that the interest in and willingness to process our experiences is a powerful prerequisite for how we shape our relationship. We each value processing experience, a trademark of a "Case" education.

We like looking at and trying to understand the differences that are occurring in front of us and exploring the "undersides" of an issue. At times, this observation involves acknowledging aspects of our self that we may feel unsure of or ashamed about and/or disclosing feelings of anger and resentment toward the other. But our experience has been that we come out of most of these explorations feeling satisfied with how we were heard and understood by the other. And many of these times, we've moved to a new understanding of an issue as a result of a blending of our different perspectives on it. We each feel respected by the other, and that comes out even when we are fighting with each other.

### Strategies for Stepping Back From the Issues

One thing we do is employ strategies that help us step back from our dynamics and take stock of what is happening. More often than not, this stepping back comes in the form of taking time out to make

sense together of what was happening with each of us in the situation—
that is, how we felt and thought about what the other was doing.

Another thing we do is use our experiences for our own and others'
professional development. For example, we have regularly used the
Organizational Behavior Teaching Conference as a forum for working
on some of the more thorny issues we have faced over the various
stages of our diversity work together. This kind of stepping back and
taking stock in professional forums helps us "disembed" ourselves from
some of the difficult dynamics we have encountered and can push us
to different levels of understanding. And it is always helpful to realize
that one's own problems have significance for others.

We both experienced the writing of this chapter as having a powerful
effect on our understanding of the patterns in our interactions. In the
2 months of drafting different parts of it, we lived out a running analysis of our colleagueship day by day. It felt like a rich opportunity to
"unpack" some of our operating assumptions about ourselves and the
other and to deepen our considerations of what goes on between us.

### Evaluations of the Other

The complexity of our interdependent roles requires that we become vulnerable to the other's view of our ways of thinking and behaving. We each share stakes in the other's "performances" at Bentley.
But we also have differences in how we think certain issues should be
handled. We often seek feedback from and offer feedback to each other
and see this process as fundamental to the quality of our work and our
own professional development.

But a significant process issue we sometimes bump up against re-
volves around how we each respond to what we think the other person
is thinking about what we are doing. Having worked together for more
than 14 years, we can predict what the other's reaction will be in certain
circumstances. (In some sense, we have each internalized the other's
evaluation of certain aspects of self [e.g., our teaching style]. So, it is
as if we don't have to ask the other what he or she thinks; we just insert
what we think the other thinks.) But carrying this internalized-views-
of-the-other can become irritating at times. For example, in discussing
an argument we had had about one of our classes, we agreed that we
both had felt as if we were being held hostage to the other's evaluation
of our own "way." We felt constrained by what the other thought about

what we were doing in the moment (e.g., in class, in a meeting) and fell into the following spiral: "I should be doing this differently, but I can't/don't want to, but s/he thinks the way I do it isn't good enough but I disagree with him/her about this but maybe there is something to what s/he is saying but it's making me feel like I'm 'less than' and that pisses me off!" So we talk some more.

## Final Thoughts

We have found this colleagueship very rich ground for much of our growing, separately and together. And, we believe that there are beneficiaries from this partnership besides ourselves. Perhaps for some of our students and colleagues we have modeled one kind of rewarding male-female partnership. Certainly, we have helped birth a new diversity course at Bentley, have supported numerous related presentations and publications, and have helped stimulate the evolution of a diversity change project at Bentley.

But it occurs to us, looking back over the story we have told, that some academics may not desire the kind of colleagueship described above. It is clear that not all successful collaborations require the intensity of relationship presented here. This style of intimate colleagueship has risks. Such intimacy is not always wanted or effective in getting work done. Expectations for closeness and self-disclosure may, in fact, hinder the accomplishment of some kinds of tasks. It also takes a lot of work to set the ground for a close relationship that feels "safe" for the personal explorations involved. And this kind of intimacy adds to the complexity of the work one does, because of the time and energy required to inquire into each other's feelings, assumptions, and perceptions.

Writing this chapter together felt like a significant intervention in our relationship. It came along at a time when we were each feeling great tension from the challenges we described above. The writing process forced us into having the kind of conversations we value having but had been avoiding because of the combined pressures of the tensions we felt with each other and the press of our work commitments. Working on the chapter gave us a space in which to investigate, appreciate, and learn from some of the conflicts we were experiencing. In effect, we were applying our craft to our own relationship, hanging in to work through the differences we had been encountering. Instead of just staking out our positions to one another, we were revealing our "backstage" feelings and concerns about the interactions we had been having. We became less polarized around our differences. Instead of seeing the other's position of "traits" as negative, we were able to integrate these differences into the work of the moment. We were reminded, for the millionth time, of the value of open and honest dialogue in maintaining a strong colleagueship.

## Postscript

After sending off the first draft of this chapter to Peter and Rae *after* the deadline, Marcy said, "After all this work, I hope they still take it." Duncan replied, "If they don't, it would be OK with me. I now feel a new peace with the relationship." Thinking about his response later, Marcy smiled and said to herself, "That's something I would have said!"

# 15 Teaching as Leading

## DONALD C. HAMBRICK

I was startled by my silence. I didn't like my colleague's idea, but I couldn't verbalize why. Those of us who teach the required MBA strategy course at Columbia were discussing possible modifications, both in content and delivery. My friend suggested that we should exploit our respective strengths by having each of us be responsible for teaching one module of the course to all sections each term, in a form of team teaching. This idea was logical; it was on the side of efficiency; it was on the side of comparative advantage, something we strategy types relish. But I couldn't warm to it; I knew I couldn't even consider it. I sat quietly, not able to say why the idea seemed so unappealing. Only later did I see what my problem was. Aside from not wanting to deliver class sessions—not even one, and certainly not several—to six or eight sections of 55 students, I couldn't picture myself in a "modular" capacity as a teacher, a mere cassette cued up and ready to roll, in between other cassettes.

AUTHOR'S NOTE: Eric Abrahamson, Ming-Jer Chen, James Kuhn, and Hugh O'Neill made valuable comments on earlier versions of this chapter.

Teaching isn't just the conveyance of information. If it were, few of us should have jobs, because textbooks and articles can impart knowledge just fine. Teaching isn't a dazzling show by an expert. If it were, we would all be replaced by Tom Peters's and Mike Porter's videotapes.

Rather, to teach is to enter into a relationship. To conduct a course is to orchestrate students' knowledge, motivation, anxiety, and energy. To teach is to understand the pulse in the classroom, the emotional and intellectual ebbs and flows, how far students can stretch, and how they can learn the most from each other. The loftiest aim of teaching is not to impart to students a new block of knowledge and skills, but rather to maximize their readiness and eagerness for further, lifelong learning. In fact, I have long thought that the ideal course evaluation question—the litmus test for how good a job the instructor did—should be, "How did this course affect your eagerness to learn more in general and in this topic in particular?"

To me, teaching is leadership. We teach leadership in our management classrooms, but we rarely think of the importance of manifesting it there.

## Getting Hooked

I first became aware of the power of great teaching as an MBA student at Harvard Business School (HBS). I had had good teachers in college but, honestly, no great ones. At Harvard, known for its teaching, a steady stream of remarkably effective teachers intellectually grabbed my classmates and me, caused us to work harder than we thought we could, caused us to take risks in the classroom, and left us wanting more.

There are jokes about a cookie-cutter teaching style at HBS (sleeves rolled up, pacing the aisles of the tiered classroom, exaggerated gestures; "Why, in all photos of HBS professors in the classroom, do they have their hands outstretched? Because they're embracing 'the big picture'!"). But I saw numerous styles, from the quiet to the bellicose, from the warm to the stern, from the abstract to the concrete. What they *did* have in common, I now see, is that they all conceived of teaching as leadership.

My classmates and I got our money's worth at Harvard. And, without knowing I'd ever need it, I got even more—an immense mental scrapbook full of images of great teachers at work.

But soon I did need it. I went to Penn State to be the director of their MBA program (a newly created "general management" position that somehow seemed more exciting, though far less remunerative, than corporate alternatives), but I was drawn quickly into teaching. Bob Pitts, who coordinated the undergraduate policy course, asked whether I would be willing to teach one section of 40 students. Why not? I remember working very hard at it but enjoying it. The students showed a gratifying level of interest, and the course evaluations were favorable. (In response to the question "What did you like most about this course?" however, one student wrote, "When it was over." That unknown student, whom I call "The Crusher," rears his ugly head from time to time in course evaluations to this day.) Bob Pitts, a superb teacher himself, made a point of telling me I had done extremely well, especially for the first time. I was hooked. I liked teaching, and it looked as if I might be able to become adept at it. I also became involved in some research projects at Penn State, and I became captivated by that side of scholarship too.

I had applied to Ph.D. programs at three prior stages, each time deciding to follow a different path.[1] But now I was ready. I had a taste of teaching and research, and I was sure the agony of a Ph.D. program (is there any other way to put it?) was worth enduring. I needed to be a professor.

I applied to Ph.D. programs, sure this time that I was not just forking over more application fees.[2] But it was the Penn State program I enrolled in, and not just out of inertia. Rather, Penn State had assembled an extraordinary management group—Max Richards, John Slocum, Bob Pitts, Chuck Snow, Don Hellriegel, and others—that I thought would be difficult to beat anyplace else. That proved to be correct. I learned a great deal from these Penn State mentors, not only about theories, analytic methods, the craft of research, and teaching, but also about the ethos of scholarship—responsibility to one's field, to one's colleagues, to one's students, and to one's institution.

From Penn State, I went to Columbia, where I have been since. I teach primarily in the areas of strategy and top management processes, and I feel blessed to have a varied portfolio of courses in our MBA, Executive MBA, senior executive, and Ph.D. programs. I savor this wide spectrum, transferring what I learn from one audience to another and enjoying the alternating focus on theory and practice.

As a further piece of background, I should say that I am a case teacher. This reveals Harvard's further influence on me. I am a believer in tangible application and experiential learning, and I have always found cases an ideal vehicle for achieving these.

I am not a "purist" case teacher, however. Under strict Socratic dogma, an instructor doesn't reveal his or her own line of thought; doesn't try to fit a class discussion into a conceptual framework; doesn't conclude a class by telling the students what they should have learned; and, above all, doesn't reveal the aftermath of a case—that would encourage the students to conclude that one course of action might be better than another. I do all these things. I also weave my own and others' research into the classroom, and I liberally sprinkle "lecturettes" into class sessions.

I make a point of noting this because of a discussion I had when visiting friends at Harvard a few months ago. I was having lunch with a professor who had been on the faculty when I was a student there, himself a great teacher but clearly a member of the old guard, the Socratic purists. With a combination of wonderment and clear disdain, he noted, "These days, whenever I walk by one of our classrooms, the professor always has the goddamned overhead projector on." To some at HBS, I have strayed.

## The Teacher-Leader

In referring to teaching as leadership, what do I mean? Leadership implies many things. Indeed, the literature on leadership is replete with definitions, dimensions, examples, and exhortations. I could use the frameworks of any number of leadership thinkers to make my case, but I am particularly taken by the concise and powerful portrayal of leadership laid out by Warren Bennis in *Why Leaders Can't Lead* (1989). He speaks of four competencies of highly effective leaders: management of meaning, management of attention, management of trust, and management of self. Although I won't claim to carry this framework in my head when I teach, I find that almost everything I believe about teaching and what I try to do in the classroom—particularly in the MBA classroom—aligns very closely with Bennis's four leadership competencies. Nor do I begin to believe that I fulfill these qualities. But to do so is my continuing, elusive aim.

## Management of Meaning

Students must be able to attach significance to what they are doing. Otherwise, their learning will be mechanical, compartmentalized, and begrudging. As a leader, a teacher cannot simply deliver material but must also cause students to see the meaning of the material from the very outset. Why is this course a profitable way for them to spend about 150 hours? How will the course affect their short-term and long-term professional competence? How will the course build on or create a foundation for other courses? Students need these questions answered.

On the first day of class, most teachers carefully walk the students through the objectives of the course, the outline, requirements, materials, and so on. But students need more than that—not only on the first day, but throughout the term. Why does the course have these objectives? Why is this stuff important? What will I do with this new material? Why does this course even exist? Particularly if it is a required core course, the instructor has an obligation to justify the material for the students.

I always spend at least 20 minutes on the first day of class strictly trying to establish the larger meaning of the course. I try to identify several potential professional benefits from taking the course; I discuss how the material aids in the interpretation and understanding of one or two current business situations that are highly visible in the news; and I draw links between the course and the other courses the students have taken and will take.

The management of meaning is also greatly enhanced by the use of experiential materials. As I've said, cases are my favorite vehicles, but simulations, role playing, and field projects are also very effective. Students cannot truly comprehend material unless they have a chance to apply it.

Simply providing the application opportunity is still not enough, however, even though Socratic purists might claim that. The teacher needs to help students extract and assemble meaning from an experience. I try to wrap up case discussions with the chief learning points, drawing linkages to conceptual frameworks presented during the term, as well as to prior cases that have been discussed. Establishing meaning for students is a day-in, day-out endeavor, not simply an opening day task, and certainly not just a closing day summarizing task.

Establishing meaning for a class can be exceedingly difficult for teachers because the material has so much obvious meaning for them. Deeply knowing the significance and range of application of course material can be a liability because these become taken for granted and obvious. Even the flow of material can become so second nature for a teacher that he or she has difficulty building bridges and linkages for the students. This is one reason why I never use textbooks. They are too preset. They don't force one to think about the flow, the transitions, the punctuation of the material. I only use loose cases and readings based on my own current model (which changes somewhat from year to year) of what topics ought to be in the course, in what sequence, and with what supporting material. In short, to convey meaning to students, a teacher must establish for himself or herself a vivid and compelling personal case for the material.

### Management of Attention

Students have many competing pressures, ranging from the legitimate to the frivolous. All leaders face the challenge of focusing the energies and creativity of organization members on the mission at hand. They must engage in the management of attention.

I consider it a critical part of my job to get my fair share—and even more, I hope—of my students' time, thoughts, and emotional energy. To do that, I have to have their attention. Let me emphasize that I have no natural endowments in this regard. I am not colorful; I have all the pizzazz of 1950s suburbia where I was raised. I am not particularly warm; the most common suggested improvement I receive on course evaluations is "loosen up." And, I am not eloquent; just ask my wife.

I try to capture the attention of students, first and foremost by establishing meaning for them, as discussed above. But I also engage in very deliberate efforts on two other fronts: (a) I make it clear to students that I care about their attention, their learning, and their performance; and (b) I try to avoid pedagogic routines and ruts.

Students will attend to you if you attend to them. I try to learn all the students' names, even in a class as large as 60, in the first 3 weeks, becoming able to address them by name without their name cards in the classroom and in the halls. This task is particularly essential because

I grade class participation and can only do so credibly if it's clear I know who's who. When students do a particularly terrific job in class discussion—especially students who seem generally reluctant to talk—I try to grab them after class or put notes in their student folders, saying what I liked so much about their contributions. I've also been known to communicate similarly with students who are a drag on class time.

I might also comment on my approach to class attendance—the basic ante in a student's attention. I want students to attend class because they feel it's time well spent, indeed better than any other possible use of those 80 minutes. And I try to design and deliver a course that will exact those feelings. At the same time, however, I essentially compel attendance by saying something like this:

> You have to make a good-faith effort on every requirement of the course in order to pass it. One of those requirements is class participation; and if you're not here, you're not participating. I recognize that you will have the occasional conflict and may have to miss class. But if you miss more than five or six classes, that would be less than a good-faith effort.

I justify this on two grounds. First, as a case course, the payoff for all students hinges greatly on the preparation and insights of their fellow students. If students don't show up, the course unravels and all students lose. Second, I am psychologically frail, taking absences very personally, becoming morose and ineffective in the process. And we don't want that.

If a student misses two classes in a row, I put a handwritten note in his or her student folder, expressing my concern: "Linda—We missed you in class. Hope all is well and that you'll be back with us on Monday." Very often, the student will then stop by to say she's fine—had an interview, had the flu, or whatever; or sometimes it's serious, and I can express my regards and sometimes even be of some help. The student often will also say that this is the first time an instructor has *ever* expressed an interest in his or her whereabouts. And I *am* interested. Students—I need their attention and they need to know that, day in and day out.

The management of attention requires the minimization of tedium and routine. We all have our own ways of enlivening classes so that students stay invigorated and fresh. The use of guest speakers, video conferencing with actual case protagonists, and role plays are among the ways that many instructors add spice to the classroom. I do those things, but I also make a point of doing two other things.

First, I try to conduct every case discussion with a different flow and cadence. Instead of having a sacrosanct order of march (e.g., "What are Mr. X's problems? Why do these exist?"), I vary the sequence, especially the opening question. One day, we might start off with students' votes on courses of action, another day on a discussion of a specific event or exhibit in the case, another day with a discussion of the contrasts between this case and the previous day's case, and so on. In part, this change reflects my deep belief that there is no universally correct sequence for thinking about business problems. Great managers are flexible "loop" thinkers and enter the loop at different places for different problems. This variety in discussion format, however, also serves to minimize any lockstep, humdrum routine in class.

Second, I rarely talk longer than 10 minutes (the -*ettes* in the above-mentioned lecturettes) without inviting responses, questions, or ideas from the students. (In executive programs, I try never to go longer than 7 minutes.) Granted, I am full of terrific ideas and material I want to impart, but as I said earlier, I'm not that easy to listen to. (As a regular listener to academic presentations, let me say that I am not alone in this regard.) More fundamentally, students stay more alert if they know the ball is going to be thrown into their court at any minute.

### Management of Trust

Trust is essential in any shared enterprise, including—and maybe especially—learning. To give a course their all, to open themselves intellectually, and to take risks, students must be able to completely trust their teacher. And the fact that the university has seen fit to give the teacher an appointment is not sufficient evidence of trustworthiness. Each teacher must earn his or her students' trust.

Teaching and learning are two sides of a reciprocal relationship. As a teacher, I must be able to expect effort, imagination, and intellect from my students. I must trust them. But, more important, because mine is the leadership position, they must trust me. They must have every indication that I am giving my all to the course and to them.

It seems all too common—perhaps it is a never-ending fashion—for some professors to bemoan the abilities and motivations of their students. I feel very sorry for these professors, not only because they have to teach students they don't respect but also because they are prevented from delivering a course built on trust. They don't trust the students; that will surely show; and the students won't trust the professors. Their classrooms will be arid and the learning sparse.

I must say that I have an abiding general respect for my students. Even before I've met them, I think highly of them. These are people with exceptional undergraduate records, very high GMAT scores, and, typically, numerous other evidences of leadership and professional promise. They are making huge investments to be in our classrooms. It is very hard for me to be skeptical about them.

The core ingredient in trust is reliability. Students must be able to count on teachers to hold up their end of the educational bargain. They need not always *like* where you stand, but they absolutely must *know* where you stand. You must have a constancy of outlook, effort, and behavior.

Any leader has a multitude of fronts on which he or she can exhibit reliability or, conversely, unreliability. This is why leaders make so many missteps; leading requires constant vigilance of one's own actions and their potential effects on the led. Accordingly, the teacher has many ways in which to build—or diminish—trust. Here are some of the more important points of trust I try to keep in mind.

- You can count on me to put together a well-conceived, contemporary course. At least 25% of the material will be new each year. When I use dated materials, I will go to lengths to say why.
- You can count on me to be fully prepared for each class. No one in the room will know more about that day's case and readings than I.
- You can count on me to listen attentively to your class comments and to acknowledge them in some way.
- You can count on me to respect your point of view but also to register, at the time or possibly later, my own point of view. You will know what I think, although you need not agree with it.
- You can count on me to evaluate your written work promptly and constructively. You will have feedback within a week; I will make substantive comments in the margins. If you write a major group report, you will receive a typed page of comments from me.

These are examples of how I strive to keep my end of the teaching-learning compact. I wish I could say I execute these items unfailingly. I don't. I know that my mind sometimes darts around when students make comments in class and that I fail to give them due acknowledgment. I know that, from fatigue or time pressure, I sometimes become stingy in my comments on students' papers. When these happen, the trust between my students and me has been chipped away at, and I know I must work hard on some other front to restore it. The basic challenge is always to be mindful of the type of implicit contract we wish to have with our students.

## Management of Self

Leadership begins and ends with one's self. A leader is capable of introspection and self-diagnosis, can hear and weigh criticisms and suggestions, and can change and grow. All of these apply to the teacher as a leader.

A teacher must know his or her own strengths and deploy them effectively. For instance, I am very organized—probably too organized. So, I try to exploit that competence in the management of class time, the distribution of supporting materials, the promptness of my feedback, and so on. However, I know I'm not a dynamic speaker or a relaxed conversationalist. Therefore, I tend to avoid long lectures and social lunches with groups of students. Other teachers would have, and deploy, different strengths.

We teachers receive criticism and suggestions all the time, at a minimum through formal course evaluations. Criticism is humanly difficult to deal with, and psychological defense mechanisms tend to spring into action. The particular tendency is to rationalize away or discount students' suggestions because the students are literally in a role signifying their incompleteness and lack of knowledge. But, in my estimation, students tend to know whether they have learned very much, whether the teacher was a help or a hindrance to their learning, and whether they are interested in learning any more. Thus, I try to take students' evaluations very seriously. I have adopted as a general rule of thumb that if at least three students in a class register the same criticism or suggestion in the open-ended items on our evaluation form, then I have to give serious attention to a change. If only one or two students register a given criticism, I generally let my defense mechanisms prevail.

Teaching well is extraordinarily hard work. At Columbia, we have a very successful executives-in-residence program, and sometimes the executives do more than just give the occasional guest lecture, teaching entire courses. When they do, they almost invariably declare their shock at how much effort teaching takes. These highly accomplished executives, accustomed to massive work loads, come to recognize quickly that teaching—at least teaching well—is not like rolling out of bed in the morning. The teacher, as leader, must manage the big picture—the course outline, materials, and requirements. But managing the details—the rhythm of each class discussion, reactions to students' comments, transitions from one topic to the next—is every bit as important. Teaching requires great personal discipline; it takes management of self. Indeed, management of self is certainly the foundation for the other competencies of the leader-teacher: management of meaning, management of attention, and management of trust.

## Teaching and Research: How Symbiotic Are They?

By now, I hope it is clear that I love teaching. I also crave research and writing, however; and because Columbia is a research-oriented institution, I spend at least twice as much time on research as on teaching. Because of this time investment in research, I should ideally capitalize on it in the classroom, seizing synergies between the two major domains of academic life. Indeed, I see three possible levels of beneficial connection between research and teaching.

The chief benefit my research has for my students is that it keeps me fresh and energized. Without research, I would be stale. Teaching is great, and it can be a source of short-term energy, but it is essentially an emptying activity; replenishment must come from somewhere. I don't know whether evidence would bear me out, but I would guess that teacher burnout is far more prevalent and severe among professors without active research programs than for those who are significantly involved in original scholarship.

A second benefit from research is that it leads to more current, cutting-edge ideas and materials in the classroom. I rely on the latest frameworks, concepts, and findings in my teaching, and if I were not active in research, I am sure I would have difficulty staying current. Although I am a believer in some classic, time-tested concepts of management and strategy, I am also aware of huge changes in the landscape for business and the options and issues facing managers. I feel an obligation to provide my students with the most current perspectives possible. Again, I will confess to being without data, but I am quite sure that professors with active research programs provide more current, up-to-date, and relevant material to their students than those not involved in research.

The third benefit is that my research allows me to build a discerning awareness and appreciation for research among my students. As managers, they will be confronted with "studies" all the time, some valid and some not. Their companies will engage in collaborative research projects with universities. And, as potential citizen-leaders, they simply need to have an understanding of the process and nature of advanced inquiry. Therefore, at least three times a term, I spend 20 to 30 minutes of class time describing one of my research projects that ties into the course topic at hand. I try to capture the students' attention by prefacing my remarks with something like this: "One reason for attending business school at a leading research university is that you will be exposed to cutting-edge material, often before that material is in the public domain." I always enjoy these discussions, and it seems that the students do as well; these research presentations are consistently favorably noted in my course evaluations. This is a delight to me because it signifies the benefits of direct cross-pollination between research and teaching.

However, some risks are associated with being exceedingly expert on a topic you are teaching. The chief risk is that you will lose all sight of what a newcomer to the material most needs to know and how it is best imparted. I am feeling some of this frustration right now with a new course I am teaching, Executive Resources and Firm Performance. This is an experimental MBA elective course, the first one I have ever designed specifically around my major research interests. My problem is that I know too much about this domain. So, I find myself assigning too many readings, discussing advanced concepts without first covering more fundamental issues, and drawing the students to nuances when they need to comprehend more basic patterns. A basic challenge in teaching is to draw a distinction between what you know about a subject and what is important for your students to know. The more you know, the more complicated this challenge.

A second risk, related to the first, is that in-depth knowledge about a topic may cause a teacher to focus on minutiae, special cases, conditional circumstances, and subtleties—all the things the scholar loves and knows to be true about the matter at hand. It is hard to forsake the points of subtlety if we know them to be the case. But very often, they are not the most important or useful information to convey to students.

In sum, I am very high on the synergies between research and teaching. I encourage any teacher to be more assertive in bringing the world of scholarship into the classroom. The risks of swamping students with the arcane should always be borne in mind, but those risks can be managed. The benefits can be substantial, both for the students and the teacher.

One friend says with exasperation,

> Business schools are having thrust upon them all sorts of metaphorical models for conceiving of themselves. They're supposed to think of themselves as stores, with the faculty as merchandise and the students as customers. They're supposed to think of themselves as factories, with the faculty as craftsmen and the students as products. I have an idea: How about if we think of ourselves as *schools!* The teachers will be teachers and the students will be students.

This plaint resonates with me. We are supposed to be teachers. And I am aware that by introducing one more metaphor—the teacher as leader—I run the risk of confusing our role in yet one more way. But I worry not at all about this. Great teaching has *all* the qualities of great leadership. Indeed, they are not separable images. Our students will be well served when we merge them in our philosophies and actions as educators.

### Notes

1. I applied to Ph.D. programs when I graduated from college (Uncle Sam had other plans for me), when I completed my military tour (a Harvard MBA seemed more practical), and after I finished my MBA (I decided I needed a paycheck). Somewhere in a basement at Northwestern is a particularly thick file on me and my false steps toward a doctorate.

2. Yes, the Northwestern file grew some more.

### Reference

Bennis, W. (1989). *Why leaders can't lead.* San Francisco: Jossey-Bass.

# IV

## Leading the Learning Experience

Effective leadership is most useful under conditions of uncertainty and ambiguity, when novelty is needed and rehearsed, or when programmed responses to stimuli will not work. Leadership is needed, too, when a reality that is not yet apparent to the followers or even to the leaders must be invented, discovered, conveyed, and incorporated into the repertoires of those involved. Leadership is useful also for creating conditions in which excitement about and commitment to ideas and applications need to occur. Many of the authors in this book talk implicitly or explicitly about leading and the learning experience. Afsaneh Nahavandi (Chapter 12) and Donald Hambrick (Chapter 15) directly link teaching and leading activities and processes. Other authors have discussed ways to help students grasp new ideas and knowledge, to find meaning in the material being learned, and to think about phenomena in very different ways. There is little here to suggest that leading learning is either an authoritarian or a laissez-faire process. Even the most apparently unstructured approaches to teaching others have some underlying intention and order to them, although no one here seems to be suggesting that the teacher/leader knows all the answers or even all the questions to ask about what is being learned.

In this section, the eloquence and insights of Peter Vaill, Karl Weick, and Darlyne Bailey help us see the richness and variety that can be associated with leading the learning experience. The reader will find echoes here of ideas expressed by many of our other authors.

Peter Vaill connects teaching and leading quite directly. "All management is people management, and all leadership is people leadership. The reason for this is that there is nothing that a manager or a leader can do that does not depend for its effectiveness on the meaning that other people attach to it." If students are unable to attach meaning to what the teacher is communicating and vice versa, it is unlikely that much learning will take place. Vaill's priority is to engage in conversations about organizational behavior with students (he calls them participants). His aim is to engender in them the same fascination and passion he has for the subject. He is unabashed in arguing that organizational behavior, as a discipline, has an exceedingly wide reach.

Karl Weick uses rich narratives to reveal meanings and connections among diverse concepts and to link them to the personal lives of his students. He discusses the importance of creating conditions for learning that are challenging yet sufficiently safe to allow both teacher and student to take risks in their learning. Participants are thus able to move beyond simply reproducing already overlearned responses that mask the fact that they are repeating old ideas in a new setting. Leadership of learning, from Weick's perspective, requires that both teacher and student have the courage to engage in learning in public.

Darlyne Bailey's intention as a teacher is to develop in her students an appreciation of the importance of dialogue ("an interactive act of creation"). She brings into focus a spiritual dimension of teaching that is implicit in other chapters in the book. Developing dialogue with students as a "teacher-learner" involves awareness of the need for humility (recognizing "just how naive and truly *interdependent* on one another . . . we all are"); faith, a willingness to trust in the inherent goodness of the world, thus allowing people to take risks in their learning; hope, that joining with others in learning will lead to a better, more enlightened world; and love, as unconditional caring for all others, which Bailey sees as "at the heart of our choice to be educators."

These provocative authors provide differing yet interconnected ways of thinking about the learning process. Each has an intriguing vision for education, and each strives to model the essentials of his or her beliefs. All are willing to take risks with what they teach and with what they reveal of themselves to students. They all lead by example as much as through the content of their courses.

 **16** Meditations on a
Poet's Overalls

PETER B. VAILL

## Introduction

When the editors invited me to contribute to this volume, I thought
it would be an easy and enjoyable writing assignment and accepted
their invitation immediately. The task intrigued me because, although
I had spent thousands of hours thinking, talking, and musing in my
journal about teaching, I had never taken the time to spell out my basic
attitude and ideas about it. I also was reminded, as the editors' invitation began to settle into my mind, that some of the most interesting
and, I think, valuable things I have ever written were as contributions
to edited volumes of original essays (Vaill, 1971a, 1973, 1978, 1983,
1984, 1985, 1989b, 1990a, 1993). Such pieces have the virtues of being
brief enough to complete in a fairly short period of time and being
likely to get fairly wide distribution, without the feelings (to me at
least) of struggle and powerlessness that go with playing the refereed
journal game. Finally, the opportunity to appear in print with the other
contributors to this volume was very attractive.

Most of the above assumptions, except for the pleasure of appearing in this company, have proved to be wrong. If you are reading this chapter, it means that I did get it done and that it was above the editors' threshold of minimum acceptable quality. But it also means that what follows is not at all what I expected it would be when I accepted the assignment and that I'm not sure I would have accepted the assignment had I known the task was going to be this difficult.

Simply put, I was not able to extract from the flow of my career a written statement of my philosophy of teaching that I felt good about. Everything I tried felt wordy and preachy, abstract, unauthentic, and basically banal. I thought I would be able to write systematically about my approach to teaching, but I could not. As an INFP on the Myers-Briggs Type Indicator, I am not a very systematic person in the first place. More particularly with respect to my teaching, I am not able systematically to account for an academic career that reached 32 years as of mid-1994—a career that furthermore has been marked from the beginning with a great deal of personal intensity, variety, creativity, and, I think, achievement.

In my favorite poem, "Corson's Inlet" (which I managed to get *Organizational Dynamics* to publish in the summer of 1986 as an extraordinary example of systems thinking), the poet faces the same problem and concludes in this excerpt as I have:

> I allow myself eddies of meaning:
> yield to a direction of significance
> running
> like a stream through the geography of my work:
> you can find
> in my sayings
> swerves of action
> like the inlet's cutting edge:
> there are dunes of motion,
> organizations of grass, white sandy paths of remembrance
> in the overall working of mirroring mind:
> but Overall is beyond me: is the sum of these events
> I cannot draw, the ledger I cannot keep, the accounting
> beyond the account:
>
> *Ammons, 1977, p. 43*[1]

"Overall," I'm afraid, is beyond me too. Somehow, though, amid all the false starts that plagued this chapter, I managed to stumble my way to a fairly simple yet basic question: As someone who stands in front of groups of people and offers ideas about organizational behavior and leads discussions of it and suggests activities that will stimulate further discussion—who "teaches," as we say—what do I think I am doing in the midst of all of this? What am I displaying about me, and what am I hoping will happen to all of us involved in the process? It wasn't my official philosophy of teaching in the sense of a worked-out doctrine I was after, but a more implicit image or frame of what all this activity has really been *about* for me. What is its validity for me? How can I keep doing it without boredom or shame or anxiety?

These questions can be asked of any occupation or career, I am sure, but I have never before asked them very insistently of myself. One reason I have not is that, at some deep level, I am OK with this way of spending my life professionally. Lots of things are wrong with the field of organizational behavior and with the actual human behavior that is the basis of the field; and certainly plenty about my way of being a professional academic is far from perfect. But, I think I can say quite honestly that I have never regretted involving myself in this work. It keeps meeting my needs—all of them. For me, being a professor of organizational behavior is "autotelic" (self-justifying). I realize it is a wonderful blessing to be able to say that after 32 years at any occupation. It is not something I particularly think I can take much credit for, but for however it has been possible for me to sustain a high level of interest and engagement in this work, I am very grateful.

Before I discuss what I think I am doing as a teacher, I need to say more about the kinds of settings I work in. My main activity has always been classroom teaching in schools of business and management, of which I have served on the faculties of five. Mostly I have worked with MBA and Ph.D. students, but I have taught perhaps half a dozen undergraduate courses over the years and have been a guest speaker in many other undergraduate courses. The MBA and Ph.D. students I have worked with have been predominantly adult students going to school on a part-time basis. I think this involvement with older students going part-time has profoundly shaped my attitudes about teaching and about my field—something I will say more about below. Another important characteristic of the students I have worked with is that they have not been only business students. I have taught hundreds of students in educational administration, public and military administration, health services administration, and nonprofit voluntary associations, usually because of their enrollment in business courses as electives. My students, furthermore, have come from all over the world because I have, for the most part, worked at quite cosmopolitan universities. Once again, my perspective is strongly influenced by the challenge and opportunity of making my ideas about organizational behavior relevant across this range of institutions and cultures.

Beyond the ivory tower, out there in that mythical "real world," I have functioned as a teacher/speaker/presenter/workshop leader/ facilitator on the average of at least 2 or 3 times a month for my entire career. I think I have been involved with just about every type of organization one could name, including many outside the United States. The opportunity to present my ideas to working adults who are my peers rather than my students has been an unbelievably stimulating experience. Not only has it shaped and tempered my style as a presenter, but I can also truthfully say that all my best ideas about leadership, management, and organizational behavior have arisen, not in college classrooms, but "out there" in the world of work, talking about the live issues of leadership and management in real organizations. I would not claim that all this experience is the same as 9-to-5 employment as a leader/manager in an organization, but in its own way all this presenting has taught me many of the same lessons and has regularly brought me into close contact with the very men and women whom I am professing about back in the university.

I should also note that, throughout my academic career, I have almost always been an administrator concurrently, usually with little or no course relief. I have been a dean, an associate dean, a department chair, academic director of various degree programs, and chair of various major administrative committees. As a nontenured assistant professor at UCLA, I was the head of the Behavioral Science group in the Graduate School of Management with the rather remarkable title of Acting Associate Vice Chairman—a title that captured quite nicely the relative impotence of academic managers!

To capture the diversity of my experience in this chapter, I do not use the words *teacher* and *student* and *classroom* to talk about my work. I refer to myself as a *presenter,* to those I am presenting to as *participants,* and to the settings in which I am doing it as *sessions.* These words, for me, do better justice to the range of my experiences and to the fact that so many important learnings have occurred outside my role as a teacher of students in classrooms.

## A Conversation and Three Motives

Let's get back to the main focus of this chapter. What do I think I am doing with all this presenting to all these different participants in all these different kinds of sessions? This, as I said, is a question I have never asked myself very insistently before. As soon as I asked the question, though, a broad answer came very quickly, undergirded by three motives that also popped into my mind almost immediately. I know that I carry this broad answer and these three motives into every session I conduct as a presenter regardless of who the participants are or what the occasion is. What I'm after, what I think I am engaging in, is a *conversation about human beings as they are in organizations.* The key term here is *conversation.*[2] I am sure that, at times, my behavior in a session seems to be at the outer limits of what a conversational style could be—either lecturing in a one-way mode ad nauseam or acting so laid-back and hardly "present" as to cause participants to wonder whether I'm paying attention at all. But my inner image of what's going on, regardless of my outward demeanor, is that we're having a conversation about organizational behavior.

I can sharpen my meaning by saying what images I do not have of what I am doing, images I personally reject even though they are all respectable and plenty of my colleagues may hold one or more. I am not, in the first place, literally "instructing." Instructing—"structuring in"—is almost the opposite of what I think I am doing. For me, the word means about the same thing as *indoctrination.* I am horrified if someone perceives me as indoctrinating, and I become depressed when a participant reveals a desire to *be* indoctrinated. I also reject, for the most part, a softer meaning of *instruction* that many might subscribe to—the teaching of theory and models and concepts and ways of thinking. Certainly, we talk about theory and concepts and ways of thinking in sessions where I am presenting, but my inner image of what I am doing is using a preexisting idea as a way to start the conversation, not as a way to end it or as necessarily the main subject of the conversation. Many academic friends would be shocked to discover how unimportant I think most of our theories are except as vehicles to get further thinking and conversation started, although some, I'm sure, would say they've always suspected it about me.

"Instruction" focuses, for me, on what the current theory is. In its drive to get theories and concepts and models ("the material") effectively presented—"covered," as we say—instruction often forgets two other categories that are of equal or even greater importance, especially to a manager or leader. One is the issue or problem that gave rise to the theory, why the problem is a problem and how it gets framed. The other is the processes of thought and action by which the theory was created (theorizing). For me, theorizing has always been at least as important as the theory or model that results. Bear in mind, though, that my participants are men and women preparing for leadership in unstable and rapidly changing environments where the issues hardly ever bear much resemblance to the problems that gave rise to published theories. My participants have to be able to theorize as they go along. Theorizing processes are almost never effectively presented to participants, even in Ph.D. programs.

"Conversation," for me, is more likely to give balanced attention to all three legs of the stool: problems/issues, theorizing and modeling processes, and resulting working theory. Because conversation is both more democratic and more free-flowing, it is easier for any of these categories to surface and receive attention in the real time of the conversation.

So, I am not an instructor. I am also not a therapist. To say I am not a therapist raises a tough issue for me and, I suspect, for many other presenters on human behavior subjects. The issues we deal with in organizational behavior can be explosive. They can be upsetting. They can cause crises of meaning and values both in me and in participants. It can be argued quite persuasively that if a presenter is going to deal with matters that are disturbing to participants, he or she has to be willing to help them work through not only the ideas but also the personal feelings, especially the anxieties these matters trigger. I agree with this and am willing to help as much as I can. But I don't think of myself as professionally qualified to help, and I struggle with how far my responsibilities go. Many painful dilemmas arise for participants when all I can say is, "Yes, I can see how you feel." Sometimes that itself is helpful, but sometimes it is not enough.

I hope I am communicating here; I fear that I may sound callous or cavalier about what are, in fact, very deep issues. In saying that my image is of a conversation, but one in which I am not a therapist, I am saying that I want to push issues as far as they go both externally in their implications for organizations and internally in their implications for ourselves, and I want to give support and, I hope, to receive it in the process. But if the participants or I "get into trouble," if we are unable to process the feelings we are having and need help to bring us back into a condition that allows us to function by ourselves, I have only very limited ability to give that help, to others or to myself. I will give what help I can, but sometimes this means helping a participant or me find someone else who can be more thoroughly helpful than can I.

Not an instructor and not a therapist. I am also not an entertainer— something we're accused of a lot in management education, especially those of us who deal with the human behavior subject matter. I don't think it is my job to be personally entertaining, and I don't think my sessions should feel like "fun and games." I am able to be very entertaining, very dramatic, and often funny in the context of our conversations, and when I am being this way I like myself a lot. But my *focus* is on what we're talking about, not on being funny about it. I don't have to tell a joke to make my points—something I see a lot, particularly in training and development sessions in organizations.

The "entertainment factor" has skyrocketed in the world of work over the course of my career, but I don't think it has enhanced the quality of what is being presented. In fact, I would say that, as we have sought to make our graphics more "professional" and our "platform skills" more stylish, we have had to trivialize content. I wonder whether participants realize the shallowness of the content they're getting in the midst of all this glitzy instrumentation. Or let me put it a little more fairly: The trouble with some carefully crafted slide presentation or an elaborate computer-based interactive exercise or a book that is really a indoctrination machine even though it looks like a book is that participants can't have a *conversation* about it or with it. They can't modify it. They can't affect it, teach IT anything. All they can do is experience it from the outside as a closed system of ideas embodied there on the screen or in the four-color, 800-page textbook. They can't participate in it; in fact, they really are no longer participants; they are passive consumers *even if the system is interactive!*

I would probably reject other roles and images as part of the conversation I want to have with participants, but these three modes of instructor, therapist, and entertainer—and their combinations—will do for now. To say more positively what I think I'm doing as a presenter-conversationalist with participants, I need to describe the three motives that underlie my image of a conversation. These motives are what drive me as a presenter.

## Fascination With the Subject

A professor, so the old joke goes, is a person who believes that the human race would be a great deal better off if it just knew a little more about his/her subject. Ever since I sat in the Harvard Business School's [beginning] course in 1958-59, I have believed this about Organizational Behavior. I simply can't imagine an academic field which lacks any of the components of OB: its interest in action and its connections to the world of affairs; its eclectic intellect and relative freedom from preoccupations with the fine differences between psychology, sociology, philosophy, history, political science, and economics; its pragmatic approach to methodology and avoidance of formalism; its devotion to fostering true learning in the student and the experimental spirit this has produced; its location in management schools where, in my opinion, most of the "action" has been for the last quarter century; its fundamental concern with the person. These characteristics have been articles of faith for me, the source of the high quality pleasures and pains which I think go with being fully alive. OB has been attacked by many, but if it really is a cancer on the *corpus universitas,* then I plead guilty to having been four-square a carcinogen. (Vaill, 1979, p. 3)

Organizational behavior as an academic discipline has always encompassed a huge range of subject matter. I have never had any trouble getting interested in all of it.[3] For purposes of this chapter, though, I focus on a few aspects of the field that are especially important to me as a presenter and that infuse all the thinking, speaking, and writing I do on the subject of "OB." When I am having one of my "conversations" as a presenter, the few themes described below are winding through my awareness in endless permutations and manifestations.

When I arrived at the Harvard Business School in the fall of 1958 as a new MBA, I had no plans for an academic career, nor had I any awareness—despite an undergraduate major in political psychology—of the application of the social sciences to formal organizations. I went to Harvard because I was fascinated with administrative processes on college campuses and because I wanted to be some kind of an educational administrator.

Harvard had a required course in its first-year curriculum called Administrative Practices. It was a yearlong course meeting in three 80-minute sessions per week, and it was almost exclusively taught by the case method of instruction. Taking this course meant that three times a week for about 35 weeks, my 80 section-mates and I chewed over some practical problem of leadership, management, and organization as described in a written case. I was only an average student, at best, in all my other courses in the Harvard MBA program and alternated between the states of confusion and cold fear most of the time. In Administrative Practices, though ("Ad Prac," we called it), I thrived. I loved the cases, loved the class discussions, loved the *ideas* about organizations and human behavior that kept bubbling up out of parts of myself I hadn't known existed, hung on Professor Charlie Orth's relatively few words from class to class, and even found myself predicting quite accurately what he was going to say about one case or another. Harvard's normally terrifying exam format of a sit-down, timed, written analysis of a case was, for me, an opportunity under a little pressure to push myself to deeper insights and more interesting ways of saying things than I might otherwise have achieved. Vain as it may sound, I believed that my bluebooks would be learning experiences for the graders.

Despite the intensely competitive atmosphere of the Harvard MBA program, I also found that I knew how to be a "star" in this course in a way that was interesting rather than irritating to my student-colleagues. It would have been easy for me to come to be perceived as a show-off and an apple-polisher or a hopeless "behavior wonk," but this did not happen. I mention this because my desire to act collegially is my second major motive as a presenter, to be discussed at greater length in a moment.

My perception is that the fundamental rationale of the case method is to give learners experience in thinking through complex, true-life organizational problems and coming to a decision about what they would do next and why if they were the key executive in the case. In many ways, this learning can fail to occur. One, students can fail to take the case seriously and never really experience the imperatives and painful dilemmas the case presents. Such students frequently say things like, "I'd never have gotten into this mess in the first place." Two, the student can become preoccupied with hearing the "school solution" and thus miss the personal puzzling and thinking-through process the case invites and, not having made the struggle, then ironically fail to appreciate the wisdom of any school solution that might be offered. Some students can get lost in analyzing the data and never make it to a decision point. Others are saddled with an instructor who doesn't know how to help them avoid any of these traps. Three, for both students and faculty, some very attractive theory seems to explain what has gone wrong and how to make it right, with the result that the discussion becomes occupied with fitting the case data into the theory's categories. Once again, the uniqueness and ineffability of *this case* gets missed, and over time, students become desensitized to the empirical nuances of particular situations. More important, they become desensitized to ethical nuances.

None of this happened to me in Ad Prac, although these distorting forces were operating and indeed did capture many of my colleagues. In a way that I can't explain very well, though, I did get it: I understood and fairly quickly internalized the link between theory and data and action as it plays out in human relationships in organizations. Somehow, I saw that it was not "one right answer," but rather a mood, posture, and way of being that would mark the approach of whoever was going to act in the particular situation. It had to be personal. It had to be a way of *living* with oneself and in relation to others. It couldn't be just a "style." The fabled "course of action" one was supposed to develop could not, in other words, be an artificial suit of clothes that one merely donned for this "managerial occasion."

From the outset, then, my interest in organizational behavior was a blend of the academic, the practical, and the personal, and this early integration has stayed with me throughout my career. My fascination is in the *intersection* of the academic, the practical, and the personal. I have never been so interested in theory that I forgot that some person was going to have to find it meaningful enough to let it infect his or her action in a real situation. And I have never been so interested in a practical problem that I thought it could not be illuminated by theory and research. Nor is it just personal growth and personal expression that we can be content with—an attitude, by the way, that was a bit out of step with the prevailing climate in the Southern California of the 1960s where I assumed my first academic position.

My fascination and my energy are in the balancing and the interrelating of the academic, the practical, and the personal modes. Whatever is distinctive about me as a presenter and as a person derives primarily from this synthesis. It is the key to my ability to work across a wide variety of organizations with a great diversity of participants concerned with a wide range of types of human problems using a pastiche of theories and research findings of my own and others.

One other thing I got from those early years at Harvard: I realized that *all* the cases we were given in *all* our courses were varieties of organizational behavior. This fact was not stressed by the faculty, although I am sure many of the OB faculty felt the same way. Certainly, it was not granted by the great majority of the other subject matter professors. But it was clear to me as I read through the cases. Over the years, I have been able to formulate this insight with increasing clarity. I put my current best statement of the idea in my first book:

> All management is people management, and all leadership is people leadership. The reason for this is that there is nothing that a manager or a leader can do that does not depend for its effectiveness on the meaning that other people attach to it. How and why people attach meanings to things, how and why these meanings change, and how and why people's meanings and people's actions are interconnected are the subjects that managers and leaders should be concerned with. (Vaill, 1989a, p. 126)

I am fond of saying to my students, "You think you're majoring in accounting," for example, "but you're actually majoring in human behavior in organizations where the vocabulary that people use and the concepts that they employ are from the accounting profession. You are not exempt, though, from understanding all this as forms of human behavior in organizations and accommodating this fact in your practice of these ideas toward and with other people." I believe this statement is true for every academic subject. I can't say that I get wild agreement and effusive thanks from students or faculty, but I like to think that some, anyway, get the point.

The experiences I talk about here were as an MBA student. My doctoral work was hardly an afterthought, but it did build on this basic posture toward the phenomena that I got as an MBA. I have said many times since that I think a solid MBA experience should be a prerequisite for anyone planning an academic career in organizational behavior. I became a doctoral student and settled on an academic career because I wanted to keep thinking about these insights I had had as an MBA.

I began doctoral work at Harvard in the summer of 1960. The year 1960 was one of those storied moments in fields of knowledge when forces that had been building up for 20 years or more rather suddenly coalesce in a new set of frameworks, research questions, and controversies. In a memo to his Harvard colleagues that summer, Fritz Roethlisberger tried to synthesize all these trends by proposing the content and the boundaries of a new academic field that he suggested be named "Organizational Behavior." Major statements by Argyris and McGregor (Argyris, 1957; McGregor [1957] in Boone & Bowen, 1987, pp. 126-138) were still not very well digested. The first statement of so-called situational leadership by Bob Tannenbaum and Warren Schmidt had appeared in 1958 in the *Harvard Business Review* (Boone & Bowen, 1987). McGregor's (1960) book was just out and beginning to have its revolutionary effect on both academicians and practicing managers. The field was already abuzz with basic new theories, published or forthcoming, of Likert (1961), Blake (Blake & Mouton, 1964), Herzberg (Herzberg et al., 1959), Bennis (Bennis, Benne, & Chin, 1961), the Tannenbaum group at UCLA (Tannenbaum, Wechsler, & Massarik, 1961), and Trist (Trist, Higgin, Murray, & Pollock, 1963). Homans, in a dramatic (and, to the Business School faculty, somewhat shocking) reversal, abandoned the theory that had made him famous for a decade (Homans, 1950) and, rather loudly and dogmatically, adopted Skinnerian operant conditioning theories as explanations for interpersonal and group behavior (Homans, 1961). Maslow, it seemed, issued an exciting new book every year or two (Maslow, 1962, 1964, 1965).

Altogether, this was a lot for a new doctoral student to digest. For me, though, the ideas of Carl Rogers had the greatest impact (Rogers, 1961). His connection to the Mayo-Roethlisberger tradition at Harvard is too complex to discuss here (see Athos & Gabarro, 1978; Turner & Lombard, 1969), but his ideas about nondirective listening and how acceptance of another person would foster learning and growth and change in them excited me like nothing I had ever encountered before. I studied the self theories and the perceptual psychology of Rogers and others (e.g., Bugental, 1965; Combs & Snygg, 1959; Goffman, 1959; Jourard, 1964; May, 1953; Moustakas, 1956) more thoroughly and intensively than anything else I did as a doctoral student. Following the lead of Roethlisberger and George Lombard in particular, I thought I had hold of a set of ideas that helped me (a) understand the leader-manager as a person, (b) understand how and why the leader-manager did or did not understand others (c) understand how a leader-manager might improve his or her understanding of self and others and while doing all this, (d) retain my own "humanness" as a person and let the leader-manager retain his or hers since all we had were our own and each other's perceptions of the world. Finally, these ideas of Rogers' and his colleagues gave me a way to (e) do research that I liked and could do pretty well: "organizational research" was not "fact gathering," but instead was the process of developing my own perceptions of the perceptions that organization members had of themselves, of each other, of their organizations, *and* of me.

It has to be quite an extraordinary set of theoretical ideas and research findings to cover the five functions I have just mentioned. The orientation toward the phenomena fostered by these ideas is something I carry everywhere with me. In the language of chaos theory, Rogers's idea that everyone has a unique, personal point of view that has validity and is of intrinsic interest is my "strange attractor": I come back to it again and again in my presentations, my research, and my writing.

One other set of ideas I encountered in my doctoral years has continued to energize my thinking and my ability to work effectively with participants. I refer to what is known as *general semantics,* a school of thought created by Alfred Korzybski in the 1930s and popularized by Wendell Johnson, Irving Lee, and S. I. Hayakawa (Hayakawa, 1963; Johnson, 1946; Korzybski, 1958; Lee, 1952). Hayakawa's interpretations were particularly memorable. General Semantics is too complex to discuss here, but what it did was give me a way to understand just *how* the communicative function of language can be affected by the psychological needs of the user. General Semantics put meat on the bones of the idea that we frequently use language to bamboozle both others *and* ourselves, painting ourselves into verbal corners without even realizing it. As such, these ideas fit beautifully with Rogers's ideas because his philosophy and method depend on our being able to understand what the other person *means,* even if expressed in a very interior and personal way. General Semantics was also invaluable in helping me understand how people were and were not able to communicate successfully with each other in organizations.

In the ensuing 30 years, my interests have gone in many directions that I could not have foreseen as a student. I have spent much time on *organization development (OD)*, a term I never heard as a doctoral student (Vaill, 1971a, 1971b, 1973, 1983, 1989b). Leadership has become more and more interesting to me. I spent 15 years fascinated by what I called "high performing systems" (Vaill, 1978, 1982, 1989a, chap. 3). I have gotten very interested in turbulence and accelerating rates of change—what I call "permanent white water," although I can trace my interest back 20 years to Eric Trist's early work (Emery & Trist, 1964; Vaill, 1989a, chap. 1). Since the late 1980s, I have become increasingly interested in spiritual issues in organizational leadership (Vaill, 1989a, chap. 14; 1990a; 1990b). Throughout all of these evolving interests, though, my early fascinations continue to manifest themselves.

As a presenter, all these fascinations from my early years in the field take the form of being able to get easily interested in the organizational worlds of participants and in their particular interpretations of these worlds. They take the form of me trying to make various organizational worlds interesting to participants, trying to offer interesting and unusual interpretations of what is going on in these worlds. It is easy for me to remember, given my fascinations, that participants want to *do* things in these worlds; they want to "succeed" in these worlds, which leads me to work with them on the various things *succeed* can mean and what the pros and cons of various images of success might be. My fascinations take the form of me trying to cook up new ways for participants to *experience* organizational worlds, which has led me to being an advocate and, I think, an innovator in what is known as *experiential education*.

In this section, I have tried to portray myself as a person who exudes an intense, if somewhat unconventional, interest in organizational behavior. Although these ideas are central to my thinking about organizational behavior, only occasionally do I directly discuss and argue for the bodies of thought I have sketched above. In a curious way, the three-way synthesis I have said is my passion works against writing purely academic analyses of these theoretical ideas. I feel them and express them, but I have not been as motivated to talk about them for their own sake. This chapter is the first time I have tried to put them down in any connected way. The main thing I want to convey, though, is how powerfully they influence everything I do as a presenter. I practice the three-way synthesis by formulating original ideas and insights that I share with participants. But without the background ideas mentioned above, or with only a passing familiarity with them, I could not possibly have had the insights I have had, and I am certain I could not have served participants nearly so well.

## Collegiality

The second motive that I bring to my work as a presenter is a desire for a collegial relationship with participants. The role of "classroom professor" provides one of the last true thrones of Western society regardless of the motives or values of whoever plays the role. I have spent my entire career trying to reduce the power and status imbalance between myself and participants—particularly university students over whom I hold the power of the grade. I do not mind evaluating people, and I do not mind being held accountable for the grades and other evaluations that I give—by students, occasionally by parents or employers, even by courts on a few occasions. What I do not like are all the ways the academic environment (whether in the university or the training room at the workplace) disempowers the learner, makes the learner dependent on me the presenter, and diverts the learner's attention from what can be learned to what I-the-presenter apparently want the learner to learn. Whatever accountability I hold for myself toward the learner is accountability I personally have had to define. The structure of the system is one in which I-the-presenter am not accountable to the learner in any material way. Officially, the learner is pretty much at my mercy. (Granted, this gross imbalance is changing, but not very fast and not very much—certainly not enough to keep up with the extraordinary decline, over the past 20 years, in the credibility of my profession.)

In a system organized to shield me from true accountability, yet with me being a person who believes in it, my resolution has been to act as collegially as I can toward participants. As anyone who has tried it knows, the attempt to be personally collegial in an environment of great power imbalance leads one into all sorts of puzzling and uncomfortable situations. I would be the first to say that I am a continual learner and a very uneven performer of real collegiality. Some of my friends and former participants might even be astonished to learn that I've been trying!

Real collegiality is the key to these conversations I say I am trying to have. As the one who starts with most of the authority and power in a session, it becomes my task to take the initiative to try to ameliorate all the factors that the traditional hierarchical model of education has built in over the centuries. These factors include whom I let into my sessions and what "prerequisites" I require of them; how the room is set up; how we address each other; how much we discover about each other as persons; how much personal interest I take in participants and model for them to take in each other; how much "required work" I put in and how I present the requirements; how I conduct myself in real-time interchanges with participants, particularly when they want to take exception to what I am saying; how I evaluate performance and what kind of participation I invite in the evaluation process; and how I respond to the inevitable exigencies of a particular session where one participant or another will need a special favor, exemption from a requirement, and so on. These are a few topics where collegiality can be developed or suppressed.

Most generally, I think we are talking about freedom: Can I act in such a way that freedom is felt by participants? The kind of freedom I am talking about is not a laissez-faire, do-whatever-you-please atmosphere. Rather, I want participants to need to spend as little energy as possible figuring out how to "play the game" of one of my sessions. For me, the "game" is that there is no game apart from our mutual engagement with each other through the subject matter. My hope is that this will free participants to focus on the subject matter that brings us together. So, I try for as much clarity and fairness and negotiability as I can in whatever requirements I do have to impose. I work very hard at assigning or suggesting activities that are intrinsically interesting and that invite, even require, a lot of individual embellishment.

I suspect that these ideas will resonate with many of my academic and professional colleagues in the OB/OD field. A healthier, more collegial relationship with students and other participants has been a core value of this teaching field for 30 years or more.[4] Yet, I also have to say that I am not comfortable with my progress in this area. I have to work harder to achieve a feeling of collegiality today than I did when I was closer to my participants in age and when the idea of collegiality in the learning setting was more in the air as a desirable thing. I remain as committed as ever to being a co-learner with participants and to acting like one, but the vision I have of what that might actually be like seems more remote, and the pursuit of the vision feels more of a strain.

This unfulfilled vision has been having a good news/bad news consequence for me. Unlike many other subjects, the OB/OD material, being about what goes right and wrong among human beings, is alive right there in the session. The question for me and for any presenter is, Am I walking the talk? Am I honoring the behavioral principles I am talking about in my own behavior toward participants? I quote here from an earlier essay that makes this point quite nicely:

> Since a significant portion of the subject matter has been about improving human relationships, the subject matter has acted back on the modes of teaching and research and intervention themselves. It is one thing to teach traditionally about participation and quite another to teach participatively about participation. . . . It is hard to be ethically powerful about the ethics of power, hard to be accepting of feedback about one's lecture on feedback. (Vaill, 1985, p. 549)

Even when I did not feel gaps of age and culture between myself and participants, I was never very satisfied with my ability to walk the talk, or even to "stumble to mumble," as a friend at a government agency likes to say. As time has gone on, as I say, it feels more and more difficult. That's the bad news. Yet, ironically, this increasing difficulty in walking the talk has also had a positive effect on my ability to act collegially. Collegiality is about humility to a greater degree than I realized when I was younger. In fact, collegiality without humility can easily turn into condescension. My very feelings of awkwardness in behaving collegially across age and culture gaps empower my collegiality. The main thing, as with all attempts to attain an authentic relationship with another person, is not to give up just because it is so difficult. In my case as a presenter, it is tempting to fall back into the cocoon of eminence and authority that society grants me as a senior academic. But to take that fallback is to sacrifice an open collegial relationship with participants in my sessions.

Just to tie this to the main point of this section: If I give up my desire for a collegial relationship with participants, I think the fascination with the subject I discussed earlier is much less likely to have the energizing effect on participants that I want it to have; and it is more likely that my fascinations will just increasingly be seen as rather arcane and superannuated.

## The Same Two Motivations for Participants

I have said that what I bring in the first instance to the conversation I want to have with participants is my fascination with the subject matter; and second, I bring a desire for a particular relationship with them—an adult, collegial relationship wherein participants are not distracted from their learning opportunities by the "noise" of my authority or eminence. What I want for them is the third thing. The best way to express it is to say that I hope, as a result of sessions where I am a presenter, that participants will become fascinated in their own ways with this incredibly rich and diverse field of organizational behavior and that they will see that this field tends to encourage and inspire a collegial attitude toward others rather than an exploitative or a scientifically objective attitude.

Let's explore in more detail each of these two things I want for participants.

Under what conditions might a participant become fascinated with the OB/OD material? That has been a career-long question for me. Doubtless, there are many different conditions, but one that stands out in my experience is when the material I am presenting connects to experiences participants have had, puzzles they have *felt* about human behavior, areas that are "charged" for them with personal significance. It is somewhat banal to say that learners are captivated by material that is relevant to their experience. It is not so banal to declare that I take the *discovery* of relevance to the learner to be my chief objective and responsibility as a presenter. It is an article of faith with me that the connection can be made. Here are a few examples:

- Convinced that everyone knows more about leadership than they may think they do, I have asked participants to think about leadership experiences that they had before the age of 12; I have gotten very rich and delightful results.
- To make my ideas about high performing systems more real, I ask participants to describe in their own language the nature of the best groups, teams, or organizations they have ever been a member of. They end up saying all the things I and others have merely said in more abstract ways.
- In relation to participants' familiarity with excellent organizations, I have discovered if you ask them to describe the most motivated person they have ever known, they will list most of the characteristics the literature mentions, and they will find themselves discussing the dark side of extremely high motivation as well as the positive aspects.

- Beginning management students need to learn that a "managerial point of view" is somewhat different from that of a detached observer, a nonmanagerial member of the system, or a client of the system. Early in a semester, all students have just gone through registration, with its frustrations and red tape. Most of them have not thought about the problem of registration of a diverse student body from a manager's point of view. I ask them to discuss the managerial challenges that each of their special circumstances presents the university—the G.I. Bill, foreign visas and currencies, part-time enrollment, transfer credits, advanced standing, course waivers, overloads, all kinds of different financial aid, and so on. Wallowing in the real managerial problems of university registration is an enlightening and sobering experience.

- Most presenters struggle with making "systems thinking" understandable and intriguing. I found it very difficult until I hit on the hypothesis that any activity that we know well, that we are intimately familiar with, we probably have a "systems view" of. We understand the complexities and interdependencies, what counts a lot and what counts less, how to tell when the system as a whole is in a stable state and when it is not, and so forth. Over the years, I've heard wonderful systems analyses of, for example, sailing a boat, cooking and serving a multi-course dinner, teaching foreign languages, hitting a golf ball, debugging software, building a house, training a dog, and writing a book. It is always an illumination and sometimes quite a shock to a participant to discover how much he or she already knows about systems thinking.

- Literally within 2 weeks of beginning my first teaching job at UCLA in 1964, I discovered that cases do not "work" as well outside the case-steeped Harvard environment. Without the external "case ideology" from the school and without the cutthroat competition with each other, UCLA MBAs did not put in enough time studying cases to get very much out of them. I thought UCLA's was a healthier climate than Harvard's, but I had to find ways of making cases more involving. I remembered that my case-*writing* experiences at Harvard had been actually more powerful than my case-reading, and so I began having MBAs write cases. This meant, then, that the case writer would be sitting in the class discussion where his or her case was discussed. The involvement and intensity reappeared. Having students write cases had the additional benefit of setting up a discussion of field research methods and how they might be useful to a manager. It also makes it very clear to students that a "case discussion" is really an inquiry into the perceptions and values of the case writer as well as the case characters.

- A few years later, I added a wrinkle that has become the most involving student exercise I have ever used. I ask students to write short 2- or 3-page cases on various subjects (e.g., teamwork). Six or seven students will produce short cases on that subject. I write commentaries of 100 to 200 words on each case and then feed the cases back to the class for discussion at the next session; at the end of the class session, I distribute my commentaries. This design produces "ownership" because we talk about cases that class members have written; it permits comparative discussion because a *set* of cases has been written on the topic; I have a chance in the commentary to direct the class's attention to various aspects of the cases that I think warrant special attention; and all the other benefits of the case method of instruction are retained. This format, repeated over 12 weeks or so, results in an extraordinary course and more than makes up for the lack of a "case tradition" in the school.

- I am conducting a new exercise with a cross-cultural management class in which I ask each student to formulate examples of "tacit knowledge" in his or her own culture ("what everybody understands"). The various examples that participants create each week are circulated to the whole group at the next session for 9 consecutive weeks. The point, of course, is to portray culture in all its richness, its concreteness, and its power. The first 24 contributions convince me that this is a very effective way to portray culture in terms that everyone can connect to. It is also an effective method of helping this diverse group of participants become acquainted with the subtleties of each other's cultures.

- Another exercise I invented for this cross-cultural management course is to ask participants to talk about the cultural significance of their names. The idea occurred to me originally because I was concerned about how little most Westerners know about the names of students from Asian countries. Because the names have no cultural meaning, Westerners can't remember them, can't associate them with personal qualities of the individuals possessing the names, and basically just "tune out" on this crucial matter. The exercise does help individuals' names become distinctive and meaningful, but I was surprised to discover that it also teaches a great deal about the culture a name comes from. I also learned that Asians have the same kind of trouble with Western names, so the benefit of the exercise is multidirectional.

- I use various instruments to make some behavioral concept real for participants. I, and I imagine many others, have used such instruments as the MBTI, FIRO-B, and Rokeach's Dogmatism Scale this way. But, I have found it even more powerful to create an instrument for a particular occasion, even involving participants in designing the items. The group then "takes" the test and discusses the results. It is important that participants understand I am not doing research to them or on them, but rather am helping them express things about themselves that we can all learn from.

I call it an article of faith that a connection can be made between the material I am presenting and the experience and concerns of the participant. I believe this to be true for all subject matter, but I am sure it is true for organizational behavior subject matter because organizational behavior is the stuff of existence for all of us.

Furthermore, I have another reason for using personal experience as a vehicle for presenting these ideas: A meta-objective of all teaching in this area is to help participants think differently about their future experience as a condition of increased effectiveness in leader-manager roles. It has become commonplace in the past few decades to say that we want leader-managers to be able to *reflect* more regularly and fruitfully about what is happening to them in their organizations. We know that modern organizations are not very friendly to reflection, given the pace at which things move, the competitiveness of the climate, and the pressure everyone is under to look good and never to be in doubt. Yet, reflection is more important than ever under these conditions. The more I can convince participants of the value of their personal experience for understanding organizational behavior, the more likely they will be to reflect creatively in the future. The question of how we can help participants become more reflective without undercutting their ability to act is a subject for a whole essay unto itself. Suffice it to say for the moment that the question is high on my list of priorities.

My first hope, then, is that participants become fascinated with organizational behavior. My second hope is that my presentations will help them understand and value collegiality in their relationships as a leader-manager with others. I said above that I think the field encourages and inspires a collegial attitude rather than an exploitative or a scientifically objective attitude. To be more accurate, I should say I want the field to encourage and inspire a collegial attitude; I want my presentations to strengthen the collegial attitudes that participants have toward others. My attitude is thus frankly normative. I don't conceive of myself as just presenting facts about organizational behavior. I don't think I can be value-neutral about these materials, and even if I can, I don't want to. The purpose of the field is a normative one—to improve human relationships in organizations and organizational effectiveness; the purposes of the schools that harbor the field are normative too; and participants' reasons for studying the field are also normative—to be more personally effective as leader-managers and to be mentally and spiritually healthier as well (even if participants don't phrase it that way). In view of this, I-the-presenter am not just a neutral instrument in the participants' quest.

But my role as a presenter is not just a license to preach my personal philosophy. I am responsible for grounding my thinking in the best research and theory I can find, and I am responsible for submitting my thinking to the criticisms of my professional colleagues, as well as to the participants in my sessions. This is why I view my presentations as conversations: They have to be conversations if the fine balance is to be discovered and kept among the impersonal theories and research findings of the field, my norms and ideals as a person, and the norms and ideals of participants. A session in organizational behavior is nothing other than the ongoing interactions of these diverse elements. What else can it be but a conversation?

I cannot compel a democratic spirit in participants. But, somewhere in his writings, Walter Lippmann once observed that the last 300 years of history is a history of the inevitable failure of unilateral power. I think our field of organizational behavior contains ample support for that idea as applied to organizations. I can't prove it; I can't—and wouldn't want to—force participants to believe it because it would be anticollegial to try to force belief in collegiality! But organizational effectiveness and personal well-being, I believe, are fostered more by collegiality than by unilateral control, for inevitably fear and game-playing ensue from unilateral control. What I can do is keep the question constantly before participants and try to help them see that one's attitude toward power and control should not be a matter of whim.

## Conclusion

"Overall is beyond me . . ." I quoted the poet Ammons as saying, and truly I have felt that as I have tried to describe my attitude toward teaching and other kinds of presentations. He finds a beautiful note of hope in this truth as he closes his poem, however, and it will help me close this chapter:

> I see narrow orders, limited tightness, but will
> not run to that easy victory:
>     still around the looser, wider forces work:
>     I will try
>   to fasten into order enlarging grasps of disorder, widening
> scope, but enjoying the freedom that
> Scope eludes my grasp, that there is no finality of vision,
> that I have perceived nothing completely,
>     that tomorrow a new walk is a new walk.

*Ammons, 1977, p. 46*

Each conversation is a "new walk," a walk I have been taking for my entire career with participants in my sessions in organizational behavior. I have said that within the broad framework of a conversation are three motives that are always present in my behavior as a presenter: (a) my own fascination with the subject matter, (b) my desire to achieve a genuinely collegial relationship with participants, and (c) my desire that participants acquire their own forms of these same two motives at least partly as a result of their presence in my sessions. Part of the "overall" that is beyond me is the question of whether I do any of this very well. I have the usual evidences that every presenter has of various strengths and weaknesses in my approach and my style, and I suppose it is true that I have never been so inept that I had to do something dramatic about it. Still, I don't know, really, whether I am consistently living out all the noble sentiments of this chapter or not. The motives and philosophy described in this chapter keep me going, and I guess that is about all I can ask—all I even *want* to ask.

Finally, a story that captures all the paradoxes of my experience as a presenter: Some years ago, I was invited to our medical school, where a group of young physicians was going through a Robert Wood Johnson Foundation program in "executive medicine"—that is, a crash course in everything else besides medicine one needs to know in order to be the leader of a health organization. Several medical school faculty were also in attendance. My job was to survey, in 2 days, the organizational behavior topics for them. I gave them 2 days of vintage Vaill and was feeling pretty good about the job I'd done. Then, in a last hour of free-flowing Q & A, the most senior faculty member rose in the back of the room and said something like this: "These two days have been really interesting. All these ideas about leadership and groups and organizations, technology, change, interpersonal skills. It is all obviously terribly important to anyone who wants to run an organization successfully. But let me make sure I understand something. Over in the business school . . . do you actually give academic credit for this stuff?"

All kinds of learned answers went through my mind concerning the nature of science, the differences between biomedical and social science, theory and practice, the dilemmas of action-takers in live situations—all the things my life and this chapter have been about. But, time was short, so all I said to my interlocutor was, "Yes."

# Notes

1. In her keynote to the 1993 National Meetings of the Organization Development Network, Margaret Wheatley read the last stanza of this poem as the epilogue to her remarks. I have included the same stanza at the end of this chapter.

2. Gareth Morgan (1983) makes research a conversation in the same spirit.

3. I realize that others are not as interested. The field, in fact, has theories about why people have trouble thinking flexibly and imaginatively about organizational behavior. If everyone were as knowledgeable and skillful as our theories say they need to be, we wouldn't need the field!

4. A wonderful early discussion of the dilemmas of creating a collegial learning climate in a power-oriented academic setting can be found in Roethlisberger et al. (1954).

# References

Ammons, A. R. (1977). Corson's Inlet. In *The selected poems 1951-1977*. New York: Norton.

Argyris, C. (1957). *Personality and organization*. New York: Harper.

Athos, A. G., & Gabarro, J. J. (Eds.). (1978). *Interpersonal behavior: Communication and understanding in relationships*. Englewood Cliffs, NJ: Prentice Hall.

Bennis, W. G., Benne, K., & Chin, R. (Eds.). (1961). *The planning of change*. New York: Holt, Rinehart & Winston.

Blake, R. R., & Mouton, J. S. (1964). *The managerial grid*. Houston: Gulf.

Boone, L. E., & Bowen, D. D. (1987). *Great writings in management and organizational behavior*. New York: Random House.

Bugental, J. F. T. (1965). *The search for authenticity*. New York: Holt, Rinehart & Winston.

Combs, A. W., & Snygg, D. (1959). *Individual behavior: A perceptual approach to behavior*. New York: Harper.

Emery, F. E., & Trist, E. L. (1964). The causal texture of organizational environments. *Human Relations, 18*(1), 21-32.

Goffman, E. (1959). *The presentation of self in everyday life*. Garden City, NY: Doubleday.

Hayakawa, S. I. (1963). *Language in thought and action* (2nd ed.). New York: Harcourt, Brace & World.

Herzberg, F., et al. (1959). *The motivation to work* (2nd ed.). New York: John Wiley.

Homans, G. C. (1950). *The human group*. New York: Harcourt, Brace.

Homans, G. C. (1961). *Social behavior: Its elementary forms*. New York: Harcourt, Brace & World.

Johnson, W. (1946). *People in quandaries: The semantics of personal adjustment*. New York: Harper & Bros.

Jourard, S. M. (1964). *The transparent self: Self-disclosure and well-being*. Princeton, NJ: Van Nostrand.

Korzybski, A. (1958). *Science and sanity: An introduction to non-Aristotelian systems and general semantics*. Lakeville, CT: International Non-Aristotelian Publishing.

Lee, I. (1952). *How to talk with people*. New York: Harper & Bros.

Likert, R. (1961). *New patterns of management*. New York: McGraw-Hill.

Maslow, A. H. (1962). *Toward a psychology of being*. Princeton, NJ: Van Nostrand.

Maslow, A. H. (1964). *Religious values and peak experiences*. Columbus: Ohio State University Press.

Maslow, A. H. (1965). *Eupsychian management.* Burr Ridge, IL: Irwin.

May, R. (1953). *Man's search for himself.* New York: Norton.

McGregor, D. (1960). *The human side of enterprise.* New York: McGraw-Hill.

Morgan, G. (1983). *Beyond method: Strategies for social research.* Beverly Hills, CA: Sage.

Moustakas, C. E. (1956). *Self explorations in personal growth.* New York: Harper.

Roethlisberger, F. J., et al. (1954). *Training for human relations.* Boston: Harvard Business School, Division of Research.

Rogers, C. R. (1961). *On becoming a person: A therapist's view of psychotherapy.* Boston: Houghton Mifflin.

Tannenbaum, R., Wechsler, I., & Massarik, F. (1961). *Leadership and organization: A behavioral science approach.* New York: McGraw-Hill.

Trist, E. L., Higgin, G. W., Murray, H., & Pollock, A. B. (1963). *Organizational choice.* London: Tavistock.

Turner, A. N., & Lombard, G. F. F. (1969). *Interpersonal behavior and administration.* New York: Free Press.

Vaill, P. B. (1971a). Organization development: Ten new dimensions of practice. In G. L. Lippitt, L. E. This, & R. G. Bidwell (Eds.), *Optimizing human resources.* Reading, MA: Addison-Wesley.

Vaill, P. B. (1971b). *The practice of organization development.* Alexandria, VA: American Society for Training and Development.

Vaill, P. B. (1973). Practice theories in organization development. In J. D. Adams (Ed.), *Theory and method in organization development.* Alexandria, VA: NTL Institute.

Vaill, P. B. (1978). Toward a behavioral description of high performing systems. In M. McCall & M. Lombardo (Eds.), *Leadership: Where else can we go?* Durham, NC: Duke University Press.

Vaill, P. B. (1979, Winter). Cookbooks, auctions, and claptrap cocoons. *Exchange, 41*(1), 3-6.

Vaill, P. B. (1982, Autumn). The purposing of high performing systems. *Organizational Dynamics.*

Vaill, P. B. (1983). OD as a scientific revolution. In D. D. Warrick (Ed.), *Contemporary organization development.* Glenview, IL: Scott, Foresman.

Vaill, P. B. (1984). Process wisdom for a new age. In J. D. Adams (Ed.), *Transforming work.* Alexandria, VA: Miles River.

Vaill, P. B. (1985). Integrating the diverse directions of the behavioral sciences. In R. Tannenbaum, N. Margulies, & F. Massarik (Eds.), *Human systems development.* San Francisco: Jossey-Bass.

Vaill, P. B. (1989a). *Managing as a performing art.* San Francisco: Jossey-Bass.

Vaill, P. B. (1989b). Seven process frontiers for organization development. In A. Drexler & W. Sykes (Eds.), *The emerging practice of organization development.* Alexandria, VA: NTL Institute.

Vaill, P. B. (1990a). Executive development as spiritual development. In S. Srivastva, D. L. Cooperrider, & Associates (Eds.), *Appreciative management and leadership* (pp. 323-352). San Francisco: Jossey-Bass.

Vaill, P. B. (1990b). The rediscovery of anguish. *Creative Change: The Journal of Religion and the Applied Behavioral Sciences, 10*(2), 18-24.

Vaill, P. B. (1993). Visionary leadership. In A. Cohen (Ed.), *The portable MBA in management.* New York: John Wiley.

# 17 The Teaching Experience as Learning in Public

KARL E. WEICK

I teach like I write, which means, if you've read my analysis of the Tenerife air disaster (Weick, 1990), you've experienced what it is like to attend one of my classes. The article and the class are built around the story of a vivid event. The story is linked to a diverse set of concepts. Each concept by itself is enlarged through nuances in the story, and the concepts are themselves linked with one another. These connections are then tied to the student's own personal life, and the story is seen as a microcosm of the human condition. Typically, the lesson is that small events can have large consequences, which suggests that life is a struggle for alertness, acceptance, and enactment.

This same sequence occurs whether the audience is undergraduates, doctoral students, or executives, and I stick to it because it satisfies six assumptions I make about teaching and living:

1. *People see what they believe.* Ideas, concepts, and beliefs are the means to improve observation. The Tenerife disaster, seen through the idea of regression to older, stronger, first-learned tendencies, becomes a different event, as does one's own reactions when under pressure.

2. *No explanation can be simultaneously general, accurate, and simple.* Any class and any explanation will disappoint. Something will always be left out, but that is no reason to discount learning and ideas. The Tenerife disaster may well be a clear instance where a person falls back on an old habit with disastrous results (a pilot accustomed to giving himself clearance for takeoffs in a training simulator gives himself clearance to take off at Tenerife while another aircraft is on the runway). This is a general-simple explanation that says nothing about cockpit crew interaction and the mitigated speech of the copilot, which are both accurate pieces of the story that are lost in the regression explanation.

3. *Complicated people see more.* If believing is seeing, then more variety in beliefs will enable people to see more. My articles and my classes are purposely dense with concepts, in the interest of improved observation. The Tenerife analysis highlights the concept of regression but also suggests that interactive complexity, discretion, and obedience are important concepts as well.

4. *Overlearned skills are resistant to stress.* People who act under pressure are more likely to enact old, overlearned, prior, less adaptive responses and less likely to enact newer, complex, tentative, recently learned responses. The primary way to block the regression that killed 583 people at Tenerife is to practice new responses beyond the point where they are first grasped. In the classroom, this means I encourage people to impose the same new concepts over and over until they can do so automatically.

5. *People know what they think only after they see what they say.* Everyone has to risk sounding stupid in order to learn something that isn't. We may not discover what a seminar was about until its final 5 minutes, just as any participant may not discover the meaning of an analysis until the final sentence. The copilot at Tenerife who told controllers, "We are at takeoff," may have tried to warn people listening to the radio that something nonstandard was about to happen. But no one else had ever heard that phrase, they couldn't see the thought behind the words, and so events rolled on just as if two 747s were not racing toward one another on the same runway.

6. *People who play the percentages solve more problems.* If one tries many solutions and analyses and has many projects and ideas floating at the same time, one of them is bound to be successful. Ideas create possibilities. And the more ideas, the greater the number of possibili-

ties. At Tenerife, the very preoccupation with just one idea—"get out of this airport before the weather falls below minimums"—kept people from seeing other possibilities.

When I combine these six assumptions with a format built around memorable stories, scenes such as the following develop:

Scene 1: I arrive at the University of Utah to talk with a group of doctoral students in Organizational Communication who have been studying *The Social Psychology of Organizing* (Weick, 1979). In preparation for my visit, each student has been asked to create a metaphor that captures his or her experience reading the book. The students voted the following statement as the clear winner: "Reading Weick is like running over something on the road at night: You know you hit something, but you don't know what the hell it was." That's the first time I ever heard *Organizing* described as roadkill.

Scene 2: I am reading in my office at the University of Minnesota's Laboratory for Research in Social Relations. My reading is interrupted when Dr. Mary Gergen, a visiting faculty member, comes in to introduce herself. Several years later, in a casual conversation, Gergen says, "Do you realize that when we first met, you stuck your finger into the book you were reading to keep your place and kept it there the whole time we talked?" I didn't remember that. But she certainly did.

Scene 3: I am stuck for a way to introduce the topic of organizational change in an executive education course I am co-teaching with four other faculty. I scan Kurosawa's stunning film *Dreams* with my wife, Karen, to see whether there is something in it I can use. She spots a segment called "The Peach Orchard," in which a small child grieves over the uprooting and loss of a favorite peach orchard, only to have his appreciation rewarded near the end of the film by new growth of a peach tree. The bulk of the segment is a sequence in which dancers in elaborate traditional costumes simulate the lost beauty of the orchard. I played the segment, asking only that the executives be prepared to discuss "what can we learn about change from the experiences of this small child?" My four colleagues gasped when they saw this segment because it was so far afield from anything we had used so far. As one of them put it, "When I saw that segment, I wondered what you had been smoking." I too was scared that I had gone over the top and might never recapture whatever hard-won credibility I had built with the participants. But during the follow-up discussion, the executives listed every insight into change that all five of us could think of . . . and several more.

Scene 4: I am having trouble sleeping because I keep getting awakened by unsettling dreams. The most unsettling dream is of a doctoral student who comes into my office to hand me a completed dissertation—except, when handing the document to me, the student says, "I want to present my devastation to you." I awake with a start, write this phrase on a Post-it that is next to the bed (and that is in front of me as I write this), and then fall back asleep.

These four experiences speak to the theme of "integration," which is the focus of this volume. When one teaches content that matters, the teaching experience invades everything, including audience feedback, first impressions, interactions with loved ones, and even those private moments when one tries to regroup. The trick is to integrate the invasions.

My teaching experience feels integrated because it doesn't involve teaching at all. Instead, it involves learning in public. By teaching, I mean transmitting knowledge and information in ways that help people acquire what has been prestructured. Teaching is about imparting information, direct showing, furnishing necessary knowledge, instructing, and realizing specific a priori intentions. Teaching resembles training rather than discovery. I understand learning to have a different character. Learning is about creating knowledge, structuring, punctuating information out of a stream of experience, imposing structures on experience, connecting, experimenting with language that captures novel nuances, and disorganizing in the service of restructuring. Learning relishes the multiple meanings that unsettle teaching. Learning complicates; teaching simplifies. We all do both, but we also tend to favor trading off one for the other. Faced with the choice, I opt for learning, and this creates many of the problems with teaching that I discuss shortly. These contrasts between teaching and learning may well be idiosyncratic, but idiosyncratic or not, they provide the context for this chapter.

To return to the issue of integration, whether I study, gather data, write, teach, administer, or live other activities, all of these sites are simply different places where learning takes place. Thus, integration is no big mystery. Sites and activities are tied together by ongoing efforts to relieve puzzlement.

But public learning is a lot more complicated than it looks. And, it is subject to many more unsettling moments than one might suspect. Just look back over the four scenarios I started with.

## Uncertainty in Public Learning

Take Scene 1. The *Organizing* book *is* tough. Parts of it are no easier to comprehend than is roadkill. I didn't intend it that way, but, consistent with the sense-making focus of the book itself, the content represents my ongoing effort to discover what I think by seeing what I say. The puzzled students who see a resemblance between roadkill and enactment caught me in the act of learning. If people know what they think only after they see what they say, then the early chapters in the book should be more puzzling than the later chapters. Unfortunately, if there is a primacy effect, then first impressions of the book as roadkill should be lasting impressions and color the interpretation of later chapters. The message of the book may have become clearer to me, but not to those who see my early saying as riddled with complex thought.

Suppose, to make matters more interesting, students were unsure what they hit when reading the book but made some interesting guesses. Should I tell them they are wrong? Should I listen to their interpretations, enlarge them, and claim that we both may have been saying/seeing something closer to their guess than to mine? I tend toward the latter style, which drives people—including myself—nuts when the question is, What *is* the *Organizing* book about? Nevertheless, so long as people keep wrestling with that question and keep inventing answers and keep looking in the world to see whether those answers make any sense, then the *Organizing* book, which is *about* sense making, has come to be its own experiential exercise. How the people use the book *is* what is being described in the book. They are learning in public by virtue of their grappling with a document that itself epitomizes learning in public.

What I have just described illustrates an occupational hazard of public learning. My certainty collapses into a hedged statement. And in reply to a student's question, "What do you really mean by that concept," I am no longer completely sure. To admit to that uncertainty while still retaining the reader's interest is not ideal for teaching, although it is the very essence of learning. Because learning is often tough, unpleasant, riddled with failure, and disorganizing, there is no guarantee that when one publicly invites people to join in learning rather than teaching, they'll agree to do so. If they do, there are also no guarantees that the outcome will be anything less than "a devastation."

## Anxiety in Public Learning

Scene 2, which involved socializing as an interruption of reading, speaks to the private side of public learning. The highs in my teaching experience come as often in private moments of reading, connecting, writing a syllabus that creates a pattern, discovering a sequence of readings from which a new pattern emerges, simulating an exercise in my mind, or enacting a virtual classroom, as they do from the actual delivery of these discovered connections. I like interaction and being "onstage" as much as the next person. But that's not the impression I gave Mary Gergen, nor is it the impression I sometimes give to other people. That's because I spend lots of time stockpiling ideas, findings, concepts, stories, and puzzles and sometimes get edgy when this process gets interrupted. Accumulating fragments, in fact, is what I do for a living. These fragments are investments that may produce unexpected connections when I interact with people who see things differently. Therein lies the rub. If I stockpile too zealously, I lose my chance to find a public forum where others can breathe some life into the fragments. For example, if Mary Gergen thinks I would rather read than talk, then her first visit becomes her last visit and I lose a chance to known another human being better and to see a different side of the world that is connected in different ways. Potential co-learners disappear, as do chances to learn in one another's presence. And, with fewer opportunities for public learning, our skills at doing so become rusty and our preferences for doing so weaken. As a result, we learn in private, teach in public, and no one sees how others actually learn on their feet. Without these data, it's easy to conclude that others have more effective learning styles than we do, a conclusion that reduces self-confidence.

That's one kind of instability in public learning, but there is an even more insidious one. This one derives from Zajonc's (1965) finding that when an audience is present, this facilitates performance of well-learned skills but inhibits the learning of new skills. The explanation is that acting in the presence of an audience is arousing and people get anxious. When people are anxious, they tend to emit dominant, overlearned responses. This dominant tendency interferes with efforts to learn newer, less familiar, more complex responses.

If Zajonc is right, then my description of my own teaching experience as "public learning" is an oxymoron. I may *think* I'm learning, but in actuality my learning in public may be nothing more than saying the same old things that I mistake for new things simply because I can no longer remember that they are old things that I've said before.

I'm more intrigued by a different possibility. Some audiences create more arousal and stress than others. In my teaching, I spend a great deal of time learning people's names, interests, and experiences so that I can use this material to illustrate abstract concepts. I use here-and-now classroom events to illustrate concepts, and I disclose personal setbacks and successes that illustrate concepts. All of these tactics personalize my teaching. But more crucially, they may lower the level of arousal in the classroom to moderate levels, and in doing so, lower the likelihood that old, overlearned reactions will interfere with learning new, more complex possibilities.

With greater familiarity goes less anxiety and less domination by responses from the past. If this line of argument makes sense, then it again suggests that public learning, for both the students and myself, is more likely the more familiar we are with one another and the more we trust one another. These are not just "feel good" outcomes. They are essential to the very thing we are doing.

We should also learn more in the later stages of our interaction than in the earlier stages. All of us should be at our most typical in our earliest, most anxious contacts when we run off well-learned routines that we mistakenly call teaching and learning. My routine output is your novel input from which you may learn something. And vice versa. Initially, we each watch smooth, overlearned performances that reaffirm and restate things we have known and stood for all along.

If we want to move beyond these performances and learn and fail in public, we've got to lower the costs of doing so. If the costs stay high, all we can count on are the same old dominant responses. So public learning, as an interpretation of the teaching experience, can be a recipe for failure. One way to avoid this outcome is to keep arousal levels modest.

But another way to evoke something more than overlearned responses is to learn privately in the presence of *imagined* others. If I read a new idea and then connect it to current events in an effort to test the power of the idea, I can imagine what Karen or Mary Gergen or Peter Frost would say about the connection. I can then "listen" to my reply, and as these "conversations" unfold, I learn. I learn because neither the stakes nor the arousal levels are as high as when I try to learn among strangers. Furthermore, my dominant responses are less intrusive, and newer, more complex responses feel more plausible and more capable of being retained and implemented in the future.

My point here is that public learning is possible in private if one relies on resources of imagination, role playing, rehearsing, and arguing. If public learning in private moderates levels of arousal, then the pace of learning should accelerate. And accelerated learning should produce more novel ideas that can be taken public and either taught or co-learned.

## Improvisation in Public Learning

Scene 3, choosing Kurosawa's "The Peach Orchard" to prime a discussion of change among executives, illustrates several points. First and most important, it is a good example of how I integrate teaching and living. Karen and I spend a lot of time together discussing and trying out platforms for learning. Our own private learning becomes more public. We share an enlarging set of common examples, and we have lots of fun as well. We too "play percentages" (see assumption 6 above), and our simulations that fail are hilarious pretexts for learning. In a profession where it is often difficult to share activities and content, these joint explorations have been increasingly rich and welcome.

The peach orchard experience also is representative of my recent discovery that executive education is, for me, a wonderful arena in which to work. I say that against the background of a lifetime spent doing advanced doctoral-level teaching of high abstractions. I haven't simply moved my doctoral syllabus intact into a classroom of executives. They wouldn't let me. But neither has much changed. Vivid stories, multiple connections, ideas that are surprising and powerful, generalizations that work, and personal relevance are no less interesting to people who are paid to focus narrowly, fight fires, avoid reflection, assume the jobs of others who were downsized, and who try in the midst of all this to love as well as work. As long as I know my material—which doesn't mean it has to be right, only that it be an intact, rich exhibit they can get their own minds around—model a respect for ideas and learning, listen to what people say, and connect it to the issues we're discussing, things go well.

Finally, "The Peach Orchard" makes clear the very real sense in which my public learning is best understood as improvisation. Jazz improvisation has been an anchor for me in several ways (Weick, 1993), the most relevant for this chapter being as a metaphor for what happens in the classroom. Jazz improvisation involves composing on the spur of the moment, using whatever resources are at hand, such as an agreed-on melody, conventions for alternating among soloists, and some way to begin and end together. The danger in jazz improvisation is that people will produce "spontaneous prattle" or simply play what they already know, which prevents them from exploring new ideas and techniques.

The tension and challenge of jazz improvisation are best seen if we visualize improvisation in other media.

> Imagine T. S. Eliot giving nightly poetry readings at which, rather than reciting set pieces, he was expected to create impromptu poems—different ones each night, sometimes recited at a fast clip; imagine giving Hitchcock or Fellini a handheld motion picture camera and asking them to film something, anything—at that very moment, without the benefits of script, crew, editing, or scoring; imagine Matisse or Dali giving nightly exhibitions of their skills—exhibitions at which paying audiences could watch them fill up canvas after canvas with paint, often with only two or three minutes devoted to each "masterpiece." (Gioia, 1988, p. 52)

Jazz involves a unique solution to problems of organization. There is no division of labor because composition and performance, creation and interpretation, and design and production are all done by the same person. Furthermore, the improviser does not work from blue-prints the way an architect does, but instead, the jazz performer "can look behind at what he has just played; thus each new musical phrase can be shaped with relation to what has gone before. He creates his form retrospectively" (Gioia, 1988, p. 61).

Unique though jazz improvisation may be, it is not that different from other forms of public learning. People have little choice but to wade in and see what happens. What will happen won't be known until it is almost too late to do anything about it. The focus is on justifying and making sensible, after the fact, whatever becomes visible in hindsight. Because that residue is irrevocable and public and results from choice, the performer is bound to those prior actions, which means improvisational teaching (a synonym of learning) is designed to produce commitment, at least for the teacher (Salancik, 1977). In teaching, as in jazz performance, people may be better off when they do such things as articulate their goals as late as possible to allow for the largest number of actions to influence the choice of goal; impose more interpretations on elapsed experience so that it can become more things in the future; strive for richness in what is said to increase the richness of what is thought; and focus on the task rather than on the self so that the lag between prior actions and sense making is held to a minimum. The more fully I incorporate implications such as these into my teaching, the more it becomes a chance to learn.

In jazz improvisation and in teaching, two additional qualities make both work. One is how people react to errors and mistakes. Jazz performances and learning in public can both look like haphazard art.

> Errors will creep in, not only in form but also in execution; the improviser, if he seriously attempts to be creative, will push himself into areas of expression which his technique may be unable to handle. Too often, the finished product will show moments of rare beauty intermixed with technical mistakes and aimless passages. (Gioia, 1988, p. 66)

To appreciate work that may be riddled with errors of reach, people need to adopt an aesthetics of imperfection. Such an aesthetics involves a mind-set in which observers are alert to what performers start with, what they make of what they start with, and what they do with imperfections once they occur. In an aesthetics of imperfection, errors are interpreted differently. People say essentially, given all the errors you could have made under these conditions, the ones you actually made were novel, were errors of excessive reach, were untypical for you, were effortful, were original, and could not have been made by someone who is lazy or unimaginative. Errors are not failures so much as experiments, challenges to be normalized, evidence of intensity, and testing of one's limits. These are not alibis and excuses. Instead, they represent acceptance of the fact that jazz improvisation, like teaching or cinema or dance, is a temporal art forms involving activity spread over time. This activity cannot be grasped in an instant. And while it unfolds, some experiments don't work. That any of them work at all is reason enough for awe and appreciation.

The second quality that makes for successful improvisation is that structure of some kind is crucial. A little structure goes a long way, but there has to be some structure. Typically, in the case of jazz, this structure is provided by a melody. As Sudnow puts it,

> Song is a social organizational device par excellence, a format that quite elegantly coordinates the movements of two or more individuals. Its metrical structure, with a beginning and an end and a definite number of grouped pulses, furnishes a planful means for coordinating simultaneous movement and allocating little batches of talk among various players over the course of on-going play. (1979, p. 105)

What is interesting about melodies, as with their counterparts in teaching such as studies, theories, concepts, and ideas, is that many younger players do not know either songs or studies. In the case of young jazz musicians, they grew up learning music by listening to jazz records. But what they learned were chord changes, not melodies. Even worse, they do not know lyrics, which means they don't know how to phrase the melody properly (Davis, 1986, p. 87). The point is that public learning as improvisation makes sense only when people have an anchor they can explore through elaboration and enlargement. Furthermore, they need to know their craft, they need to have confidence in their ability to listen and make do, and they have to trust the company they are in to support the learning process and to be inventive in their use of the failed experiments that are inevitable.

Showing "The Peach Orchard" to 30 impatient people who have invested 2 precious weeks of their time and several thousand dollars into learning works only when all of these factors line up.

## Voice in Public Learning

Scene 4, in which the doctoral student hands me a "devastation" rather than a dissertation, hints at the darker side of public learning. There are several downsides to public learning, but I sample only three: (a) imitation as an unreasonable goal, (b) unstable class content, and (c) generalizing from rare events.

Most people who work closely with me start out with a self-defeating agenda. Eventually, but not always, that agenda changes and then becomes doable. But an invitation to devastation lurks in the innocent opening phrase, "I want to do what you do and think as you do."

I hear that a lot. But I'm not always successful at alerting people that this is a shaky basis for a relationship. The problem is obvious. I write about what I think as a result of seeing what I say. But what I write and think and say and see are influenced by who I am, where I've been, and how I've spent my time. I write and teach close to my own experience, which means those who don't share that experience can never do what I do or think as I do even if they go through the same motions. It's trite to say that my voice is not their voice, but it seems to take a long time for this lesson to get through to people.

Most of my students don't do what I do, sound as I do, or build on what I've done. That could mean I've failed as an advisor if success is defined as perpetuation of my point of view. That very lack of perpetuation, however, could also mean I've succeeded as an advisor because, just as I struggled in the critically supportive company of people like my master's advisor, Harold Pepinsky; my dissertation advisor, Douglas Crowne; and a key mentor, Marvin Dunnette, to find my own voice, students who have struggled in my company have also discovered what really matters to them. One never knows for sure about these things. And that creates plenty of devastation to go around.

A second downside of public learning, one that is less devastating but no less nettlesome, is that there is no such thing as previous lectures, *the* syllabus, or standard boilerplate for a course. When teaching becomes learning, then once something is learned, it is time to move on to something else. Each year, I throw away most of my lecture notes, syllabi, and exercises. And each year I vow never to do that again. And each year I build most of my courses from scratch. This makes it tough to build a reputation for a course because, whatever new students expect on the basis of the experience of previous students, they seldom find. Students arrive eager to grapple with the topic of escalation in the book *Final Cut,* only to find that the book is missing from the syllabus precisely because people *did* grapple with escalation and *Final Cut* and it's time to move on.

I believe strongly that there *are* such things as classics (recall my earlier lament that younger faculty never learn "melodies" in organizational studies), yet I often act like a hypocrite. In the interest of learning, I treat nothing as classic, but I do smuggle in classics such as Salancik (1977), James (1890), Follett (1924), and Meyer (1982). And I'm eternally on the lookout for unexpected classics (my current favorite is Frank, 1992). But even the classics disappear for a year or so, only to reappear mysteriously and seemingly at random. What is constant amid all this shuffling is learning in real time.

One consequence of zero-based course construction in the interest of learning is that I often assign things I don't understand. What is truly unexpected is that, invariably—and I use that word intentionally—when I own up publicly in class to disappointment or bafflement with a new, untested item, someone defends it passionately and helps me and the rest of the class see what we have been missing.

I'm fond of the story about a regiment of soldiers that gets lost in the Alps and finally finds its way out by using a map that turns out to be a map of the Pyrenees. The moral I draw is that when you're lost, any old map will do because it calms you down, you pay more attention to what is around you, and you think more clearly. It just may be that the same holds for public learning. When you're lost, any old article will do because it calms you down, you pay more attention to what is around, and you think more clearly.

A third downside of public learning involves those memorable stories that I mentioned at the start of this chapter. Memorable stories often are vivid precisely because they portray rare events. I have great classes when we take apart the Tenerife air disaster, or the grounding of the *Enterprise* on Bishop Rock, or the failure of Expo '86 in Vancouver, or Francis Ford Coppola's filming of *Apocalypse Now,* or the Bhopal disaster, or Dee Hock's start-up of VISA. But then we face the question,

What do these events have to do with dull, normal days in Cody, Wyoming, servicing accounts for Frito-Lay?

To answer that question, we spend lots of time using theories to connect the large with the small, the rare with the commonplace. We treat our everyday living as if it were a scaled-down microcosm of the same forces for miscommunication that were operating at Tenerife. We put ourselves in the command positions at Bishop Rock and discover that we too might have grounded the vessel. We probe our past experience to extract what happened to us personally that is closest to the event we want to understand. We question the fact of rarity itself and often find that what we thought was rare, in fact, is surprisingly common. We struggle to identify boundary conditions. We do all of this and much more. We make an uneasy peace with the fact that, rare as such events may be, we can learn things that apply to the commonness of our everyday lives.

And yet, we all know in our hearts that, with all this focus on that which is rare, we may be neglecting that which is more common. We act as if the common is implicit in the rare; but then, we aren't so sure. The issue never settles down and has to be argued and examined again and again. Repeatedly, we have to reaccomplish what we think we have learned. Reaccomplishment, however, soon becomes indistinguishable from learning, which, after all, is what we are about.

## Guides as Guidelines for Public Learning

Given the preceding as a slice of my teaching experience, the questions become, How did it get that way? and What does that experience suggest by the way of counsel for people just beginning to amass their experience? This chapter concludes with a discussion of these two questions.

In an autobiographical essay (Weick, 1993), the closest I came to describing the antecedents of my teaching experience is this reflection on undergraduate life as a psychology major at Wittenberg University. I quote that passage because it captures accurately the meaning I associated with teaching.

> I have often suspected that when I decided to go for a Ph.D., the life in academia that I envisioned was modeled very closely after the life I saw at

Wittenberg: easy conversations at frequent intervals between faculty and students, earnest discussions of weighty issues while seated around the fireplace at a professor's home, fascinating things to read, humanities as the foundation of everything, easy movement among disciplines, and the discovery of patterns among seemingly unrelated elements. The world I envisioned was a world of teaching with incidental research, a world that is quite different from the one in which I now live. Maybe Allport's concept of functional autonomy really works. I conducted research in order to teach, but over time, doing research became an end in itself and I lost sight of the original instrumentality. But not quite.

There is a mixture of wistfulness tinged with anger when I see people get turned off to the world of ideas when their window on this world is an overworked researcher. I suspect that my longstanding fondness for the world of Wittenberg is most visible when I write articles which teach rather than present new evidence, and when I give speeches that do the same thing. Not only do the speeches let me teach, but they also let me re-enact my days as a radio announcer and experience something of the excitement surrounding improvisation and one-night stands that I associate with jazz musicians. (p. 291)

In that essay, I also described the person who most clearly served as my mentor, Harold Pepinsky, a demanding professor of counseling with a legendary ability to spot nonsense. My description of Pepinsky will sound several themes already evident in this chapter.

My work to this day shows the extent of Pepinsky's influence. He is fanatic about clear, graceful writing, he reads everything he can get his hands on, the bibliographies of his papers have a startling range of citations, he is eclectic and interdisciplinary, he has a longstanding interest in language and productivity, he always wants to know what's new, he has ties to Minneapolis, his wife gives him some of his best ideas, he is a therapist at heart, and half of the time people have no idea what he is talking about. If that doesn't describe me, I don't know what does. I feel sorry for anyone who tries to tackle academia without a model like this. (Weick, 1993, p. 294)

If I move to the present (November 1993 at age 57), I still think of myself as someone who has mentors, although those who now serve this role have changed. My mentors now include Harry Gisborne, Gary Marx, and Harry Wilmer.

Gisborne is the fire science researcher made famous in Norman Maclean's *Young Men and Fire* (1992) who revisits the scene of the

Mann Gulch fire to test a theory of how wind patterns forced it out of control. Despite a severe heart ailment, Gisborne wanted to visit the scene of the fire in 1949 before winter washed away crucial evidence. He and a ranger named Robert Jansson hiked into the terrain, which was nearly impassable, and alternated between periods of climbing and resting, stopping exactly 37 times to talk (data are from a report filed for insurance purposes, Maclean, 1992, p. 137). Gisborne grew visibly weaker as the climb progressed. At Stop 32, Gisborne saw evidence of a fire whirl that destroyed his theory of how the fire had blown up. Gisborne and Jansson then traced the path of the whirl, and at Stop 35 Gisborne said, "I'm glad I got a chance to get up here. Tomorrow we can get all our dope together and work on Hypothesis Number One. Maybe it will lead to a theory" (p. 138). At Stop 37, one-quarter mile from their truck, Gisborne sat down and said, "Here is a nice place to sit and watch the river." As he got back up, Gisborne fell over and was dead in a minute. Before he ran for help, Jansson put Gisborne's "glasses back on him so, just in case he woke up, he could see where he was" (p. 138).

What is so striking about Gisborne is that he wasn't bitter when his theory proved to be wrong. Instead, he was excited that tomorrow he would assemble the new evidence, build another theory, and possibly come closer to a better explanation. Subsequent work showed that Gisborne was on the right track, and the next day, had he lived, he might well have found the right answer for what precipitates a fire blowup. Embodied in Gisborne is a complex mixture of stubbornness, love of inquiry, desire for firsthand evidence, optimism, resilience, ability to evaluate ideas independent of self, and absorption in the world, all of which seem worth working for. Gisborne's inquisitive ascent up Mann Gulch is the essence of public learning.

I have never met Gary Marx, just as I have never met Gisborne, but I have learned and continue to learn a great deal about integration in academic life from Marx's candid autobiographical essay "Reflections on Academic Success and Failure: Making It, Forsaking It, Reshaping It" (Marx, 1992). Marx chronicles a hot start to a career at Harvard, followed abruptly by an equally startling disappearance from the limelight. The story is one of impermanence, journeys rather than destinations, transient success, intensity, volatility, and the tough search for anchors. To paraphrase the moral Marx draws would do a disservice to the complex, nuanced integration he has made of these experiences.

It is sufficient to note that integration of a sort does occur, that it is continually reaccomplished, and that the teaching experience is no more buffered against the jolts Marx describes than is the research experience. Marx too had to learn in public, against his wishes. He had to learn that there is life after one is rejected for tenure at Harvard and after telephone calls from the White House dry up. What Marx teaches me is that the process of creating is an end in itself.

This same emphasis on the process as the end is visible in Harry Wilmer's work as a Jungian analyst. He comprehends more and more events of the world within this powerful set of ideas (Wilmer, 1987). Gisborne teaches me to be wary of my tendency to look for confirming evidence, whereas Wilmer teaches me not to overthrow completely that tendency.

After 30 years of teaching and learning, my ideas have been subject to lots of winnowing. Superficial simplicities, which gave way to tortured complexities, now begin to give way again, this time to a smaller number of profound simplicities that have the power to connect. What used to feel like a confirmation bias now begins to feel less like a bias and more like validation. That doesn't mean the doubt so crucial to public learning has disappeared. What has shifted is the target of that doubt. To reverse a well-known phrase, no longer do I seek simplicity and distrust it, but I also seek complexity and distrust it as well. I look for the old easy answers and distrust them, just as I more recently look behind the complexities I relish and discover that, as I comprehend them more fully, they can be understood more simply. Whenever I "teach" these days, I am caught midstream in these shifts. If anything, more of my time is spent learning, not less. The same is true for Wilmer, as it was for his mentor, Carl Jung.

Not Gisborne, Marx, or Wilmer would wow people with their platform manner, their zippy stories, their choreographed classes, their awesome overheads, their animation during class, their props, their acting, their sense of drama, or their cleverness. What would wow people is their willingness to make public their struggles for understanding. Struggles are themselves not especially pretty or orderly or entertaining. But they do constitute moments of integrity. And they do constitute moments in which wisdom triumphs over hubris. Those things matter to me these days when I learn in public. And that's why these mentors matter to me.

## Conclusion

What kind of advice do I distill from all of this? Partly, I trust whatever conclusions and morals readers draw on their own from this account. I say that, however, with one big caveat. And that caveat comes from the brilliant pen of William Gass (1978). He concludes a discussion of Wittgenstein's style of public learning with the observation that a whole sentence can never come from half a person (p. 252). That's why the editors of this volume are so concerned with integration. Without it, we are doomed to partial sentences, incomplete insights, and cryptic concepts. The remedy is not to work on substance, but on self. If readers pull bits and pieces from my account that help them fill out their own development as persons, then the sentences they subsequently utter in their teaching and learning will take care of themselves.

## References

Davis, F. (1986). *In the moment.* New York: Oxford.

Follett, M. P. (1924). *Creative experience.* New York: Longmans, Green.

Frank, A. W. (1992). The pedagogy of suffering: Moral dimensions of psychological therapy and research with the ill. *Theory and Psychology, 2*(4), 467-486.

Gass, W. H. (1978). A memory of a master. In *Fiction and the figures of life* (pp. 247-252). Boston: Nonpareil.

Gioia, T. (1988). *The imperfect art.* New York: Oxford.

James, W. (1890). *The principles of psychology* (Vols. I & II). New York: Holt.

Maclean, N. (1992). *Young men and fire.* Chicago: University of Chicago Press.

Marx, G. T. (1990). Reflections on academic success and failure: Making it, forsaking it, reshaping it. In B. M. Bergen (Ed.), *Authors of their own lives* (pp. 260-284). Berkeley: University of California Press.

Meyer, A. D. (1982). Adapting to environmental jolts. *Administrative Science Quarterly, 27,* 515-537.

Salancik, G. R. (1977). Commitment and the control of organizational behavior and belief. In B. M. Staw & G. R. Salancik (Eds.), *New directions in organizational behavior* (pp. 1-54). Chicago: St. Clair.

Sudnow, D. (1979). *Talk's body.* New York: Knopf.

Weick, K. E. (1979). *The social psychology of organizing* (2nd ed.). Reading, MA: Addison-Wesley.

Weick, K. E. (1990). The vulnerable system: An analysis of the Tenerife air disaster. *Journal of Management, 16*(3), 571-593.

Weick, K. E. (1993). Turning context into text: An academic life as data. In A. G. Bedian (Ed.), *Management laureates* (Vol. 3, pp. 285-323). Greenwich, CT: JAI.

Wilmer, H. A. (1987). *Practical Jung.* Wilmette, IL: Chiron.

Zajonc, R. B. (1965). Social facilitation. *Science, 149,* 269-274.

# 18 The Power of Dialogue

*Celebrating the Praxis of*
*Teaching and Research*

DARLYNE BAILEY

My life's work has been and will continue to be the exploration of the interrelatedness among the individual, group, and organizational units of a system. Therefore, my activities both within and outside the classroom concurrently attend to multiple levels. In teaching, this attention translates into ensuring that my management students grow to appreciate the needs and aspirations of each staff member for whom they are responsible while learning how to form and sustain alliances between organizations. In research, I draw on the literature from various schools of thought as I explore the theme of collaboration through dialogue in the building of theory and in the developing of strategies for practice.

Wow! That sounds so simple, so clear. But I know it was not always that way. In the next several pages, I attempt to recapture my academic journey, a process that has led me to the realization of the praxis, or the powerful connection, between teaching and research. My intent is to share my perspectives in a way that serves two purposes: (a) to normalize the experience of the bumpy roads of academia and (b) to propose that the process of dialogue and praxis can serve as beacons on the crossroads of teaching and research.

## The Journey Begins

Not too surprisingly, the seeds for my belief in the power of interconnection through dialogue were planted quite early in my life. Being a member of a family that identifies as African American yet embraces the other ethnicities that make up this "us" undoubtedly helped form my appreciation for interconnection. Growing up in a town that actively supported the rights of individuals and groups by, for example, being among the first in the United States to radically desegregate its schools, further validated the importance of integration through exchange among all parts of the whole. As an adult, the combination of the following learnings led me to my current place in life: the intrapsychic and small-group course work at Columbia University, the Lenox Hill Psychoanalytic Psychotherapy Program (both in New York City), and the doctoral studies in organizational behavior here at Case Western Reserve University, and discovering the real meaning of leadership through the W. K. Kellogg National Fellowship Program.

At Columbia, I learned about the power and challenge of seeing oneself as the primary tool for intervention; recognizing and working through one's "blind spots" and working with one's acquired and innate skills continue to be requisites for effective relationships with others. The message was repeated at Lenox Hill Hospital. Yet, there I also learned that I was verbal and needed mutuality/reciprocity/interactive exchange in my relationships—too much mutuality to fit the profile of a "traditional" psychoanalyst.

As a doctoral student at Case Western Reserve, I realized that this self-learning needed some alone, quiet time but that real learning could only take place in the context of others. Sides of the all of who I am were most fully realized in the emotionality of our "Groups" class, in the cognitive aha! experiences (and lack thereof) in our Multivariate Analysis class, and my spiritual awakenings in our 4- to 5-day-long retreats.

My 1993 acceptance into the W. K. Kellogg National Fellowship Program has provided the resources of space, time, and people to fully integrate my learnings about the power of interconnection. In the community of wise and passionately caring Fellows, advisors, and staff, I have had the opportunity to do intense self and other work and to pursue a learning plan for exploring the role of spirituality in community building. The synergistic impact of these professional (yet highly personal) markers has produced the following: I am a university dean and associate professor with appointments in the schools of social work and management who maintains a multilevel, multidisciplinary perspective of the world.

My entrance into academia, with its traditional boxes of professional identities, was quite awkward at first. The reasons for this discomfort were largely twofold: One, the solid lines that made for professional boundaries seemed to hold little respect for "nonpurists" such as myself; and two, the ways to simultaneously excel in both teaching and research posed a great mystery for me. In my first year, when asked about my area of research and scholarship, I could easily talk about my interest in the nonprofit sector; the vast majority of my paid and volunteer experiences to date had been within the world of not-for-profit organizations. And although this topic was not a "real area" in either school, it was a primary link between social work and management. Shortly thereafter, I was asked to be a member of the teaching faculty of a new center on nonprofit organizations (ironically, a joint venture of the social work, business, and law schools). My acceptance was reaffirmation of my commitment to this "stepchild" area.

Accepting the resultant status of marginality in the professional schools of business and social work, I began to see that being on the *edges* of these disciplines offered me the freedom to question and challenge both while also drawing attention to their areas of complementarity, compatibility, and overlap. Such use of my marginality eventually led me to recognize myself as a boundary spanner with all the rights and responsibilities of such a role. For the past 7 years, the content and process of my teaching have reflected a synthesis of learnings from both departmental "camps," while for the past 5 years this has also been true for my research projects and writings. A description of my thoughts and practices in teaching and then research will be helpful here.

## The Teacher-Learner

Several months into my role as teacher, I realized that (a) teaching was a combination of art and skill that far surpassed one's knowledge of course content and (b) I loved it! Through an interesting series of events, I had twice, during the past several years, spent time in the company of Paulo Freire (1970/1981, 1993, 1994). Freire is the Brazilian educator who, from 1964 to 1980, was excommunicated from his homeland for teaching the peasants how to read. In my first few months in the classroom, I discovered that Freire's theories about liberatory education (e.g., in which both teacher and students are learners) best resonated with my beliefs about mutual empowerment through interconnection and with what has emerged as my philosophy of teaching.

One of the most impactful aspects of Freire's work has been in my operationalization of the concept of dialogue. Dialogue à la Freire is more than a conversation between two people; dialogue is an interactive act of creation. It happens like this: You and I come together and discuss a certain topic. I have opinions B, and you have opinions A. In true dialogue, we both are willing to share our opinions and simultaneously be open to the opinions of the other. In true dialogue, there is mutuality of respect (of self and other), trust (in self and other), and unconditional caring (of self and other). Freire talks about these as humility, faith, hope, and love.

Let's look more closely at these words—*humility, faith, hope,* and *love*—as the critical elements of dialogue. Being unassuming and unpretentious in presentation of self and genuinely respectful of others is what is meant by *humility.* Two years ago, my fellowship colleagues and I relearned the meaning of this word while in the mountains of Leadville, Colorado. We had all been recently accepted into the Kellogg National Fellowship Program and were told at that time that we had been identified as the future leaders of the world. Representing many lifestyles and professions, we all shared the feelings of being honored by this fellowship, proud of our accomplishments that led to this award, and eager to see what this 3-year journey would be all about.

We all knew that a week-long Colorado Outward Bound program was part of this experience. Expressing varying degrees of anxiety about the described "physical-ness" of this week, some of us worried about our physical strength, asking, "Would I be able to hike with a 40-pound pack on my back?" Others wondered whether their physical endurance would be enough to allow them to hike with this pack for 4 to 9 hours . . . largely uphill. And still others were uneasy about their physical health—sleeping outside on the ground in temperatures under 20°F. Truthfully, I worried about *all* of these issues! Without going into all the details, let me say that I don't think *any* of us were prepared for our biggest learning from this experience. We learned that the person smallest in physical stature and perceived strength could turn out to be the hardiest in determination and persistence. We learned that the person with the greatest physical challenge (in this case, over 70 years of age and with one leg) could be the one with the greatest amount of courage. And we were constantly reminded of just how little we all are in the real world—just how naive and truly *interdependent* on one another, the air, the trees, and the rivers we all are. In a word, our greatest shared learning was one of humility—humbled by one another and even more so by the strength and endurance of the mountains—majestic yet unassuming testimonies of life.

Dialogue also requires faith—not a religious faith, but definitely a spiritual belief in others, in their right to "be," an unswerving conviction and trust in the inevitability of the rightness of the world. This is not to suggest that all is now right with the world. But the faith I am describing knows that all *can* be right if we try to be the best human being we can be and support similar efforts of others along the way. The only thing that can stop this faith is fear . . . of the known or unknown. As a dear friend of mine reminds me, faith and fear *cannot* coexist. True faith leaves no room for fear. Martin Luther King, Jr., used to recite a motto that can still be found on the walls of homes of some of our elders:

> Fear knocked at the door.
> Faith answered.
> There was no one there.

And this leads to hope. Hope is rooted in recognizing our incompletion—a realization that more and better can and will come for us all. Hope begins our search for the fullness—a search that can only be carried out in communion with others. This wish, this longing, this yearning is what makes up the core of the lives of all those you and I consider heroes—the well-known ones and the ordinary ones. Hope is the driving force in our going to school, looking for a job, and working hard. Hope is actually the wind in the sails of faith.

The last critical element of dialogue is love. Love is the *foundation* of dialogue. Love is the core of life itself. Love is ever present; it gets covered up by acts of manipulation, antagonism, hate, and oppression, but it is always there for us.

The Greek New Testament has three words for love. One is the word *eros*, which refers to a romantic, aesthetic love. Some of the most beautiful love in the world has been expressed this way. The other Greek term for love is *philia*. This is a type of intimate love. This is the type of love you and I share with those with whom we feel very close.

That leaves the term *agape*. Agape is more than romantic love and more than even a deep friendship. Agape is an unconditional caring for all. Agape is my wanting *your* life to be one of "good" for you simply because you exist. Agape is an overflowing love that seeks nothing in return. Agape is a term and a way of being that is best evidenced in the lives of Jesus, Martin Luther King, Jr., Gandhi, and Mother Teresa. I believe that agape is at the heart of our choice to be educators. This agape love is critical to dialogue.

These elements of dialogue—humility, faith, hope, and love—outline my lifelong strivings, which are reflected throughout my classroom activities. For example, classes begin with a formation of our individual objectives for the course and an identification of our theoretical perspectives of the subject about to be studied. Most students initially get anxious here, believing that "theories" must be scientifically tested and unchangeable; such a big word for their seemingly small thoughts! After a discussion about guiding principles and core values, however, these same students are most energized about the power of their ideas, and everyone can begin to join me in seeing all as teachers and learners in this class.

The next step is usually my asking folks to buy into some ground rules—the four C's—that underscore the expectations of unconditional trust and the search for completeness and of self in the context of others. The four C's are *caring* (about oneself and others' opinions and questions), *candor* (in presenting one's ideas and feelings and in responding to those from others), *confidentiality* (of exactly what was said or done by whom in the class) and working together to lay the foundation for the class as a *community*, an emergent system that collectively works toward the course objectives in a dialogic culture that values the process of teaching-learning as much as its products.

Through dialogue, we are best able to conceive and explore theory. In true dialogue, we take on some opinions of the other. The synergy of the unassuming presentation of self, profound respect for and trust in the right of the other to "be" with his or her thoughts and feelings, allows us to be transformed by the dialogue. As described, we have together engaged in critical thinking about our A and B perspectives and have created an opinion C on this subject.

I now know that I am a teacher who is also a learner who encourages creativity and the continuous enhancement and use of self through dialogue. I strongly urge students to play with their ideas by risking asking questions, offering their thoughts, and trying out new modes of behavior. Through experiential exercises and lecturettes, I actively discourage my co-learners from memorizing just my ideas and then simply depositing them for me in their class assignments. By asking students to explore the whys underlying their questions, rather than simply give answers, I facilitate and model dialogic interactions. This process is designed to help all of us take concepts and think them through so that each person comes to own and therefore be best able to act on the knowledge generated in the course.

Thus, this practice of dialogue and philosophy about teaching-learning necessitated that I abandon the illusion of being the expert in the classroom. Although I accept ultimate responsibility for the class meeting core content requirements, my co-learners and I collectively create and monitor the course work. In these classes, I develop a bare-bones, skeleton syllabus and co-develop the specifics of the course with the students. Combining individual objectives for the course, we create community-level objectives that become the blueprint for the course experience. Although, initially, these classes were anxiety-inducing for me, I have found that spreading the responsibility for and authority over the process of learning among all in the room not only has pushed me to "walk the talk" of interconnection and dialogue but also has demonstrated that learning is lifelong and can be fun!

Most important, this process has elicited a spiritual reawakening for me. I have come to know that effective educators must reframe the focus from leading to being led. We must recognize our lives as journeys that are most exciting and fulfilling when mortal fear of the unknown can be cast aside or worked through; when we can walk with faith, trusting in the divine rightness of life. This fundamental faith makes room for our hesitations and even regressions, but when followed it is so powerful that it allows each of us to be truly authentic with others. As teacher-learners, we must be able to acknowledge our questions and confusions and even admit to not knowing the answers. This is more than modeling for our students; this is honoring ourselves.

Being true to others means that I have to risk being open and attentive, rather than just passing judgments. Some may see this uncritical, unconditional openness as giving away the power of being "The Teacher," but so far on this journey, I have found that openness is much more potent than any system of judgment ever devised.

### The Teacher-Learner as Researcher

As may be apparent from my earlier statement, I spent the first 2 years of my professorship cultivating my teaching-learning abilities and seeing research as a competing demand on my time. During the 3rd year, I suddenly realized that some of the unanswered questions I had stumbled upon when preparing to teach served as excellent research questions that, when explored, generated theory to use in teaching.

I then rediscovered Freire's concept of the *praxis*—the union of reflection and practice. The core of the praxis is the belief that theory without action is a form of mental game playing and that action without theory is simply flying by the seat of your pants. We need both. The praxis is where true learning takes place. The praxis for me was in the interweaving of my research ideas and questions with the application of such in the classroom. From that moment on, the cycle of theory-in-action through dialogue continued.

In my research, I operationalize the concept of dialogue through participatory action research. Striving for a true dialogic experience, I work with the "subjects" of my projects to co-inquire into the areas of study. I have used this methodology, working with single organizations as well as with community-based consortia. For example, in evaluating a 5-year federal grant from the Department of Health and Human Services to reduce infant mortality by 50% in Cleveland by 1996, my graduate research assistant and I established three co-inquiry teams. These teams were made up of project staff, social/health/educational service providers, and community residents. Each team worked with us as we collected data about the initiative by using the elements of dialogue as "ground rules."

The data from this project have led to the proposal of new theory in the literature about the development of community-based consortia, as well as to the suggestion of practice models for evaluating this interorganizational unit. These theories and models have, in turn, collectively formed the core content for a graduate course new to the schools of social work and of business.

Another example of this dialogic style is in the 3-year, $50 million federal initiative called Hope VI. I am the principle investigator for the evaluation of this project, which was designed to reconstruct the physical and social structures of public housing in Cleveland. My two student assistants and I are recruiting housing residents to partner with us in assessing the effectiveness of the project changes on the lives of all the residents and the surrounding social service and business providers.

In both projects, our team members helped us understand and validate the data and, in so doing, came to realize their true ownership rights to this project. After all, as researchers, no matter where our hearts are, we are still temporary members or guests in their communities.

The challenges in this research approach are similar to those found in the classroom. Because of the different roles and role expectations we "educators-researchers-students-community citizens" bring to the process, the issues of power and control most always surface. Freire states that true dialogue cannot take place between "oppressors" and "oppressed" peoples. A belief in the equality of the parties involved must exist. This is not to say that there are no legitimate power differences and that Party A doesn't know more about a particular subject than Party B. Rather, in true dialogue, A recognizes that there is still much to learn from B . . . and vice versa. This stance requires a fundamental belief in the *need* for all involved to be active participants in order for the process to be optimally successful—where the research and the class uncover and discover knowledge to be applied.

Within this reconceptualization of interactions are several small but practical and effective steps that the teacher-learner-researcher can take. What follows are some of my learnings to date.

1. *Risk being the teacher-learner-researcher . . . the educator,* or *Yes, Virginia, power need not be a four-letter word.* Risk putting out what you believe are good ideas, insightful questions, disturbing thoughts,

and thoughtful decisions. I am ever reminded by and grateful for the words of Freire, when I asked him the summer of 1994 about leadership. He said, "A good leader doesn't have to have all the questions." Rather, I take that to mean, a real educator has to make sure that the right questions are on the table.

A great educator has to realize the meaning of true power. And yes, my comrades were also socialized to view power as synonymous with unfeeling control; great educators do realize their power. This doesn't mean being perfect, but caring about the difference between right and wrong in dealing with others and taking stands on issues that have been worked out from inside out. It means being honest, not lying even when one seems better served in the short run by misleading others. It means not *always* having one's own way, but being able to *compromise* when that is appropriate. It means being comfortable with all the ambiguities of life. It means a lot. Power used for good means being *worthy* of trust and respect even from people who may disagree with us.

True power can be freeing. First is the fear of losing oneself, of being some type of "political animal" that co-learners, family, and friends wouldn't even recognize, much less want to be around. I now recognize that true power comes through collaboration from interdependence and that interdependence can be recognized through our simply working together for the greater good. Paradoxically, power is freedom that comes from recognizing and actually *obeying* the realities of interdependence and collaboration.

2. And yet, I have also learned that I am much more effective as an educator when I *do less and simply be more*. Admittedly, I haven't quite got the first part down yet. I'm still working somewhere between 70 and 80 hours a week, but I have seen that when I'm with my colleagues and I'm more of a facilitator than, say, a used-car salesperson, the whole school becomes more spontaneous. As a group, we become simply brilliant in our words and our deeds. "Being more," to me, means taking time to be still, to be in a state of what the Zen-Buddhist monk Thich Nhat Hanh refers to as "peaceful mindfulness," to remember to breathe deeply and let my mind and my thoughts just wander.

I have found that because life gets very busy very shortly after I wake up—the early morning hours (literally before getting *out* of bed and getting *into* the world)—if I just lie still for a while, I get my best ideas,

ideas that, at best, are received and built upon by my co-learners in classes here at the Mandel School and in the community or, at worst, when brought in, spark a whole new series of different ideas. It's important for us to figure out when, in each day, it's good to *just be*—to just follow our inner wisdom and allow ourselves to both think and feel at the same time.

3. *Be fully human.* It is imperative that we also allow ourselves to feel our full range of emotions. Say "I don't know" when you truly don't know something . . . and scratch when you itch. Seriously, being who you are as you are creates the space and gives permission for everyone else to be fully present. And, do we ever really want anything less from the people we work with? I think not! Rather, I believe we would all benefit from experiencing our full range of emotions. I would rather deal with someone else's anger (one of the tougher emotions both to have and to experience) than deal with his or her apathy. Anger can be worked through, worked with, and the underlying energy can be used. Apathy is empty.

4. And yet, the paradoxical learning here is that a good educator really needs to *strive for transcending oneself.* True leadership is service *to, with,* and *for* others, not selfishness or even self-centeredness.

Despite the good and bad press you get about yourself, remember not to get too consumed with yourself. Hold both praise and criticism lightly because, for the most part, they are fleeting.

I am not saying don't strive for a good reputation, but if you *cherish* your reputation and try to *preserve* it, you actually lose the freedom and honesty and spontaneity that's necessary for continued development. I value and, yes, even sometimes feel humbled by, my life's work in academia, but if I take it too seriously, I get overwhelmed by the multiple demands. I have found that my keeping everything, even this job, in perspective, that by striving to transcend myself, as an educator I am actually able to enhance myself and therefore my teacher-learner abilities for the good of all.

5. Last, I have been reminded that an effective educator must *fully embrace the fragility and magic of life.* I believe that each moment is a blessing meant to be lived to the fullest. Whether making a tough budgetary or personnel decision or giving or getting some difficult feedback, we need to care about others just because they exist and not get blinded by what we may experience as their "flaws." What helps me here and helps me remember the magic of life is knowing that life

is a series of interconnections. It is organizational systems thinking at its best.

In sum, recognizing and then working from the interrelatedness of research and teaching has strengthened the process and "products" from these efforts, heightened my enthusiasm for both, and greatly enriched my life. Those of us who see our journey as following the roads of academia need to salute the natural interconnections in life. In this time of global transition, the walls surrounding our disciplines, as well as those delineating the components of our professions, must come down. We must strive for true dialogue to fully use the praxis of our teaching and research. The future of education depends on this achievement. The future of our world depends on this education of all.

## References

Freire, P. (1981). *Pedagogy of the oppressed.* New York: Continuum. (Original work published 1970)
Freire, P. (1993). *Pedagogy of the city.* New York: Continuum.
Freire, P. (1994). *Pedagogy of hope.* New York: Continuum.

# V

# A Look at the Future
## *Some Questions*

The chapters in this book were written by people who love to teach. These people are also scholars who take a keen interest in exploring ideas, who see value in remaining intellectually vital and in being accomplished both in and out of the classroom. We would like to think that these authors represent the majority of academics. Yet, although many colleagues are like them, other scholars do not follow this integrative model. They either spend most of their time teaching or are mostly engaged in research. Furthermore, in our opinion, the deck has been stacked against those who want to make strong contributions to both research and teaching. Rewards systems in institutions and in the professions tend to give more weight to research productivity than to teaching proficiency. We think there are barriers to even thinking about or recognizing how each of these activities can feed the other even though both are at the root of the academic goal to facilitate learning.

Having had the opportunity to read all the chapters in the book and to think about their impact as a whole, we found ourselves asking questions about the teaching process and about the nature of integrative links between teaching and research. We note them here to help surface issues, to stimulate debate and discussion, and to help begin a dialogue that may move us forward in the quest for a better understanding about effective university education.

## Overall Impact

What might the impact of the ideas expressed in this book be on those who read it? What will other academics, our fellow teachers and researchers, make of it? How will administrators respond? Will it resonate with students? Could anything change in the academic system if the ideas, experiences, and messages from these authors were taken seriously?

Undoubtedly, some scholars will see themselves in the stories in the book. We will be preaching to the converted in such cases. Not that this is a bad thing, necessarily. Reading about others struggling with similar issues, experiencing the highs and lows of the learning process, trying the same or similar kinds of techniques, and expressing the same kinds of values can be heartening. It can inspire one to continue to strive to create meaningful teaching and learning milieus, to take risks, and to make the effort. Moreover, academics seem always to be looking for ideas and insights from others that they can borrow and adapt. That's the nature of the game. But we need to ask the question, Are we capturing some of the important parameters of good teaching in academia through these self-reports, or is this a slice of teaching life that can only be applied in a behavioral science arena? We think the authors' insights and experiences are generalizable to the wider academic enterprise. Notice, for example, the following comments from award-winning teachers (*Award Winning*, 1991):

The relationship (between teaching and research) is an absolutely intimate one. . . . If you are active in research, it also means that the science that you are teaching will always be current. There's nothing worse than the people who are the most wonderful, suave lecturers who are teaching subjects that are 50 years out of date. . . . Again, even at the first year level, I want to make sure that I try to include lecture material that was discovered last year. (p. 14)

Robert G. Gilbert,
School of Chemistry

The most important thing—in my case, teaching mathematics, anyway—is to make them aware of the beauty of the subject. It gives great motivation. (p. 8)

Humphry M. Gastineau-Hills,
Department of Pure Mathematics

When I first started lecturing I felt it wasn't really fair to talk about caves, which were my research area and my major sporting area—that caves weren't really "kosher" chemistry, I guess. I've certainly changed my views. Students know that I cave and that my research problems are interesting. I interlace my lectures, my research, and my sporting areas. (p. 25)

Julia M. James,
School of Chemistry

Administrators are facing increasing pressure from students, legislators, parents, and others to deliver excellence in teaching (as well as in research) in their institutions. Perhaps, the models and behaviors of teachers in this book can provide a basis for administrators to talk about what they are looking for in terms of commitment and to delineate exemplary actions of academics teaching in their institutions. Perhaps, they can provide a basis for constructing text that administrators can use when they are communicating with various stakeholders about their vision for teaching in their institutions. Perhaps, the approaches and techniques of the authors in the book can provide a basis for some important content and philosophy of a training program for doctoral students to help them become good teachers as well as researchers.

Some authors in this book are highly idealistic about their teaching. They have visions for what learning is and should be. They have a commitment to developing students in terms of the content of their field. Also, we think, in various ways they communicate learning that fosters self-awareness and a respect for the values and positions of others. Are their values widely held in academia? Should they be?

A related question is whether the philosophies and practices of the teacher-researchers in the book are in synch with the dominant paradigm of professional school education—the dominant milieu of our contributors—or whether they are marginal to that paradigm. We can imagine a professor in finance or accounting or in other nonorganizational science areas reading with puzzlement or amusement or even downright disdain some of the practices described in this book. Like his colleagues at Michigan, they might ask, for example, what on earth Karl Weick (Chapter 17) was trying to accomplish by showing senior executives a video scene from some esoteric movie that seemed to have nothing to do with business or the bottom line. Weick makes his own case for this as an innovation to help stretch people to learn about change, but would others from a different discipline see any connection to teaching about business? Could others with less visibility than a Karl Weick "get away" with it?

Again, would these same professors or their administrators see the value of teaching skills that enable students to critique the dominant ideologies of business and organization, as Pushkala Prasad (Chapter 13) does, or would this be seen as subversive? Would it perhaps be dismissed as marginal thinking and merely tolerated on the basis of academic freedom, or can the new paradigm that has currency in organizational research have an impact on other colleagues?

## Impact on Students

Students who read this book will perhaps point to teachers who remind them of one or other of our authors. What will their reaction be? Will students be moved in any way either to critique the teaching approaches in the book or to argue that they need more of this quality of teaching in their own institutions, that academics who teach well should receive more recognition and support? Will reading the book help students get a more informed view of what the academic profession is like for some of its practitioners? Would it make them more critical of or sensitive to the teaching and the research they encounter in their schools?

We are inclined to think that something important going on in the professional work world that requires an education has many of the ingredients captured in this book. Increasingly, managers and others in organizations are being called on to adapt to and manage change that is happening at a very fast pace. Students who are preparing to enter this turbulent environment or who are in it already must assess its underlying dynamics. They need to be sensitive to much more diversity in human affairs in and around organizations. They need to be exposed to unusual stimuli in relatively safe settings so as to learn how to respond to them effectively in their life roles. They need to seek out novel forms that might help them break through to new understandings and to read and digest information in ways that enable them to contextualize the information, to act on it with wisdom.

We know from the Porter and McKibbin report on business education (1988) that, in addition to requiring recruits with strong technical skills, hiring organizations desire that students be trained in leadership and communication skills, that they be attuned to the "softer" processes in organizations. Students being prepared for this world need to specialize in certain functions and disciplines as always, but they need also to become generalists about organizational matters. The teaching-research orientations described in this book may have an important bearing on such educational issues. Of course, that is *our* bias, so the question is, Is anyone else out there listening who might want to help change the educational content and the learning processes in professional schools?

In a related vein, we ask the question, What are the weaknesses in the orientations to teaching that are described in this book? The authors, by and large, seem enamored of teaching that emphasizes participation of others in the learning process, that draws on learning to function in groups or teams, and that includes a facilitative role for teachers. In short, they are "process" sensitive. Are these teachers ahead of or behind the curve?

We have observed that, in recent changes to many MBA programs in business schools in North America, one emphasis has been on teaching part of the program through an integrated core of material taught by teams of academics from different disciplines. We suspect that such team teaching requires that the instructors come to terms with differences in intellectual styles (their own, as well as those of students), that they find ways to ground the knowledge they are incorporating from disciplines other than their own into their frameworks. There is a necessary attention to dialogue and debate within the teaching team, as well as among the student body. Thus, the importance of processes to build a team of instructors becomes crucial to the success of the initiative. The lessons about collaborative teaching that Crary and Spelman (Chapter 14) share with us, as well as the insights and experiences of other authors, should be useful inputs to building a successful learning experience in the MBA programs of the current era.

Does the interest that many in this book have in helping students transform their understandings of organizational and personal understandings lead to too much influence being attributed to the teachers? We suspect that some of the authors are charismatic teachers. Is this healthy for those who experience the charisma? What do these charismatic teachers, who seem also to be highly sensitive to the needs of their students, do that might be mitigating possible negative outcomes from the power of their teaching? What could we learn from them? Do they model values that can make safe the transformational experiences they attempt to produce in others through the learning experience?

## Linking Teaching and Research

What exactly is the synergy between teaching and research that gives passion to our authors' experiences? We get a sense of this through their stories, yet perhaps this could be investigated more systematically. For some of them, there is a fairly direct crossover from research to teaching and vice versa. Authors Boje (Chapter 6), Crary and Spelman (Chapter 14), Gutek (Chapter 3), Mahoney (Chapter 8), Mello (Chapter 11), and Weick (Chapter 17), to name a few, discuss ways that they bring their research, their conceptual frameworks, and their values into the classroom. This is not the only connecting path. Intellectual curiosity focused on research issues can motivate the individual, as teacher, to ask challenging questions and to search for answers through the dialogues that take place in the classroom. Aldrich (Chapter 2), André (Chapter 4), Cameron (Chapter 10), Fukami

(Chapter 1), Pokrovsky (Chapter 9), and Vaill (Chapter 16), among others, capture this quality rather well. Still others let what they observe in the classroom inform what they are studying as researchers. Such links can be observed in the chapters by Bailey (Chapter 18), Frost (Chapter 7), Hambrick (Chapter 15), Nahavandi (Chapter 12), Prasad (Chapter 13), and Van Buskirk (Chapter 5). One might argue that connecting research and teaching may be more feasible for some subjects than others. Nevertheless, we reiterate our proposition that the dichotomy between research and teaching masks a common concern with learning. When learning is the purpose, then the processes of investigation and of communicating about discovery can be linked through both teaching and research activities.

## Managing the Teaching and Research Links

Qualities of enthusiasm and high energy that are evident in the teaching behaviors of our authors may be necessary ingredients in good teaching. How do we ensure that the efforts expended do not burn out the teacher-scholars? It probably makes sense to create or support ways for them to recuperate after strenuous teaching efforts. It is likely to be helpful also if we create spaces in which they can connect with their research interests. The people in this book seem to be fairly aware of the dangers of burnout and of the need to pace themselves, although we suspect that many of them stretch even their high energy levels to the breaking point. Perhaps, we can count on individuals to monitor their own energy levels. We think, however, it is also an institutional issue and needs examining. Perhaps, some people who do mainly research find that teaching simply drains their energy and that institutions could do more to nourish them when they teach.

In general, how do scholars manage the energy that seems to be needed to teach well and to engage actively in research? It is a question not only for individuals who practice these crafts but also for administrators who more than ever need to manage effectively the process of allocating faculty members to assignments. Do we create a cadence that allows some faculty members to emphasize teaching while others do research? Much of the evidence in this book suggests that good teachers can be and are good researchers and that one can have a desire to do both well rather than to be only a researcher or a teacher. The dominant academic culture and reward system in North America still seems to assign second-class citizenship to those who declare a preference for teaching or even an emphasis in teaching even when they do research, especially if the individuals do not publish frequently in the best academic journals. The task of balancing portfolios so that a greater proportion of researchers begin to take time out to seriously enhance their teaching is significant.

What is the cadence that might lead us to a time when more academics than at present are comfortable doing both crafts well? The conventional wisdom in academia seems to be that junior scholars fresh from obtaining Ph.D.s make sure they do an adequate job in the classroom but are encouraged to recognize that the more important task is research. Is this the best way for the field to prepare academics for the future? Best for whom? Will students and legislators, among others, sit still for this arrangement, and does it matter whether they do? Is it even the best way to nurture the scholars of the future so that they are competent and creative in their teaching and their research and so that they are vital contributors for the duration of their careers? Perhaps there is merit in having academics in professional schools spend time working in the field after receiving their doctoral degrees. Or, perhaps they should concentrate on teaching for a while and then increase their attention to research. Working in the field and teaching intensively are each interesting ways to learn about phenomena and about oneself that are different from and complementary to emphasizing learning by doing research.

Such strategies might give junior scholars time to reflect on what they have learned from the doctoral training process, to draw breath, and to gain perspective on themselves and the careers they are fashioning as scholars. This was the career path of at least two authors in this book. It is possible that administrators and senior academics need to review the vision for the academic and scholarly career. Valuing more varied career path options might prove beneficial to the field and to its members.

## Enhancing the Credibility of Academic Teaching

How do we bring the credibility of teaching to the level of that accorded to doing research? One way may be through clearer parameters for assessing teaching performance. The experiences described in this book suggest that such criteria need to be creative enough to capture the innovation that goes with good teaching, that build learning experiences that stretch students and require teachers to also take risks. We will need ingenuity and wisdom to develop measures that are sensitive to this issue.

We may also benefit from doing the kind of research that informs us about effective teaching and that is respected for its rigor. A call in 1995 for papers reporting empirical work on teaching effectiveness in the prestigious *Academy of Management Journal* included a request for studies that examine the role of power in the classroom and the nature of control in the teaching process; an interest in the factors that are significant in the development of effective teachers; an examination of possible parallels between teaching performance and theories and data on the practices of leadership, organizational learning, continuous improvement, communication, and the like; and an examination of the effects of different learning experiences, such as planned teaching versus improvised teaching.

When such research is done well, it can enhance the visibility and credibility of academic teaching. The rich descriptions of teaching in this book should stimulate good research ideas on teaching effectiveness.

## References

*Award-winning university teachers talking about teaching.* (1991). Sydney, Australia: University of Sydney, Center for Teaching and Learning.

Porter, L. W., & McKibbin, L. E. (1988). *Management education and development: Drift or thrust into the 21st century.* New York: McGraw-Hill.

# 19 Conclusion

RAE ANDRÉ
PETER J. FROST

We hope the outcomes and insights from this book will help re-searchers become more attuned to teaching and assist teachers to become more inclined to do research. But what else might need to be present to help such bridging? Does the book push academics more toward a center that embraces both teaching and research, or are traditional values that make research primary so strong that this and other books like it will make no more than a slight dent in the process, soon to be forgotten? It is not for us to answer these questions, but rather to hope that the accounts in this book do pique some interest among academics, students, and administrators. We hope that, as others consider questions we have asked, our understanding of the synergies between teaching and research—that very human, complex, and integrated process—can move forward and the quality of the learning experience can be enhanced for all those involved.

# About the Authors

---

**Howard E. Aldrich** (Ph.D., University of Michigan) is Kenan Professor of Sociology, Director of the Industrial Relations Curriculum, Director of the Sociology Graduate Studies Program, and Adjunct Professor of Business at the University of North Carolina at Chapel Hill. Prior to assuming his current position in 1982, he taught at Cornell University, Ithaca, for 13 years in the New York State School of Industrial and Labor Relations and also held appointments in the Sociology Department and the Business School. He has been a Visiting Scholar at Stanford University, Stanford, CA; the International Institute of Management, West Berlin; Aston University, Birmingham, England; Uppsala University, Sweden; Keio University Business School, Yokohama, Japan; and the University of Economics, Vienna, Austria; and has lectured widely in the United States, Canada, Japan, and Western Europe. He has been Associate Editor of *Administrative Science Quarterly* and has published more than 100 articles on organizations, entrepreneurship, small business, ethnic relations, and organizational strategy. Publications include *Organizations and Environments* (1979), *Population Perspectives on Organizations* (1986), and *Ethnic Entrepreneurs: Immigrant Business in Industrial Societies* (with Roger Waldinger and Robin Ward; Sage, 1990). Research projects include a comparative study of R&D consortia in the United States and Japan (with Toshihiro Sasaki and Michele Bolton), a survey of the human resource management practices of small and medium-sized firms in Vancouver, Canada (with Nancy Langton), a panel study of business performance in the Research Triangle Area (with Amanda Elam), a case of two emerging industries in the Research Triangle Area (with Ted Baker), and a study of the commercialization of the World Wide Web (with Marlene Fiol and Courtney Hunt).

**Rae André** (Ph.D., University of Michigan) is Professor of Organizational Behavior and Theory in the College of Business at Northeastern University, Boston, and has been Visiting Professor at the University of Ulster, Belfast, Northern Ireland, and the University of Waikato, Hamilton, New Zealand. An eclectic and interdisciplinary scholar, she has published 3 books and more than 40 articles; her personal favorites are *Positive Solitude* (HarperCollins, 1991) and *The 59-Second Employee: How to Stay One Second Ahead of Your One-Minute Manager* (Houghton Mifflin, 1983), her series of articles on the design of economic development organizations (some of which appeared in *Journal of Managerial Issues, Economic Development Quarterly, Journal of General Management,* and *Journal of Small Business Management*), and her articles "*Diversity Stress as Morality Stress*" (*Journal of Business Ethics,* 1994) and "The Scientist, the Artist, and the Evangelist" (*New Management,* 1985). She has also shared exercises and cases, including "The Leadership Self-Study Project" in *Organizational Behavior: Experience and Cases* (edited by Dorothy Marcic for West Publishing) and "The Self-Shaping Project as a Tool for Teaching the Managerial Uses of Behavior and Modification" (*Organizational Behavior Teaching Review,* 1987-88). Research and teaching interests include intercultural negotiation and conflict and managing people in international settings. In a former life, she worked for General Motors, IBM, and MCA, Inc., and graduated from the UCLA Film School.

**Darlyne Bailey** (Ph.D., Case Western Reserve University) is Dean and Associate Professor at the Mandel School of Applied Social Sciences at Case Western Reserve University, Cleveland, and has secondary appointments in the Weatherhead School of Management and the Mandel Center for Nonprofit Organizations. She is also a Group XIII Fellow in the W. K. Kellogg National Fellowship Program, where she is exploring the role of spirituality in building community. Research and publications focus on community-based consortium development, workplace diversity, and participative organizational redesign strategies. Most notable is her methodology of participatory action research. Her work with the Healthy Family/Healthy Start and Hope VI projects in Cleveland have received recognition both locally and nationally. She is conducting research on the development and evaluation of local and international collaborations. She is the first woman and African American to be awarded the George Washington Kidd Award of 1836 from Lafayette College in Easton, PA; this award is given to alumni to acknowledge distinguished professional achievement.

**David M. Boje** (Ph.D.) is Professor of Management and Head of the Management Department, College of Business Administration and Economics, New Mexico State University, Las Cruces; and Director of the Peace Corps Fellows Program at Loyola Marymount University, Los Angeles, which provides job development, small business consulting, recycling, and tutoring programs in two public housing developments in Los Angeles. The author of numerous articles in such journals as *Administrative Science Quarterly, Academy of Management Journal,* and *Management Science,* he also writes for magazines, is Track Chair for Postmodern Organization Theory for the International Academy of Business Disciplines, is an activist for *Electronic Journal of Radical Organization Theory,* and does tape recordings of and transcribes stories that crack the foundation of modernist science. In 1991, he assumed editorship of *Journal of Organizational Change Management,* turned it into a radical theory publication, and despite being a favorite son of two academy divisions, continues to terrorize total quality management, AACSB, and nonsustainable business practices. Books include *Postmodern Management and Organizational Theory* (with Robert Gephart and Tojo Thatchenskery, 1996) and *Managing in the Postmodern World: America's Revolution Against Exploitation* (with Bob Dennehy, 1994). He got his start as a radical theorist when Louis Pondy and Hal Leavit invited him to coedit *Readings in Managerial Psychology* (1979, 1989). Despite being the recipient of six teacher-of-the-year awards, one class project was thrown off campus when his students began distributing condoms at a Catholic university. Despite his rebellious behavior, several universities have invited him to be their department chair. Can a postmodernist be a department head?

**Beverly J. Cameron** (Ph.D., University of Michigan) is Associate Professor in the Economics Department at the University of Manitoba. Previously, she was Instructor II and Lecturer. Since 1992, she has been seconded half-time as Director of the University Teaching Services. Awards include the 3M Canada

Teaching Fellowship and several University of Manitoba and Department of Economics teaching awards. Publications are mainly in the area of teaching and learning. She has written and edited *Teaching at the University of Manitoba: A Handbook* (1993); coauthored *Economics: Understanding the Canadian Economy* (4th ed.; Dryden Press, 1993) and study guides to accompany four editions of *Economics* (1980, 1984, 1988, 1993); and authored *Economics: Reporting the Issues* (Holt, Rinehart & Winston, 1982). Articles are concentrated in the fields of teaching and learning and economics; titles include "Using Tests to Teach" (*College Teaching,* 1991), "Personal Growth as a Faculty Goal for Students" (*Accent,* January 1991), and "Effective Thinking: What Is It?" (*The Teaching Professor,* 1990).

**Marcy Crary** (Ph.D., Case Western Reserve University) is Associate Professor in the Management Department at Bentley College, Waltham, MA. She came to Bentley in 1981; in 1990, she helped create Bentley's team-taught course Managing Diversity in the Workplace, which was developed as a partnership between the college and Digital Equipment Corporation. She is a founding member of the Diversity Consortium at Harvard; this consortium is a local group of diversity practitioners from industry, education, community service, and government who meet monthly to learn with each other. She is a member of the Academy of Management Association and the Organizational Behavior Teaching Society. Her writing, research, and teaching interests concern adult development, the management of diversity issues in the workplace and the classroom, and the dynamics of attraction and closeness in work relationships.

**Peter J. Frost** (Ph.D., University of Minnesota) is in the Faculty of Commerce and Business Administration at the University of British Columbia. He holds the Edgar F. Kaiser Chair in Organizational Behavior and is a former Associate Dean of the Faculty. He is a Senior Editor for *Organization Science* and has served as Executive Director of the Organizational Behavior Teaching Society. He has published books on organizational culture, including *Reframing Organizational Culture* (with Larry Moore, Meryl Louis, Craig Lundberg, and Joanne Martin, 1992), and on management, including *Managerial Reality: Balancing Technique, Practice, and Values (with Vance Mitchell and Walter Nord, 1995),* and he has coedited a special issue of *Leadership Quarterly* titled "Leadership for Environment and Social Exchange" (with Carolyn Egri, October 1994). The recipient of a 3M Teaching Excellence Fellowship in 1988, the CASE

Canada Professor of the Year Award in 1989, and the David L. Bradford Outstanding Educator Award in 1993, he is a Fellow of the Academy of Management, has a keen interest in the politics and processes of leadership, and is working on a project about leading in times of crisis and ambiguity.

**Cynthia V. Fukami** (Ph.D., Northwestern University) is Associate Professor in the Department of Management in the Daniels College of Business, University of Denver. She teaches organizational behavior and human resource management and has conducted research in the areas of employee commitment, turnover, absenteeism, discipline, and total quality management. She was awarded the 1992 Willemssen Distinguished Research Professorship by U S WEST and the University of Denver and the University of Denver's 1992 Distinguished Teaching Award. She is a member of the Academy of Management, the Organizational Behavior Teaching Society, the Industrial Relations Research Association, and the Society of Industrial Psychologists.

**Barbara A. Gutek** (Ph.D., University of Michigan) is Professor in and Head of the Department of Management and Policy at the University of Arizona, Tucson. Among her research interests are women in management, sexual harassment, biases in performance evaluation, impacts of information technology, and service transactions. A Fellow in the American Psychological Association and the American Psychological Society, her research has been funded by the National Science Foundation and the National Institute of Mental Health. In 1992-93, she was Visiting Professor at the California Institute of Technology, Pasadena. Publications include more than 80 articles and chapters and 10 books, including *Sex and the Workplace* (1985) and *The Dynamics of Service* (1995), and she is co-editor of the Women and Work Series, published by Sage. She is Secretary-Treasurer of the 3,000-member Society for the Psychological Study of Social Issues and is on the Board of Governors of the Academy of Management. Consulting includes the Xerox Palo Alto Research Center, the RAND Corporation, and the Equal Employment Opportunity Commission. She also serves as an expert witness in court cases in the areas of sex discrimination and sexual harassment.

**Donald C. Hambrick** (Ph.D., Pennsylvania State University) is Samuel Bronfman Professor of Democratic Business Enterprise at the Graduate School of Business, Columbia University, where he teaches courses in corporate strategy, top management processes, and executive leadership. He is the recipient of the

Singhvi Award for outstanding teaching in the MBA program and the Chandler Award in the Executive MBA program. Author of numerous articles, chapters, and books on strategy formulation, organizational design, executive staffing and incentives, and the composition and processes of top management teams, his article "Top Management Teams: Key to Strategic Success" won the Pacific Telesis Award for best article in *California Management Review*. He has served as President of the Academy of Management (1992-93), on the Board of Directors of the Strategic Management Society, and on the editorial boards of many journals, including *Administrative Science Quarterly, Academy of Management Executive, Academy of Management Journal, Academy of Management Review, Journal of Business Venturing, Organization Dynamics,* and *Strategic Management Journal.*

**Thomas A. Mahoney** (Ph.D., University of Minnesota) is Frances Hampton Currey Professor Emeritus at the Owen Graduate School of Management, Vanderbilt University, Nashville. Prior to joining Vanderbilt in 1982, he taught for more than 25 years at the University of Minnesota in the program of Industrial Relations. He has published works as diverse as workforce governance, investigations of comparable worth, computer simulation of internal labor markets, work motivation, and numerous studies of employment compensation, and in such journals as *Labor Law Journal, Industrial and Labor Relations Review, Academy of Management Journal, Journal of Applied Psychology, Harvard Business Review,* and *Administrative Science Quarterly*. In addition to teaching and advising candidates for the MA and MBA degrees, he has advised numerous candidates for the Ph.D. degree who are now engaged in careers of research, teaching, and consulting.

**Jeff Mello** (Ph.D., Northeastern University) is Professor of Management in the School of Business at Golden Gate University, San Francisco, and also teaches in the Haas School of Business at the University of California, Berkeley. In 1994, he received the David L. Bradford Outstanding Educator Award, presented by the Organizational Behavior Teaching Society. Books include *AIDS and the Law of Workplace Discrimination* (Westview) and a forthcoming text on strategic human resource management. Articles have been published in such journals as *Seton Hall Legislative Journal, Journal of Individual Employment Rights, Public Personnel Management, Labor Law Journal, Employment Relations Today, Journal of Management Education, International Journal of Public Administration,* and *Dickinson Journal of Environmental Law and Policy*. He is a member of the national and regional divisions of the Organizational

Behavior Teaching Society, Academy of Legal Studies in Business, and the Academy of Management.

**Afsaneh Nahavandi** (Ph.D., University of Utah) is Director of the MBA program at the Arizona State University West School of Management. She taught at Northeastern University, Boston, from 1983 to 1987 and joined Arizona State University West as one of the founding business faculty in 1987. The recipient of the 1992-93 Arizona State University West Achievement in Teaching Award, she has teaching interests in organizational behavior, organization theory, leadership, and cultural diversity. Her research focuses on leadership, teams, and organizational culture. Her books include *Organization Culture in the Management of Mergers* (1993) and *The Art and Science of Leadership* (1997). She has published in such journals as *Academy of Management Review, Group and Organization Studies,* and *Journal of Management Studies.* Her recent article "Restructuring Teams for the Reengineered Organizations" was selected by the *Academy of Management Executive* as the journal's best article of 1994. She has provided consulting and training in the areas of leadership, teams, and culture.

**Nikita Pokrovsky** (Ph.D.) is Professor of Sociology and Social Philosophy in the Department of Sociology at Moscow University in Moscow, Russia. He also is a full professor at the government's Institute of Foreign Relations (MGIMO), where he teaches basic sociology courses. He is known for his publications in the fields of American social philosophy, history of sociology, and cultural studies. He is the author of five books and numerous articles published in Russian and American journals. He is also involved in Russian/American cross-cultural studies, mainly on the sociology of personality. In 1978, he was adviser to the first group of Russian exchange graduate students at SUNY-Albany, where he spent several months as an employee of the International Programs. He is the recipient of several national scholarly awards, including the National Lenin Komsomol Prize in the humanities for his monograph "Henry David Thoreau" (later published in English), and an award for his essay on the philosophy of Thomas Jefferson. He is also the author of the book *Early American Philosophy: Volume I, The Puritans,* the first Russian intellectual biography of Ralph Waldo Emerson (1955), and, most recently, of *Loneliness and Anomie* (1996). He is also a contributor to *Nezavisimaya Gazeta,* the second-largest Russian daily newspaper, and to other periodicals. He has participated in many international academic congresses and conventions and, in 1989, became the first Russian scholar to receive the

Andrew W. Mellon Foundation Fellowship at the National Humanities Center, Research Triangle Park, North Carolina. He has often visited the United States and Europe as a guest of leading universities and other academic institutions.

**Pushkala Prasad** (Ph.D., University of Massachusetts) is Associate Professor at the University of Calgary, where she teaches organizational behavior and organization theory and recently received the Outstanding New Scholar Award. Before coming to Calgary, she taught for 2 years at Clarkson University, where she received the Distinguished New Teacher Award. Primary research interests include the computerization of white-collar work, organizational culture and symbolism, and multicultural issues in the workplace. Her work has been published in such journals as *Organization Science, Human Relations,* and *Academy of Management Journal,* and she is currently coediting a book on the challenges of workplace diversity.

**Duncan Spelman** (Ph.D., Case Western Reserve University) is Associate Professor in the Management Department at Bentley College, Waltham, MA. His professional work focuses on workplace diversity. He played a central role in Bentley's organizational change effort centering on diversity, and he helped create and currently teaches Bentley's undergraduate and graduate courses on managing diversity in the workplace. He consults on diversity issues to businesses, schools, and governmental agencies.

**Peter B. Vaill** (DBA, Harvard Business School) is Professor of Human Systems and Director of the Ph.D. program at George Washington University's School of Business and Public Management, Washington, DC, and is also former Dean of this school. He has also served on the management faculties of the University of Connecticut and UCLA and has been Visiting Professor of Organizational Behavior at Stanford Business School. His essay "Toward a Behavioral Description of High Performing Systems" (1972) was the first contemporary description of what has come to be called "organizational excellence." He designed and taught one of the first courses in cross-cultural management offered in a U.S. management school and is well known for his ideas about what he calls "permanent white water." Articles include "The Purposing of High Performing Systems" (*Organizational Dynamics,* 1982). Contributions to edited volumes include "Process Wisdom for a New Age" (in *Transforming Work,* 1985); "Seven Process Frontiers for Organization Development" (in *The Emerging Practice of Organization Development,* 1989); "Executive Development as Spiritual Development" (in *Appreciative Management and Leadership*, 1990); and "Visionary Leadership" (in *The Portable MBA in Management*, 1993). Authored books include *Managing as a Performing Art: New Ideas for a World of Chaotic Change* (1989) and *Learning as a Way of Being: Strategies for Survival in a World of Permanent White Water* (1996). He is a member of the Academy of Management, Organizational Behavior Teaching Society, National Organization Development Network, and American Association of Higher Education. From 1985 to 1988, he was Editor of the American Management Associations's journal *Organizational Dynamics*, and he has been a member of the Board of Governors of the Center for Creative Leadership since 1990.

**Bill Van Buskirk** (Ph.D., Case Western Reserve University) is Associate Professor of Management at La Salle University in Philadelphia. He has won a best paper award from the Organizational Change and Development Division of the Academy of Management (1989) and the Roethligsberger Award from *Journal of Management Education* (1991). He has also received a Japan Center of North Carolina Fellowship (1983) and has been a Visiting Professor at Tokyo Keizai University. His research interests are organizational cultures of urban schools, appreciative inquiry, and the design of workshops to sensitize managers to their own organizational cultures. Articles have been published in *Human Relations, Journal of Management Education, Public Administration Quarterly, Project Management Journal*, and *Journal for Organizational Change Management*.

**Karl E. Weick** (Ph.D., Ohio State University) is Rensis Likert Collegiate Professor of Organizational Behavior and Psychology at the University of Michigan and has been associated with faculties at Purdue University, the University of Minnesota, Cornell University, and the University of Texas. In 1990, he received the Irwin Award for Distinguished Lifetime Scholarly Achievement from the Academy of Management and the Best Article of the Year Award for his article "Theory Construction as Disciplined Imagination" in *Academy of Management Review*. Research topics include how people make sense of confusing events, the social psychology of improvisation, high reliability systems, the effects of stress on thinking and imagination, indeterminacy in social systems, social commitment, small wins as the embodiment of wisdom, and linkages between theory and practice. His writing has appeared in numerous journal articles, chapters, book reviews, and speeches. Books include *The*

*Social Psychology of Organizing* and the coauthored *Managerial Behavior, Performance, and Effectiveness,* which won the 1972 Book of the Year Award from the American College of Hospital Administration. He consults with a variety of organizations in the public and private sectors, including Corning Glass, Narco, Cole Products, the National Science Foundation, the National Institute of Education, and the National Institute of Mental Health.